Global
Logistics
Strategies

Global Logistics Strategies

Delivering the goods

John Manners-Bell

KoganPage

LONDON PHILADELPHIA NEW DELHI

First published in Great Britain and the United States in 2014 by Kogan Page Limited

2nd Floor, 45 Gee Street
London EC1V 3RS
United Kingdom
www.koganpage.com

1518 Walnut Street, Suite 1100
Philadelphia PA 19102
USA

4737/23 Ansari Road
Daryaganj
New Delhi 110002
India

© John Manners-Bell, 2014

ISBN   978 0 7494 7023 4
E-ISBN   978 0 7494 7024 1

British Library Cataloguing-in-Publication Data

A CIP record for this book is available from the British Library.

Library of Congress Cataloging-in-Publication Data

Manners-Bell, John.
  Global logistics strategies : delivering the goods / John Manners-Bell.
    pages cm
    ISBN 978-0-7494-7023-4 (pbk.) – ISBN 978-0-7494-7024-1 (ebook)   1. Physical distribution of goods.   2. Business logistics–Management.   I. Title.
  HF5415.6.M317 2014
  658.7–dc23
                                                                                2013032117

Typeset by Graphicraft Limited, Hong Kong
Print production managed by Jellyfish
Printed and bound by CPI Group (UK) Ltd, Croydon, CR0 4YY

CONTENTS

LIST OF FIGURES

LIST OF TABLES

ACKNOWLEDGEMENTS

This book would not have been possible without significant contributions by several colleagues at Transport Intelligence.

I would like to thank Thomas Cullen, particularly for his expertise and contributions on the sections related to automotive and consumer logistics.

Also, Cathy Roberson for her contributions on e-commerce, high tech and pharmaceutical logistics as well as on the North American logistics market.

Additional thanks goes to Jola O'Hara for the work she undertook in creating the many charts and figures which illustrate the topics explored.

I would also like to extend my gratitude to Professor Michael Browne, Professor of Logistics at the University of Westminster and my former tutor who has done so much to promote the understanding of logistics and supply chain concepts.

Finally, I would like to thank my father, who by setting up a transport company in the 1970s gave me the best possible understanding of the industry, and of course my wife for her continued support and encouragement.

JMB

ABOUT THIS BOOK

Although much has been written about the various supply chain management practices which have transformed global manufacturing over the past 30 years, less attention has been paid to the development of the logistics industry which has facilitated these advances. This book has been written with the aim of going some way towards rectifying this situation by describing at some length the structure of the industry and examining the dynamics which have influenced its evolution.

To provide the reader with an indication of the content of this book, it is worthwhile examining the title, 'Global Logistics Strategies: Delivering the goods,' in a little more detail.

The analysis contained within the book takes a *global* view of the issues affecting the industry although many of the issues discussed could be said to be regional, national or in some cases local in nature. Some parts of the industry are indeed truly global – for example, air cargo, shipping or the international express sector. Other parts of the logistics industry undertake services at either the beginning or end of international supply chains, and these tend to be road-based and localized. The 'micro-economics' of these sectors, whether international or not, have gone a long way towards shaping global supply chains and, in a circular relationship, have in turn been shaped by globalization.

The term '*logistics*' is used throughout this book to refer to physical distribution and, specifically, to the 'supply-side' industry which provides transportation and warehousing services, including value-adding services. The definition may not please everyone; for example, people working within the express parcels or shipping sectors would not necessarily view themselves as 'logisticians'. Additionally, many people working within manufacturing and retailing may feel that physical distribution is just one element of their broader understanding of logistics, which encompasses many aspects of supply chain management. In fact, rather than spend much time defining logistics as a concept, this book approaches the issue more practically by defining the subsegments which together go towards comprising the 'logistics industry'.

A large proportion of this book is spent examining the *strategies* which have been employed by the management of logistics companies. Underlying every strategic decision is a responsibility to their shareholders to deliver reasonable returns on the capital invested whilst at the same time successfully providing customer-aligned services. To make these decisions, management need to be acutely aware of the global economic and demand-side trends affecting their customers as well as the unique dynamics of their own market. This book is designed to provide the necessary background to allow executives, or future executives, to confidently make these decisions.

The subtitle of the book is 'Delivering the goods' and this provides a positive assessment of the impact which the modern logistics industry has had on the global economy. The levels of professionalism, technological innovation, investment in global networks and infrastructure have ultimately driven economic development. By one measure, the globalization which the modern logistics industry has facilitated has lifted an estimated 600 million Chinese out of poverty. It has the potential to have similar effects throughout Asia, Africa and Latin America. In this respect, although much still needs to be done – not least in terms of improving its image – the global logistics industry can be rightly proud of its achievements.

Introduction

The global logistics industry is vast, both in terms of market size and the huge numbers of people employed in the sector. It is therefore surprising that its role in the development of the global economy is generally overlooked. Without the inexpensive and reliable transport of freight, manufacturers would not be able to tap into the cheap labour resources based in remote locations throughout the world. Nor would retailers be able to provide ever-increasing levels of service to their customers, ensuring shelves are always stocked whilst inventory is kept to a minimum.

In the last two decades the logistics industry has undergone a transformation, as a flurry of mergers and acquisition activity in the 1990s and 2000s led to the creation of a number of giant diversified transport-based groups. Deutsche Post DHL and TNT were at the forefront of this trend, aggressively building logistics enterprises diverse in both geographies covered and services offered. In the process many well-known, mid-sized companies disappeared but even large operators, such as Tibbett & Britten or Exel, were not immune.

The origins of the acquisition frenzy of the 1990s and 2000s can be traced back to the implementation of certain elements of supply chain theory in the 1980s. At this time there was a sea change in the way in which retailers and manufacturers viewed inventory. Just-in-Time manufacturing became the industry mantra resulting in smaller, more frequent movements of goods. Companies started to focus on the physical centralization of stock, a goal facilitated by the growth of trade blocs such as the European Union (EU) and North American Free Trade Agreement (NAFTA). Much has been written on this subject and this book does not intend to re-examine supply chain theory – only in so much that it has helped sculpt the logistics industry we know today.

As a result of these changes to manufacturing strategy, transport became critical to supply chains and the lowly freight company became a major partner in ensuring that goods reached the intended recipient on time and in good condition. It is clear that the evolution of supply chain management resulted in much higher standards across the industry, and gave the major road freight operators the opportunity to develop their value proposition.

Up until this point they had struggled to compete in a market characterized by low barriers to market entry and exit.

The intensity of the merger and acquisition (M&A) activity came about due to a 'perfect storm' of market conditions. These included the demand for higher value, outsourced logistics services by manufacturers and retailers; the availability of cheap private equity-sourced cash; the globalization of the world's economy; the liberalization of the world's postal markets; and the rise of e-commerce. This is discussed in more detail in Chapter 2.

Suddenly, the perception of the sector was transformed from being a rather boring, commoditized, low-margin jumble of transport and warehousing services, to that of a dynamic, value-adding driver of the global economy.

Since the first major acquisition which kicked off the period of frenetic consolidation (that of TNT Express by the Dutch Post Office in 1996), there have been a variety of different trends which have influenced the strategies of the market leading companies. At this time (the mid-1990s), the ability to offer global 'one stop shopping' became an ambitious goal for major logistics companies in their attempt to differentiate their services from their competition. Although no one believed that any one logistics company had a complete portfolio of services in all geographies, or in fact that manufacturers and retailers would be willing to put all their eggs in one basket even if they did, there was a trend for a rationalization of the number of logistics service providers (LSPs) utilized by a shipper, which is ongoing today.

At the same time the management concept of 'outsourcing' was taking root. It was believed that logistics companies could take advantage of manufacturers' and retailers' desire to focus on their core competences and spin off the management of their distribution activities to LSPs. By greater engagement with their clients, logistics companies had the opportunity to offer more value-adding, higher-margin services (such as postponed manufacturing, call centres, inventory ownership etc).

However, the impact of outsourcing on the logistics industry has not been entirely beneficial. There is no doubt that in revenue terms the trend has been massively important. However, the majority of contracts (especially in the consumer and retail sectors) are undertaken at low margins, and in truth there have not been as many opportunities to engage with clients at a more value-adding level. This is not to say that some sectors, such as high tech, have not encouraged innovations from their logistics providers – only that most have remained stubbornly unwilling to give up control of what they believe to be a competitive advantage.

Another problem faced by logistics operators is contract 'churn'. As markets became more mature, logistics companies were continually chasing contracts which came up for renewal once every three to five years. Contracts were awarded predominantly on the basis of price, and so the industry was participating in a race-to-the-bottom in terms of profitability. Margins on logistics contracts have bottomed out at around 3 per cent – hardly the high value, high margin business many companies had hoped for. A mitigating factor in these low margins is the fact that many logistics companies have become 'asset-light' – no longer major owners of trucks and warehouses – and that consequently return on capital is significantly better than the headline figures might suggest.

By the mid-1990s, the outsourcing argument had gained traction, and investors continued to promote companies which were heavily involved in 'contract logistics' such as Exel and Tibbett & Britten, to mention two. Others such as Christian Salvesen, Hays, TDG and Wincanton were also favoured. It is no coincidence that all these companies were British, as the outsourcing trend had started in the UK's retail industry, driven by supermarket giants such as Tesco and Sainsbury's.

Many of these companies were emboldened by positive investor sentiment to expand out of the UK and into Europe, where there was the expectation that the emerging outsourcing trend would develop at a faster pace. Although there was nothing wrong with this strategy, the execution proved to be flawed. Competition in local markets was much greater than expected, and integration of acquisitions poorly handled, which ultimately left these companies exposed financially. Consequently the only one of these players still independent today is Wincanton, albeit having sold off its extensive European network of subsidiaries.

The exception to this was Exel which was acquired due to its strength, rather than weakness. It had acquired Tibbett & Britten in 2004 and had become a powerhouse in both the contract logistics and freight-forwarding sectors (more on the latter, later). It was acquired by Deutsche Post to transform its own 'Solutions' division and this propelled it into market leadership under the DHL Exel Supply Chain brand.

At around this time, the internet or 'dotcom' boom was occurring, and this added a certain level of hysteria to the acquisition market. Logistics companies were quick to position themselves as the providers of the infrastructure enabling 'clicks and mortar' e-retailers to fulfil customer orders, both warehousing and transport. Inflated expectations arose and this translated into much higher prices which companies had to pay for even very ordinary acquisitions.

Despite the fact that it would be another decade before the dotcom expectations were realized, the pressure on companies' management to expand through acquisition was remorseless. Several years into this particular phase of the sector's evolution, there were now fewer good quality targets available to buy, and in many cases due diligence being undertaken was cursory.

It is at this point in the timeline that the bottom fell out of the market, with the bursting of the dotcom bubble. Companies such as ABX Logistics (a division of the Belgium Post) had followed Deutsche Post's lead in building a pan-European network of road freight companies and freight forwarders. The resulting European recession of the early 2000s quickly led to a reverse in strategy as bullish volume forecasts proved to be unachievable and companies struggled to pay back the loans they had taken to make their acquisitions.

It is fair to say that all logistics companies were affected by the downturn. However, those with the deepest pockets, such as DHL and UPS, were able to ride out the storm. Others such as ABX and Thiel Logistik were not so fortunate.

Although it would be too simplistic to conclude that at this point the investment community fell totally out of love with 'contract logistics' or 'solutions' as it may be called, this reversal for the sector coincided with the rise of the international freight forwarder.

Up to this point, freight forwarding had been widely viewed as a non-value-adding 'necessary evil' for moving goods across borders and booking space on ships or aircraft. Business practices had not changed for many decades, if at all since the 19th century. However, as globalization gathered pace it became obvious that the freight forwarder, with links throughout the world (and especially in up and coming markets such as China) would become a critical element in supply chains.

The race was on to build owned networks of forwarding operations. Deutsche Post had acquired Danzas (and subsequently Exel, which included MSAS); UPS bought Fritz and Menlo Worldwide Forwarding; Schenker (itself now part of Deutsche Bahn) bought Bax Global, to name just a few.

The pace of globalization translated into big annual increases in international air and sea freight volumes. Forwarders' countercyclical business model (which allowed them to make better profit margins in a downturn, and better revenues in an upturn – see Chapter 5) was applauded. Their 'asset-light' nature, managing rather than owning transport assets, provided high returns on capital expenditure. Suddenly forwarding was no longer the poor relation of the logistics world, playing second fiddle to more sophisticated, value-adding logistics.

The rise of the forwarder has been temporarily slowed by the 'Great Recession' of 2009. The 'Black Swan' event, starting in the subprime mortgage market in the United States, resulted in a meltdown of global freight volumes. Retailers and manufacturers, gripped by uncertainty, placed a moratorium on orders with their suppliers in the Far East. Volumes plunged by 25 per cent or more as they sought to run down inventories located in distribution centres in Western Europe or North America. This had a dire impact on the shipping and air cargo industry, with the spare capacity resulting in a catastrophic fall in rates and near bankruptcy for many carriers.

Since then there has been a recovery, but there are now fears in the investment community that the forwarding industry will never again regain its stellar growth trajectory. Wage inflation in China has made goods produced in the Far East less competitive and prompted some manufacturers to adopt near-sourcing strategies (sourcing goods from suppliers based closer to the major consumer markets of the West). Natural disasters have shown the fragility of extended supply chains, and risk is now being increasingly taken into account when looking at sourcing strategies. The age of cheap transport (on which globalization is predicated) is coming to an end as oil costs move inexorably upwards. On top of this, the growth of Asia as a consumer market will lead to greater levels of regionalization (as opposed to globalization) with the fastest growing sector being intra-Asia movements of goods. This will lead to the dilution of forwarders' yields.

This book will look at all the pressures which have led to the emergence of today's vibrant global logistics industry – from both the 'demand' (ie manufacturing and retailing) and the 'supply' (ie logistics provider) side perspective. In addition to the roles of the contract logistics and freight-forwarding sectors, it will also examine the dynamics of express parcels, container shipping, air cargo, road freight and intermodal industries. Whilst global macro-trends are highly important to the long-term future of these sectors, conversely it is the structure and competitive nature of these sectors which has a 'bottom up' influence on supply chain management, and hence global economies. For example, hyper-fragmentation and competition in the European road freight industry has been a key input into the formulation of manufacturers' and retailers' centralized distribution strategies.

A further section of the book reveals how this centralization of inventory has translated into the geographical clustering of logistics facilities. In Europe, the Netherlands and Belgium dominate the regional distribution centre market, although the accession of new countries to the EU means that many companies are now looking eastwards as Europe's economic centre of gravity shifts. In the United States, gateway locations are important, and the growing role of Mexico as a near-sourcing location will inevitably impact on distribution strategies. In Asia, the emergence of region-wide distribution hubs is still at a nascent stage due to lack of economic integration and weak transport infrastructure. However, the key locations for distribution property in China, the largest market in the region, are examined in detail.

The demand for logistics services over the past two decades has increased the need for high quality and well-trained employees to help in the development of the industry. This book has been written with the logistics executive in mind – those working both on the 'supply' and 'demand' side of the industry. It will allow those employed in manufacturing and retail supply chains to fully understand the background of the markets in which their logistics suppliers work. At the same time it will provide insight for managers of all levels into the workings of the freight markets and the macro-economic and supply chain trends which influence them. The information contained within the book will also prove invaluable to the next generation of logistics executives – whether presently studying at graduate or post-graduate level.

What is clear is that, after a turbulent period of transformation, there is no sign that change in the logistics industry is slowing down. A powerful mix of demand-side and supply-side factors means that further restructuring is possible, if not probable. The shift of the economic balance of power towards Asia; increasing supply chain risk; the price of oil; further mergers and acquisitions; and even near-shoring/re-shoring are just some of the 'known' issues which logistics providers will need to contend with. Twenty years ago nobody would have considered that the German Post Office would be a market leader in the international express, contract logistics, road and freight-forwarding sectors or that China would be so important to the world's logistics industry. It is likely that in another 20 years the market environment will be just as unrecognizable.

What's shaping the global logistics market?

01

The global logistics industry in its present form has come about as a result of a confluence of demand-side and supply-side trends. Political, economic, social and technological factors have facilitated major changes in the way in which multinational manufacturers supply global consumer markets and how retailers source their goods. This, in turn, has allowed many of the larger logistics service providers (LSPs) to differentiate their service offering from smaller competitors by leveraging their global scale, technological capabilities as well as financial and human capital.

FIGURE 1.1   The confluence of supply-side and demand-side trends

This chapter will be spent exploring some of the key macro-economic and demand-side drivers which have brought about today's logistics industry. It will identify how the logistics industry has gone far beyond simple transport and warehousing services, becoming the glue which holds together the systems that underpin the global economy.

Trade and globalization

One of the driving forces behind the trend towards the free movement of goods between countries has been the World Trade Organization (WTO), an inter-government organization born out of the reconciliation talks at the end of the Second World War. It essentially fulfils an anti-protectionist role, recognizing that the economic upheavals which gave rise to extremism in Europe and Asia in the 1930s were partly as a result of barriers to trade. These were created ostensibly to protect jobs, but in fact resulted in exacerbating the economic crisis and sowing the seeds of political discontent. As well as promoting free trade, the organization also provides a mechanism through which countries can settle trade disputes. The WTO has been very successful in preventing arguments over issues such as quotas and 'dumping' escalating into full-scale trade wars.

Negotiations since the first round of talks in 1947 have been aimed at reducing and then eliminating all tariff and non-tariff barriers. After many successes, the last Doha round of talks was a failure, breaking down finally in 2008 over an inability to agree on the liberalization of trade in agriculture and industrial products. In essence, developing and developed countries could not agree on the appropriate level of support for farmers.

However, perhaps the defining success of the WTO has been the development of China as the powerhouse of global industry. By acceding to the World Trade Organization, the Chinese government committed to root-and-branch reform of its economy, which has subsequently allowed it to grow to a position of global importance.

One of the consequences of China's accession, along with other economies in the Asia Pacific region, has been economic integration, which has in turn transformed the supply chains of sectors such as consumer electronics, clothing and furniture. This has had a profound effect on freight transport and brought about the emergence of large, integrated logistics providers, capable of supporting such complex, international supply chains. In turn, these new supply chains have transformed the pattern of sea and air freight routes.

However, tariffs are common on many products and some governments still turn a blind eye to anti-competitive practices. The inability of the WTO to get things done through the multilateral nature of its negotiation process has meant that developed nations have turned to direct, bilateral agreements in the hope that they will accelerate trade growth.

Below are a few examples of new trade groups:

- Following an agreement in November 2011, the leaders of nine trading partners – Australia, Brunei Darussalam, Chile, Malaysia, New Zealand, Peru, Singapore, Vietnam and the United States – announced the creation of the Trans-Pacific Partnership (TPP). It had also been announced that Japan was to open negotiations for membership.

- In March 2013, the European Commission recommended that member states give the official go-ahead for a trade agreement with the United States – the Transatlantic Trade and Investment Partnership. It said that there could be economic gains for the EU of €119 billion a year – and for the United States of €95 billion a year.

- Members of the Association of Southeast Asian Nations (ASEAN) together with the group's six major trading partners are due to begin the first round of negotiations in May 2013 to form the world's largest economic bloc by 2015. The ASEAN+6 trade deal will establish an integrated market of 16 countries in the Asia-Pacific region, with a population of more than 3 billion.

Other smaller deals include one between the EU and South Korea. An agreement between the EU and Canada is also near completion.

These deals will inevitably result in changes for the logistics sector. It is unlikely the sector will experience the sort of supply chain revolution that was seen in the 1990s, as the economies involved already have strong trade links. However, if, for example, the barriers to merging airlines in the United States and the EU could be removed, there is a major opportunity to transform the structure of air freight. Additionally, the market for integrated logistics companies might become more broad-based as economies become more interdependent.

Although the EU's remit has extended far beyond its original goal, it is, of course, the world's largest free trade area. The success of the Single European Market (SEM), which was created in the early 1990s, transformed the way in which manufacturers and retailers could supply their customers in the region. The SEM had deep-seated implications for production and distribution which could consequently be centralized and rationalized to a much smaller number of locations. More latterly the geographic centre of Europe has shifted eastwards with the accession of the Central and Eastern European economies such as Poland, Hungary and, most recently, Bulgaria and Romania.

The North American Free Trade Agreement (NAFTA) has had a similarly major impact on the flows of goods. An increasing number of manufacturers are choosing to supply the giant US consumer markets from production locations and distribution facilities in Mexico, where costs are substantially lower.

Looking ahead, trade deals which lead to the creation of single markets, whether in Asia, the Middle East, South America or Africa, have the potential to revolutionize distribution strategies in the same way in which they were in the European Union.

Growth in trade

World trade is a key driver of the freight-forwarding market. Although most elements of road freight may be dependent on domestic economies, air freight and sea freight are dominated by the performance of trade between nations – that is 'world trade'.

FIGURE 1.2   World trade growth: value of world merchandise exports, 2005–12

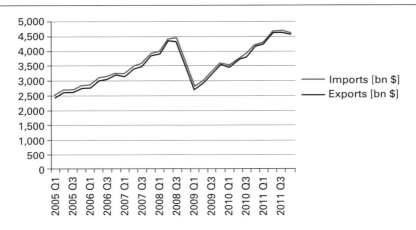

SOURCE: WTO/Ti

World trade has been very dynamic over the past decade, with underlying development being driven – until very recently – by strong growth of export and import traffic from China and related economies. To some degree the rates of growth since the end of 2009 have been flattered by an element of 'bounce-back' from the severe dip seen in the recession, but the underlying trend is still evident. Volumes have also been more recently boosted by trade between China and other emerging economies as supply chains in the region become more integrated and China's rise as a consumer market continues.

One of the most important background factors underlying the dynamics of global trade in the past year has been the depressed nature of consumer demand in Western markets. Of course, up to 2008–09 such demand was the main driving force behind air and sea volumes, moving product between the new assembly locations in China and the retail markets of the West. These trades have not gone away, however their growth has moderated.

China, the world's largest exporter, has undergone a degree of change in terms of exports. The huge leaps in volumes seen in previous years have moderated to around single digit percentages. There are indications that volumes between China and other emerging markets are filling some of the void left by lower export activity to the Eurozone in particular, but again this is a recent trend and it is unclear how prolonged this will be.

FIGURE 1.3   China exports 2009–12 US$m

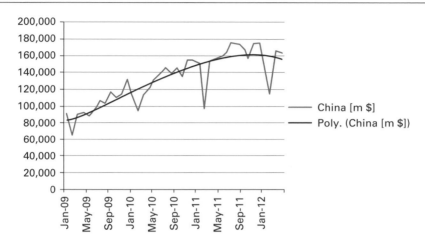

SOURCE: WTO/Ti

The growth of Asian trade

The past decade has seen a major shift in trade patterns, with traditional trade lanes, connecting China with the United States and Europe, losing some of their importance. Africa, for example, is amongst the fastest growing markets for China, as investors target mining and infrastructure opportunities. In fact, according to the Chinese government, trade with Africa was up over 25 per cent for 2012. According to China's Ministry of Commerce, it is likely that Africa will surpass the United States and Europe as China's largest trade partner in the next three to five years. As a result freight forwarders, such as DHL and Damco, are developing this trade lane by expanding multimodal products combining ocean freight and air freight services to new destinations. China is also among the largest trade partners for Argentina, Chile and Colombia. In 2009, China became Brazil's largest trade partner.

The development of the 'Modern Silk Road' between Asia and the Middle East is also resulting in increasing trade. In fact, from 2001 to 2010, trade increased over 700 per cent and now more than half of the Middle East's trade is with Asia.

Asia is not only seeking to increase external trade with potential trading partners such as South America, the Middle East and Africa but it is also turning inwards as intra-regional trade increases. However, in order for intra-Asian trade to really take off, infrastructure improvements are needed across the region. China, the dominant country in the region, is taking the lead as it assists with infrastructure projects in neighbouring countries. Along with internal projects, the linking of countries to one another and more importantly to China is resulting in a complex intra-Asian supply chain. As such, logistics providers have taken note and are increasingly positioning their service offerings to this market. Of particular note, intra-Asia trade expanded from 46.6 per cent of Asia's total trade in 1999 to almost 52 per cent by 2009. Shifts in manufacturing, supply chain interdependence and growing consumer spend have contributed to this increase.

It is estimated that by 2030, Asia's economy will be larger than that of the United States and the European Union combined, with the region's share of world GDP (gross domestic product) increasing from about 30 per cent to more than 40 per cent. Although Asia is leading the recovery of the world economy, the global crisis has highlighted issues the region must address, many of which are due to its dependence on export trade. To reduce this dependence, another engine of growth, domestic demand, is needed to sustain growth within the region. Improvements in infrastructure, financial reforms and greater flexibility in exchange rates are all needed to generate this demand.

FIGURE 1.4   Asia trade by region as a percentage of total value

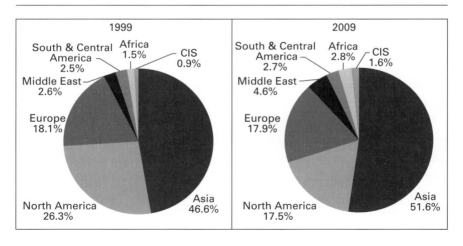

FIGURE 1.5   Increasing supply chain complexity

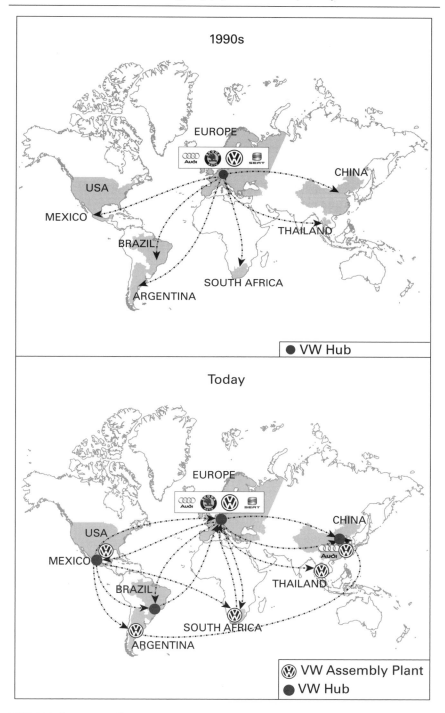

SOURCE: Volkswagen-Audi Group

Global trade networks

Perhaps the changing face of trading networks can be best illustrated by the example of VW-Audi Group. In the 1990s, flows of materials and finished vehicles originated predominantly in Europe, as shown in the first chart in Figure 1.5. However, in the past few years the company has transformed itself from a German-based exporter to the world, to a global automotive producer with a complex production footprint.

This has clearly had a major impact on its transportation and distribution requirements. Transport volumes, for instance, have increased by 25 per cent due to the multiple production locations and hubs. The company has created an intertwined network of trade lanes, supported by a range of freight forwarders and global logistics providers. This is in addition to the national and local logistics services required to support inbound logistics.

The impact of supply chain management practice on logistics

For much of the 20th century the predominant manufacturing strategy was based around creating economies of scale. This involved long production runs that created high levels of stock at low unit costs. Products were then 'pushed' out into the market, with the hope that there was sufficient demand. This was termed Just-in-Case manufacturing.

During this period the transport market was characterized by:

- full loads (inbound and outbound);
- low levels of service provision required;
- long lead times;
- regular, stochastic movements.

The problem with this approach was that demand could often be volatile, and manufacturers, retailers and other supply chain partners could tie up considerable amounts of capital in inventory. Stock itself could become redundant or be lost or stolen.

There were also other problems, not least that in fast-moving sectors such as the fashion or electronics industry, product life cycles are measured in terms of months, not years. They also need the flexibility to release new products on short lead times.

During the 1980s and 1990s, Japanese manufacturing processes were quickly adopted throughout the world – the best known of these originated in Toyota. Smaller production runs were adopted with production lines running on an 'as and when' basis depending on demand – the 'Kanban' system. This build-to-order (BTO) strategy did away, in theory anyway, with the need for buffer stocks.

This level of agility and flexibility is perhaps best demonstrated by technology company Dell. The lead time for any one computer is generally about five to six working days – two to three days for production and two to three days for shipping. Intel, the Central Processing Unit (CPU) manufacturer, estimated that the adoption of the BTO model throughout the industry took $750 million of inventory out of the system.

Along with a change in production systems, there was also the consequent introduction of Just-in-Time delivery schedules, which complemented the on-demand nature of manufacturing. This had a very major impact on transportation requirements. Suddenly freight operators were asked by their customers for more frequent services, moving smaller consignments on a less predictable basis. Efficiency was also affected as, in terms of transport costs, it is far more economic, on a per kilo basis, to run larger trucks than smaller ones.

There were also modal consequences as the flexibility of road services placed rail operators at a considerable competitive disadvantage when competing within the new paradigm. However, despite rising transport costs overall, logistics costs (including inventory financing) fell, making the trade-off more than worthwhile for shippers.

The way in which manufacturers in North America or Europe implemented a Just-in-Time supply chain strategy was very different than in Japan where manufacturers were able to achieve high levels of supplier concentration around assembly plants. For example, all 11 of Toyota's assembly and major component plants were located in and around 'Toyota City'. In contrast, Nissan's vehicle assembly plant in the UK has suppliers located in Germany, Spain and France, up to three days' journey time away.

This has put the supply chain under extreme strain, and of course makes the transport element of logistics more critical. From a manufacturer's point of view, the transport element cannot be allowed to fail, due to huge consequential loss should production be affected. This risk is examined in more detail in Chapter 13.

Figure 1.6 illustrates the impact which lowering inventory has on various parts of the production and distribution process. As the inventory (or water in the picture metaphor) falls, the business (or boat) becomes far more vulnerable to the hidden 'rocks' beneath. From a transport perspective, the hazards include mis-delivery, damage of goods in transit or late delivery.

FIGURE 1.6   Supply chain hazards of inventory reduction strategies

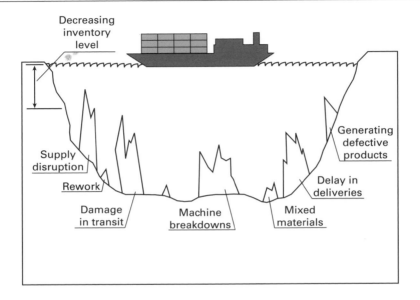

Centralization of inventory

Distribution strategies have been largely influenced by the trade-off between the cost of moving goods to market and the cost of holding inventories. The relatively cheap cost of transport has allowed manufacturers and retailers to store goods in centralized locations and supply them over longer distances. This has many advantages:

- cost of inventory holding falls;
- less buffer stock is required in each warehouse;
- there is less shrinkage;
- lower levels of redundancy occur;
- warehouse costs are lower.

Figure 1.7 shows that when goods are stored in close proximity to the end market (eg in national warehouses), transport costs are low. If a regional distribution strategy is implemented, the number of national warehouses falls and so do stock levels. However, transport costs rise, due to the increasing distance to market.

FIGURE 1.7   The transport cost/inventory trade-off

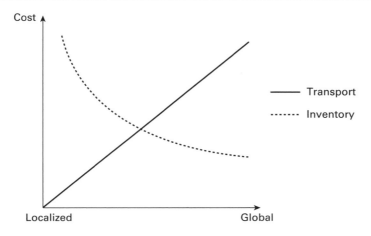

Research suggests that the cost of transport has risen from one-third of overall logistics costs in the 1980s to around two-thirds of costs in the 2010s. This has come about from an increase in transport-related costs (such as congestion, tolls, fuel costs and compliance) as well as a greater underlying demand caused by these changing distribution strategies. It has also derived from an increase in international transport, as more goods are supplied from centralized distribution facilities on a cross-border basis. Figure 1.8 illustrates this trend.

Taking Europe as an example, this has meant that there has been a surge in demand for European distribution centres in geographical central locations, such as the Netherlands. Research by Cap Gemini shows that for the high tech sector, about half of facilities are located in either the Netherlands, Germany or France. By contrast, just under one-quarter are located in large but peripheral markets in the UK, Spain and Italy.

One challenge faced by manufacturers is that while it may be possible to treat Europe as a single market, in reality there is no such thing as a 'Euro-consumer'. Many products still need to be customized to meet national regulations or take into account cultural preferences. From a supply chain management perspective it is preferable for as many goods to be produced in as generic form as possible, so they can be directed to the market where there is greatest demand. Consequently the process of customization should occur late in the supply chain. The distribution centre is often the last stage when the manufacturer can undertake an intervention, and consequently a demand for 'postponed manufacturing' activities has grown. Given that a manufacturer may have outsourced the management of its distribution facility,

FIGURE 1.8   The changing structure of supply chain costs

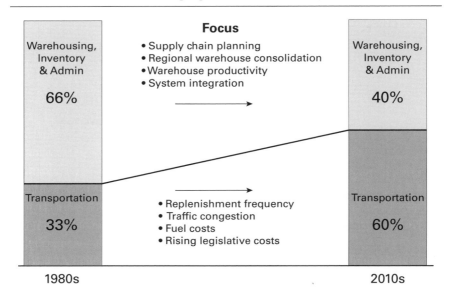

Focus
- Supply chain planning
- Regional warehouse consolidation
- Warehouse productivity
- System integration

Warehousing, Inventory & Admin   **66%**

Warehousing, Inventory & Admin   **40%**

Transportation   **33%**

- Replenishment frequency
- Traffic congestion
- Fuel costs
- Rising legislative costs

Transportation   **60%**

1980s   2010s

FIGURE 1.9   The location of high tech European distribution centres

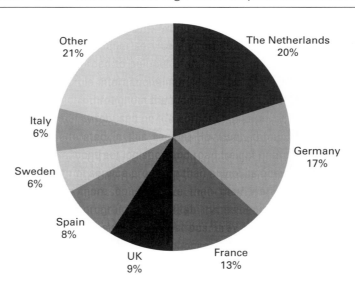

Other 21%

The Netherlands 20%

Italy 6%

Germany 17%

Sweden 6%

Spain 8%

UK 9%

France 13%

SOURCE: Cap Gemini

it is obvious that an LSP should undertake these forms of value-adding activities. In some cases they may be simple, such as 'kitting' (eg adding the right sort of electric plug to an electrical device depending on the country of destination). They may also be highly sophisticated, such as testing and configuring hard disk drives. In one contract UPS Supply Chain Solutions employed musicians in one of its European Distribution Centres to tune guitars imported from Asia to ensure that the customer took the instrument home in a ready-to-play state.

Another consequence for the logistics sector is that this intervention can only be affected cost efficiently by leaving the customization to the latest point within the supply chain. Only manufacturers that are agile enough to stay ahead of the market with sophisticated products and sophisticated supply chains are able to deliver this level of customer service. Much of the customization often occurs at logistics centres as these are closer to the customer than the manufacturers' own plants.

Outsourcing logistics

The outsourcing of logistics functions by manufacturers and retailers over the past 30 years has been one of the defining trends of the global logistics industry. The logistics provider's importance in terms of the overall supply chain has risen considerably with the ongoing trend towards outsourcing of non-core competences.

At the outset, classical outsourcing theory suggested that companies should identify those functions which were non-essential to its operation and then find service providers to take on those activities. This would provide a range of mostly cost-saving benefits as the service provider could, for example, make use of its economies of scale to provide a service more efficiently to an individual client. Outsourcing peripheral roles would also have the benefit of taking staff and assets off the balance sheet.

However, more recently many logistics managers have come to believe that it is in the best interests of their company to outsource certain core activities. This means that whereas previously a manufacturer would not have considered outsourcing its customer care, it is more likely these days to consider using a specialist contact centre provider which it believes can do the job better. It would only retain competencies in which it believed it had a competitive advantage.

FIGURE 1.10   Stages in the logistics outsourcing process

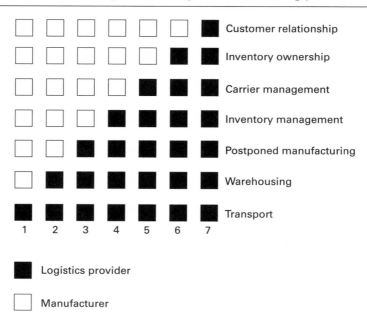

As shown in Figure 1.10 above, the first stage of outsourcing usually involves the transportation function. In many cases (although not all) LSPs will have more buying power than the manufacturer or retailer they are working for, which will allow them to get better deals for trucks and materials. They may also have invested in technology, such as transportation management systems, and be better able to hire and manage driving staff. There is also the question of managing peaks and troughs of demand; working for multiple clients, a transportation provider is better able to manage spare capacity. A manufacturer whose demand is highly seasonal or cyclical, used for only part of the year, will not want to own underutilized transport assets. Finally, outsourcing the ownership of transport assets takes them off the balance sheet, and allows the company to invest in other, more value-adding aspects of its business.

Not all types of transport are outsourced to the same extent. For example, international transport is almost entirely outsourced due to the specialized nature of the business. Local distribution is much more likely to be undertaken in-house, as utilization levels will be much higher and demand more predictable.

The next stage of outsourcing is usually warehousing. This is a labour intensive activity, and one which many companies are happy to be undertaken by a third party. The outsourcing company can also benefit from the LSPs' economies of scale, if it combines their business in a shared, multi-user facility. As mentioned above, the distribution centre can also be used to add value in the form of postponed manufacturing and other services.

These days it has become a strategic decision to outsource logistics activities (not just the transport or warehousing, for example) and the role of logistics providers has changed as they have been allowed to penetrate further into their clients' operations and supply chains.

Reasons behind the outsourcing trend

Companies can outsource their logistics functions for many different reasons, from the purely financial to the expectation of using a company as a catalyst for change management. It is essential that when they go into the outsourcing process they have clearly defined the extent that they wish to engage with their logistics provider. At the most basic level, vehicle contract hire, one of the primary aims will be to take assets off the balance sheet whilst retaining complete control of transport management. At the other end of the spectrum, high end LSPs have a greater element of strategic control, often choosing suppliers, controlling inventory management and fulfilment whilst leaving the client to focus on key competencies such as product development, marketing and production.

Although the global trend is towards more logistics outsourcing, the extent to which this has occurred differs widely from country to country. The so-called 'penetration rate' (ie the level of contract logistics undertaken by logistics service providers as a proportion of overall spend) varies from around 40 per cent in the UK to less than 10 per cent in the Asia Pacific region. In the latter region (China in particular) there is a dearth of qualified local logistics providers and this has hindered the growth of the sector overall.

It is not only countries that have differing rates of outsourcing; market sectors differ – with grocery, non-food and clothing being the most mature and pharmaceuticals and healthcare with higher levels of in-house provision.

In 2012, market research company Transport Intelligence undertook a survey of 105 logistics managers in the manufacturing and retailing sectors. The vast majority of survey participants (85 per cent) were found to outsource an element of their logistics function to a third party provider. The main reasons for this were the cost savings it provided (22 per cent) and the ability to gain access to specialist expertise (22 per cent). Financial benefits in terms of lower capital investment were also highlighted as a driver for outsourcing logistics, by 20 per cent of the sample. With the exception of Aerospace, automotive manufacturers appear least open to outsourcing their logistics operations.

Of those companies (15 per cent) that didn't outsource any logistics activities, the main reasons cited were 'to maintain control' (48 per cent) and the fact that it was considered 'cheaper to keep logistics in-house' (30 per cent).

Fifty-eight per cent of the companies surveyed expected to outsource more of their logistics function in the following year.

Even though outsourcing has now become a fact of life in most industry sectors, that is not to say that LSPs are fulfilling their customers' needs. The survey also showed that, with the exception of 'range of services' and 'geographic coverage', the LSPs used by the sample fell short of shippers' expectations. Shippers appeared to be least satisfied in the areas of price, service levels and reliability.

FIGURE 1.11 3PL/Shipper perceived user value survey

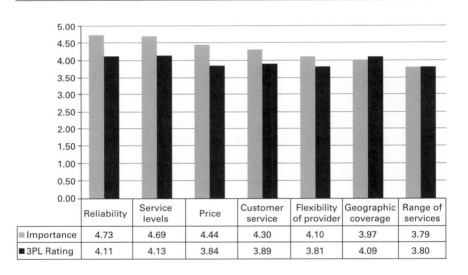

	Reliability	Service levels	Price	Customer service	Flexibility of provider	Geographic coverage	Range of services
Importance	4.73	4.69	4.44	4.30	4.10	3.97	3.79
3PL Rating	4.11	4.13	3.84	3.89	3.81	4.09	3.80

Maximum Score = 5

SOURCE: Transport Intelligence

Evolution towards value-adding services

The need by logistics companies' customers for increasing levels of value has been mirrored by an equal desire by the logistics companies themselves to improve their profit margins. Increasing sophistication and complexity of supply chains is a considerable opportunity for LSPs to achieve this goal by moving away from the provision of commoditized activities. A survey for the European Logistics Association by AT Kearney shows that value added services (VAS) increased considerably in the 2000s, whilst expenditure on logistics as a whole fell.

FIGURE 1.12   Logistics costs and value added services

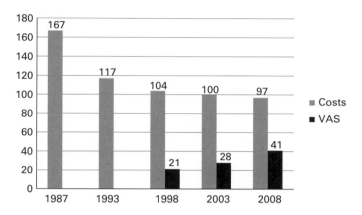

SOURCE: AT Kearney/ELA

Figure 1.13 on the following page outlines this trend, from the early days of logistics outsourcing in the 1980s within fairly simple transactional relationships towards the aspiration of deeper partnerships in which solution development and management is most important. As supply chain complexity increases, so do the services which logistics providers are asked to perform. No longer is logistics seen as a tactical activity, where the gains made are purely measured in terms of transport or warehousing cost savings. Instead, customers become more engaged in the transformational impact on supply chain competitiveness which a logistics provider can achieve.

To offshore or near-source?

As described above, supply chains have become highly globalized as manufacturers and retailers take advantage of low labour and transport costs to 'offshore' production. However, wage inflation and rising transport costs have started to rebalance this particular equation in favour of production at locations much closer to the major consumer markets in the West.

FIGURE 1.13 The evolution of the logistics industry

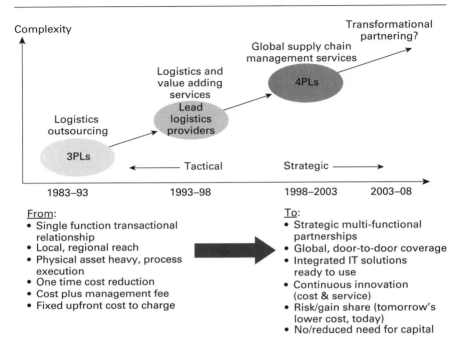

From:
• Single function transactional relationship
• Local, regional reach
• Physical asset heavy, process execution
• One time cost reduction
• Cost plus management fee
• Fixed upfront cost to charge

To:
• Strategic multi-functional partnerships
• Global, door-to-door coverage
• Integrated IT solutions ready to use
• Continuous innovation (cost & service)
• Risk/gain share (tomorrow's lower cost, today)
• No/reduced need for capital

While the BRIC countries (Brazil, Russia, India and China) have played a significant role in global growth for a number of years, other emerging markets are now showing increased promise as potential investment alternatives. There are signs that increased labour costs and skill shortages are eroding China's once-commanding edge over other markets. That said, China continues to benefit from strong domestic growth and acts as a major driver of growth in the global economy.

Separately, increasing transport costs are driving decisions about preferred production locations. 'Near-sourcing' – the effort to control costs by producing in countries adjacent or close to major destination markets – is on the rise. Markets close to the United States and Europe, such as Mexico and Turkey, are attracting increased attention.

Offsetting the near-sourcing trend is the growing attractiveness of emerging economies as consumer markets. Weakened demand in Europe, the United States and other developed economies means emerging markets have been less able to depend on these countries as export markets. This has powered increased trade between emerging markets and led to development of vibrant retail sectors, increasing opportunities for domestic-based logistics operations.

Generally, if a product has a high manufacturing cost and is not heavy, it is better to produce it in a region where labour is cheap. If it has a low manufacturing cost and the goods are heavy, it is better to produce it closer to consumer markets. In 2005, for example, it made economic sense to produce mid-range copiers and assembled TVs in Mexico. Following an increase in labour costs and oil price, however, a shift in the trade-off curve meant that it became more cost-effective to build these types of product in the United States. Likewise, the production of mid-range servers could now be undertaken in Mexico, rather than in Asia.

In the survey of manufacturers and retailers undertaken by Transport Intelligence, 70 per cent of the sample stated that they intend to adopt a hybrid model of sourcing goods from a mix of low cost markets, such as China, as well as countries closer to key consumer markets. The proportion of companies continuing to source goods solely from remote markets is relatively low (21 per cent), while 9 per cent of the survey are now actively seeking to source all of their goods from markets closer to their consumers. This switch from dependence on the more remote markets may, in part, be driven by continued increases in fuel prices.

The process of unbundling and fragmentation of manufacturing which has resulted in the globalization of supply chains is described in detail in the paper 'Relocating the value chain: off-shoring and agglomeration in the global economy', authored by Richard Baldwin and Anthony Venables.

The authors describe how over the last two decades 'unbundling' of production processes has occurred across markets. This initially occurred in Europe, with the accession of Spain and Portugal to the European Union, and continued with its expansion into Central and Eastern Europe. In North America, the establishment of maquiladoras just across the United States/Mexico border had the same effect. The facilitation of longer distance supply chains was helped by the development of information and communications technology, which occurred at the same time as falling transport costs. In Asia, unbundling has been encouraged by the huge disparity in wage costs compared to physical distances. For example, wage costs in China are far lower than those in neighbouring Japan.

In many instances it makes sense to outsource high labour-intensive processes to lower wage cost markets, although if the goods are capital intensive and transport costs high, then outsourcing may not take place. Fluctuating shipping costs can mitigate or enhance the benefits of co-locating various production stages within an end market, influencing management decisions and demonstrating the fluidity of the environment in which these decisions are taken. Timeliness, reliability, information sharing, quality and design, along with wider benefits resulting from shared labour skills and knowledge all mitigate against outsourcing to remote markets.

An interesting part of the analysis shows that in some cases outsourcing to remote locations will only work if a sufficiently large number of production stages are relocated. Otherwise remote companies have the penalty of being distanced from upstream supply partners and the end market. In addition to this, many companies are unwilling to relocate production if other companies are unwilling to follow. This will slow development of manufacturing clusters in developing markets as the necessary production eco-systems do not exist. Japanese manufacturers have been able to overcome this problem in one such developing market, Vietnam, by creating their own supplier parks. This is no doubt facilitated by the strength of the relationships which often exist between suppliers and manufacturers in Japanese supply chains.

This perhaps demonstrates that decisions on relocating production are highly sophisticated. One recent report suggested that in one sector of light manufacturing the differential in wage costs between the UK and China had shrunk from 50 per cent to 15 per cent. Other factors therefore come into play and, very rapidly, sourcing strategies can be changed. At the same time, Asia is transforming from a production market to consumer. This will add an extra layer of complexity into sourcing and offshoring decisions for Western manufacturers.

An industry in transformation: towards consolidation

02

Although mergers and acquisitions have always been a constant factor in the global transport and logistics industries, the last two decades have seen unprecedented levels of activity.

The catalyst for change was the entrance of the European post offices into the global logistics industry in the mid-1990s, in particular the Dutch and German mail operators. They brought with them considerable resources which enabled them to sustain lengthy – and costly – acquisition and integration programmes.

The present market leaders have emerged from a range of backgrounds. Post offices, railways, freight forwarders, integrators, road hauliers/truckers and former in-house distribution businesses have all built integrated service offerings in order to capture the enhanced value which can be attained through building scale operations and extensive portfolios. This has resulted in one of the most marked impacts of consolidation: the merging of traditionally discrete logistics segments.

Consolidation has also occurred within sectors, perhaps most noticeably within the shipping industry. Maersk, for example, built a market leading position through acquisition (P&O Nedlloyd, Sea-Land), although not without problems along the way.

Air transport has perhaps been the only sector to miss out on this seemingly inevitable process of merger. The only acquisition of substance has been that of KLM by Air France. However, recent liberalization of the US/Europe market could see the creation of mega-airlines with true regional and global scope.

The market dynamics of today's logistics industry have resulted from a number of trends which have created opportunity for logistics service providers. This chapter reviews these trends before examining the strategies employed by companies to exploit this opportunity.

Consolidation and fragmentation in the logistics industry

External pressures for industry consolidation

The fundamental changes in the logistics industry have been driven by a number of imperatives, both demand- and supply-side led. The speed at which change has taken place over the last decade is as a result of the mutual benefit and opportunities to both logistics service providers and users which these trends have created.

The three charts below (Figure 2.1) show how the transport and logistics industry has evolved in the last three decades. Right up until the 1970s and 80s each of the functions highlighted were largely discrete, with little overlap. The reason for this was partly due to a lack of sophistication in the demands of customers; partly due to national regulations which favoured, for example, in-house operations against outsourced; and partly due to the high levels of fragmentation which meant that few companies had the management expertise, resources or backing to expand aggressively through acquisition.

In stage 2, the largest companies, already dominating their national markets, expand into neighbouring sectors. The Dutch post office, for example, acquired Australian transport group TNT, providing it with express and logistics capabilities; Deutsche Post bought international express operator DHL and a range of domestic express parcels companies before subsequently expanding into the logistics sector; Deutsche Bahn acquired road, forwarding and contract logistics specialist Schenker and subsequently Bax Global. Management justify these decisions on the level of synergy which can be achieved. Acquisition strategies are fuelled by cheap money and pressure from shareholders.

Stage 3 shows the reverse pressures which have existed since the recession of 2008 (and in some cases before). In several instances, due to the absence of expected synergies or poor integration, companies have sold off their loss-making acquisitions. TNT, for example, sold first its underperforming logistics operations and then split its express operations from its mail. DHL was forced to withdraw from the US domestic express market (as well

FIGURE 2.1 Merger and fragmentation of logistics functions

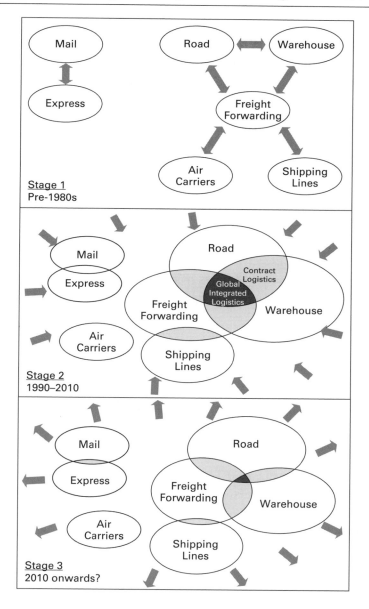

as domestic markets in the UK, France and elsewhere) losing billions of dollars in the process. The harsher economic environment could be said to have shown up weaknesses in either business models or management.

However, large diversified groups, such as DHL, UPS, Deutsche Bahn and SNCF continue to operate despite the fact that there is little integration between many of the functions they provide. This lack of synergy makes disposals more likely if and when management come under pressure from shareholders.

Putting to one side the claims of synergy, acquisitions have delivered benefits in the form of diversification. UPS, for example, has created a much more defensive business model by developing an international express offering, largely by inorganic growth. Its profits have been helped by the development of Asia as an economic powerhouse, even when the US domestic parcels sector was stagnating. Likewise, at various times in the past decade, its forwarding and logistics capabilities have proved to be a useful source of revenue and profits, despite initial painful integration.

Ambitions to build diversified transport groups still exist. French-based group Norbert Dentressangle has, for example, added contract logistics capabilities to its road freight operations, and more recently freight forwarding. However, others, despite access to capital, strong management and plenty of opportunity, have eschewed this approach. Expeditors, a pure play freight forwarder based in the United States, has successfully concentrated on organic growth within its sector and has been one of the best performing companies in the industry.

The push for globalization

Many logistics companies with the necessary resources have chosen to globalize their operations in line with the changing requirements of their clients. Manufacturers and retailers have increased both the level of global sourcing and the scope of the markets which they supply. This has been enabled by the reduction of barriers to world trade facilitated by such organizations as the EU, NAFTA and the WTO, as detailed in Chapter 1. The rising levels of international trade, and the increasingly integrated nature of supply chains, has created a need for logistics companies which can offer sophisticated services on a worldwide basis, including IT systems which can provide global visibility.

Outsourcing manufacturing to regions of low cost production has been gathering pace for many years, although the decision of where to source goods from or where to locate production facilities takes into account a wide variety of different factors, labour costs just being one.

For instance, if time to market is of prime importance then the decision may be made to 'near-source', that is, locate production in Central and Eastern Europe or in the Mediterranean region. Nowhere is this more apparent than in the clothing sector, where a whole market of 'fast fashion' has developed.

Retailers buying clothing may choose to near-source some product lines in order to meet short-term market trends. Product can be manufactured and delivered in weeks, rather than the three months which is usual for goods to be brought in from China. Of this lead time, a transit could comprise a month at sea rather than a few days by road from a comparable supplier in Eastern Europe.

Consequently, the response of logistics providers has reflected this. To continue the fashion logistics theme, logistics service providers have needed to develop operations which can move goods to Western markets in a fast and effective manner. This has meant establishing operations in Eastern Europe, North Africa, Latin America or the Asia Pacific region to undertake value-adding activities such as quality control and packing as well as having the infrastructure in place to move the goods in an appropriate manner.

Whether in Eastern Europe or Asia Pacific, one thing is certain: those LSPs which have not adapted to the outsourcing of manufacturing to remote locations face a very uncertain future. The European manufacturing sector has undergone a long-term decline, although conversely the transport and logistics costs associated with getting goods to consumer markets in North America or Europe are rising. This has provided the global operators with greater opportunities to exploit larger revenue streams whilst smaller operators have continued to struggle.

Logistics companies will in the future be expected to go even further afield by their clients. At the lower value end of the product spectrum, China is starting to lose out to even lower cost countries in Asia Pacific such as Vietnam. For low value production it could be said that a 'ripple' is moving out throughout the region, with China as its centre, although it will be many years before this trend starts to have any real impact. Crudely it could be surmised that China may end up being squeezed at the bottom of the market by lower cost rivals and in the middle of the market by its Western customers' supply chain requirements (time to market/inventory cost). This will eventually result in a focus on higher quality, higher value products where more expensive but quicker air cargo (or indeed a mix of sea and air cargo), are options. For logistics companies it will reinforce the trend to develop operations in remote and difficult countries, requiring a particular set of skills.

Liberalization of markets

The liberalization of the European postal markets has been one of the driving forces behind the high level of M&A activity in the late 1990s and early 2000s. The market has been progressively opened up to private sector competition, although it is more obvious in some markets – such as the UK and the Netherlands – than others. However, the threat of competitors entering what previously had been monopolistic markets was the key reason for mail operators to diversify their revenues. This led the Dutch, German and subsequently the British, French, Austrian and Scandinavian post offices to embark on extensive buying campaigns, which added express parcels networks and, in the case of Deutsche Post, extensive logistics operations to their portfolio.

There has also been deregulation in Europe's rail industry, which prompted some state-owned railways to prepare for a more competitive environment. ABX, a subsidiary of Belgium's SNCB, embarked on a hugely ambitious (and ultimately flawed) programme, building an extensive European logistics group. Deutsche Bahn, Germany's railways, acquired one of the world's biggest logistics companies, Schenker, and also US-based global forwarder Bax Global. This was in addition to complementary rail operators throughout Europe, such as EWS Railways in the UK. SNCF, France's national rail operator, meanwhile, has acquired logistics giant, Geodis, also French-based.

Europe has not been the only market to see major changes through liberalization. Although deregulation of the US postal market is highly unlikely, the trucking market has already seen a major transformation. The Motor Carrier Act of 1935 stipulated that companies that wanted to haul freight across state lines on a for-hire basis had to obtain authority from the Interstate Commerce Commission. Prices were determined through a collective ratemaking process made legal by federal antitrust exemption. Following deregulation starting in 1980, interstate trucking became much easier, as did the setting of competitive rates. This had the effect of a huge shake-up and it is estimated that more than three-quarters of the US's largest carriers in 1980 have since gone out of business.

There are now efforts being made to liberalize the US–Mexico cross-border trucking market – in the teeth of strong opposition from Teamster Unions. A pilot project will permit US trucks to cross the Mexican border. In return, a certain number of Mexican trucks will be allowed to deliver freight to destinations beyond the present 20-mile limit inside the US border. At the moment only a small number of licensed trucks can deliver freight between the two countries. This means that there have to be drop-off points at the border, where freight is transferred before it can progress. This results in extra trucks on the road, congestion, delays and 'over-handling' of shipments, which invariably leads to increased cost.

Even the trend towards outsourcing of logistics, one of the prime catalysts for the change in the industry in the past three decades, can be attributed to deregulation. In many markets, in-house transport operations were favoured by regulators (and to some degree this is still the case). However, since reducing the protection of in-house operations the third party logistics (3PL) sector has emerged, allowing manufacturers and retailers to focus on their core competences whilst providing new impetus to the transport and distribution industry.

In order to take advantage of this trend, logistics companies have sought to build skills, capabilities and geographic scope. The fact that in some markets (such as in the United States) it is estimated that only around 20 per cent of logistics activities are outsourced, shows that a huge potential still exists.

Product differentiation, sector focus and supplier rationalization

Many segments within the logistics industry, such as road haulage and ware-housing, are commoditized or with low barriers to entry and exit, such as freight forwarding. This has led to the market being typified at the grass-roots level by low margins and high competition.

The largest companies have sought to address this challenge by making targeted acquisitions which increases their exposure to vertical sectors or supply chain segments in which there is less competition, whilst at the same time building on their own competitive advantages, such as access to finance, intellectual capital, IT capabilities and global scale.

For example, the pharmaceutical sector has attracted considerable interest from LSPs in recent years. The sector is very sophisticated in its logistics needs, requiring high security distribution, a high degree of regulatory compliance, consignment tracking capabilities as well as, in some cases, temperature control and monitoring.

Rather than attempt to build these capabilities in-house, many LSPs decided to buy niche specialists who already had the expertise and licences. Below are some of the most recent examples of such acquisitions:

- UPS acquires Pieffe Group in Italy;
- Kerry Logistics acquires Trustspeed Medicine Logistics;
- Forward Air Corporation acquires Total Quality in US;
- Geodis acquires Pharmalog in Europe.

One of the earliest companies to enter this sector was Exel , the forerunner to DHL Supply Chain, which acquired a number of pharma logistics specialists in 2004 and in the process built a market-leading position.

In addition to vertical sectors, some LSPs have sought to add functionality at additional stages of the supply chain. Perhaps the most relevant and recent examples of this involve the e-commerce sector. For example, UPS acquired European e-commerce specialist Kiala to give it business-to-consumer (B2C) downstream supply chain delivery capabilities in Belgium, France, Luxembourg, the Netherlands and Spain. Kiala had developed a platform that enabled e-commerce retailers to offer their shoppers the option of having goods delivered to a convenient retail location.

Other examples include La Poste's acquisition of e-fulfilment specialist ORIUM and TNT Post's acquisition of e-retail company Kowin. At the time, TNT Post commented that the acquisition would, 'develop the required capabilities for the entire e-commerce chain faster and quickly expand its offering to new industries and markets'.

Additionally, logistics companies are increasingly being asked to provide a range of value-added services, rather than just one element of transportation or warehousing. Using a smaller number of logistics suppliers benefits the manufacturer or retailer, by reducing the amount of supplier administration required. It also allows them to leverage their buying power to drive down costs. Acquisition is one way in which a logistics supplier can expand its range of capabilities to meet these ever increasing demands and improve margins.

Supplier rationalization will benefit the larger logistics companies as scale players are more likely to remain on shortlists for tendering, reducing the level of competition and allowing them to access logistics spend which was previously spread over a greater number of suppliers. This helps to increase revenues as well as the bargaining power which an LSP has with its carriers. This in turn can improve transportation management margins.

Options for growth

At present, acquisition is the most favoured route towards building global portfolios of integrated services. However, there are other alternatives which are available to logistics providers looking to offer a wider range of services to clients.

Organic growth

Although organic growth is viewed as being the safest way in which to develop presence in new markets, in the race to build European and global platforms it has become increasingly unfashionable. Acquisitions delivered immediate revenue streams and an operational presence which organic growth could not. However, with the number of appropriate target companies reducing, the absence of 'cheap money' in the financial markets, and with many companies' acquisition programmes nearing completion, management are now increasingly focusing on organic growth to deliver sustainable revenues and profits.

Alliances

Alliances are a quick and easy way to offer clients enhanced services in different geographies or to add functionality. They are very common in the freight-forwarding sector as they allow national or regionally based operators to compete effectively on a global basis with owned-network providers such as DHL Global Forwarding or Kuehne + Nagel.

Examples of where an alliance adds functionality include a tie-up between express carrier TNT and US trucking company Con-way. TNT's US operations mainly consist of international express delivery services to and from the United States and Canada. For delivery within the United States and Canada, the company utilizes a combination of regional partners, own operations and a relationship with Con-way, established in 2009, that provide less-than-truckload (LTL) services from TNT's main gateways: New York, Los Angeles, Chicago and Miami.

Alliances work best in stable, conservative markets where the threat of competitors acquiring alliance members is low. This obviously has not been the case in the global logistics market in the last few years. Most recently in 2012 a forwarding network, World Air Cargo Organization, had to restructure its membership in Africa/Middle East when one of its independent members, Swift, was taken over by a global player, DSV.

Another weakness of the alliance model is the potential of a lack of strategic direction. Individual members may have different opinions on the future for the alliance as well as having their own distinct corporate priorities and identity. This often inhibits investment in the network infrastructure, both physical and IT. If this is the case, the alliance will have little chance of competing against fully owned and integrated players and can leave the partners vulnerable to acquisition.

Joint ventures

A joint venture (JV) is a formal relationship in which two or more parties create an entity with a shared stock ownership. JVs are typically used by companies which have complementary services or attributes to exploit a particular market.

Joint ventures were essential in the Chinese market, where legislation forced foreign-invested companies to partner with local companies. Since deregulation of the market this is no longer an obligation and many have chosen to establish wholly owned foreign enterprises (WOFE) or buy out their JV partners (such as UPS buying its JV with Sinotrans; and FedEx with DTW). However, many still see advantages from JVs as they provide local market knowledge, contacts with local officials and a knowledge of regulations. Most notably this includes DHL's long-term relationship with Chinese logistics and express giant, Sinotrans.

'Piggybacking'

Expansion by 'piggybacking' involves developing services geographically on the back of the needs of a key client. This has become a frequently used mode of expansion due to the internationalization of manufacturing and retailing. Using existing logistics suppliers has various advantages:

- There is already a relationship in place which provides a level of trust that otherwise would need to be developed if an unknown supplier was contracted.

- There is often a shared business culture between senior management of both companies.

- When locating production to an undeveloped, remote market, sophisticated logistics practices may not exist.

The global expansion of UPS Supply Chain Solutions, Schneider and Penske from the United States, Geodis from France and DHL from Germany has involved piggybacking on existing domestic clients. One of the obvious benefits of piggybacking is the immediate revenue stream that it brings, along with the potential to leverage the investment costs in the operation across a range of other clients.

Is acquisition worthwhile?

For many years the global logistics market has been consolidating due to the reasons outlined above. However, the risk element of the trend has never really been examined in the race for scale and global scope. The number of logistics companies which have been able to grow 'successfully' through acquisition is limited.

On the whole, large companies seem to be better at acquisitions than smaller ones, although there are exceptions to this statement. Larger companies are often already experienced at undertaking acquisitions, as well as the job of integration. They are also able employ appropriate levels of manpower to oversee the integration, thereby releasing the value of the acquisition. Being global already, they are also often better able to understand and overcome cultural barriers.

Smaller logistics companies do not have this luxury. Into this bracket must fall many of the UK companies which expanded into Europe in the late 1990s. At that time the prevailing belief was that better opportunities were to be had in the mainland European market as the domestic logistics market was becoming increasingly competitive and mature. However, providers such as Wincanton, Christian Salvesen, TDG (both now Norbert Dentressangle), Hays (now Kuehne + Nagel), and even Exel (now DHL) all at one point or another ran into problems. All these companies, with the exception of Wincanton, have now been taken over by larger European rivals.

However, being very big is no guarantee of success. DHL, for example, failed to turn around its domestic express operation in the United States and this cost the company several billion dollars. Rival logistics operator ABX Logistics (owned by Belgian Railways) also faced difficulties following its acquisition programme, and it was forced to sell off poorly performing companies, and then was sold itself. Similarly, German logistics company Thiel also expanded too quickly and as a result lost its management and then sold off many of its constituent parts.

Acquisition strategies

'Blockbuster' deals

Since the 1990s, a number of global logistics companies have undertaken one or more 'blockbuster' deals to acquire immediate scale. The acquisition of GeoLogistics by Agility, TNT by the Dutch post office, or Deutsche Post's acquisition of Danzas, AEI, Airborne and Exel are examples of these types of deals. They have then proceeded to 'in-fill' gaps in capabilities or geographies with a sequence of smaller acquisitions.

The advantage of this approach is that it gives the company immediate scale and market presence, therefore providing competitive advantage over smaller players. It also reduces the level of M&A activity required in identifying a series of potential targets, as well as approaching, negotiating with them and eventually integrating them into the parent company. It may also reduce cultural barriers if the acquisition target is from a similar business background.

However, there are many disadvantages too. Even the largest-scale player does not have consistent depth of services across all geographies and segments. Therefore, whereas small, focused acquisitions can identify high quality players, which can be easily integrated into a larger company, scale acquisitions can leave buyers with ongoing management problems due to weak or badly performing business units.

Evolution strategies

An alternative to the 'blockbuster' scenario is the evolution model. The early stages of an expansion strategy usually focus around increasing presence in the home market, and consolidating market position in a core competence. When this has been achieved, the company develops into associated competences and markets in close proximity or with similar attributes, through a range of alliances, joint ventures or focused acquisitions. In this way, a portfolio of capabilities and markets can be built without the risks involved in a scale acquisition in areas where the company has no prior experience or skills. This approach is usually termed 'bolt-on' acquisition.

In this respect post offices have a natural advantage over competitors in other logistics fields. They already have market dominance in their own sectors due to the fact that in most cases they have monopoly or near-monopoly positions. They therefore have no need to focus on building or protecting their own core businesses and can diversify, using the profits gained in their home market to fund the acquisitions.

Some companies have found that building a major global presence without solid foundations carries high levels of risk. ABX Logistics and German logistics companies Thiel and D.Logistics experienced severe financial difficulties due to the underperformance of acquired companies. In addition they did not have the resources required to integrate the group into a coherent entity, therefore unlocking the value of a global or European network. One of the major risks involved in acquisition is the migration of key employees and clients – this is especially the case with freight-forwarding companies where client loyalty often revolves around personal contacts rather than corporate relationships.

TABLE 2.1   Major acquisitions in the global logistics industry 1996 to date

Year	Acquirer	Target	Geography	Approx cost
2012	Russian Railways	GEFCO	Europe	€800m
2012	Ingram Micro	Brightpoint	Global	$840m
2010	Norbert Dentressangle	TDG	Europe	€232.8m
2008	SNCF Geodis	IBM Logistics	Global	Not disclosed
2007	Toll	Baltrans	Asia Pacific	€300m
2007	Norbert Dentressangle	Christian Salvesen	Europe	€365.1m
2007	CEVA	EGL	Global	$2bn
2005	Agility	Geologistics	Global	$454m
2005	Deutsche Bahn	Bax Global	Global	$1.1bn
2005	Kuehne + Nagel	ACR Logistics	Europe	€440m
2005	DP-DHL	Exel	Global	€5.6bn
2005	Maersk	P&O Nedlloyd	Global	€2.3bn
2004	UPS	Menlo Worldwide	Global	$150m
2004	Exel	Tibbett & Britten	Global	€480m
2003	DP-DHL	Airborne Express	USA	$1.05bn
2002	Deutsche Bahn	Stinnes (Schenker)	Europe/Global	€2.5bn
2002	Deutsche Post	DHL	Global	€2.44bn
1999	Ocean	NFC (Exel)	Global	€2.2bn
1999	Maersk	Sea-Land	Global	$800m
1999	Deutsche Post	AEI	USA/Global	€1.2bn
1998	Deutsche Post	Danzas	Europe/Global	€1.3bn
1996	TNT Post Group	TNT	Global	€1.2bn

SOURCE: Transport Intelligence

The emergence of the 'mega-carrier'

The consolidation of the global logistics industry was forecast as long ago as 1991 by Cooper, Browne & Peters (*European Logistics*). They believed that companies from a range of different logistics backgrounds would converge in terms of services offered and geographic scope. This has been shown to be the case as the largest freight forwarders, distribution companies, express operators, shipping lines, in-house operators and, of course, post offices have engaged on a strategy of developing into one-stop shop providers of multiple functions.

Figure 2.2 shows the original positioning of the major logistics segments. From their relative starting points there has been convergence towards the 'mega-carrier quadrant'. Distribution companies in particular have tended to offer clients the most sophisticated logistics activities. However, this has largely been on a regional or national basis and contrasts with freight forwarders and express operators which have large global networks, but offer limited products or services.

FIGURE 2.2   The 'mega-carrier' quadrant

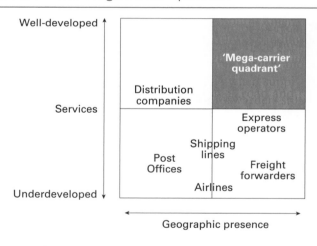

SOURCE: Cooper, Browne & Peters in *European Logistics*

As detailed above, the trend towards the development of a multi-service portfolio has been driven by a number of demand- and supply-side factors. The result of this has been a frenetic period of acquisition as companies have extended their capabilities horizontally into adjoining logistics segments as well as geographically. For many companies, with a few notable exceptions, the next step has been to integrate these capabilities in order to provide customers with cohesive solutions. Deutsche Post DHL acquired international express capabilities through DHL, land transport and freight forwarding through Danzas, air freight operations by buying AEI and distribution operations through Exel, which was itself a merger of Exel and Tibbett & Britten.

It should be noted that total integration of all their acquired distribution, forwarding, express parcels etc is not the goal of these companies. Rather they seek to have the processes and networks in place which can be used where necessary for a limited number of 'blue chip' clients with sophisticated, regional or global logistics needs.

Although to begin with many companies were aiming to position themselves in the top right 'mega-carrier' quadrant, the last two economic recessions have led to a counter trend. Falling volumes exposed poor acquisitions or weak integration and management. The figure shows that whilst some companies are still acquisitively building global presence, others including even DHL, TNT and Wincanton, have retreated towards the core competency/ home market quadrant.

FIGURE 2.3   Reversal of the mega-carrier trend?

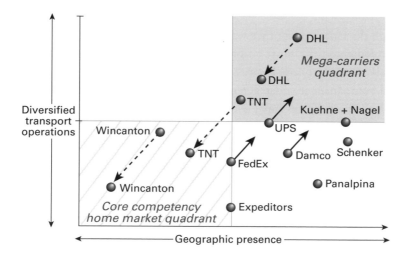

The key logistics segments

Post offices

European postal operators have been responsible for a significant proportion of the acquisition activity in the logistics market. The first post office to recognize that there was a major opportunity to develop a worldwide logistics presence was Royal Dutch Post, acquiring the express parcels and logistics company TNT in 1996.

The reasons behind the expansion of the post offices can be summarized as follows:

- Their domestic markets were in the process of liberalization and therefore the monopolistic advantage they enjoyed was passing. Diversifying into other parts of the logistics industry was a way of maximizing their brand, presence and resources, as well as utilizing the strong cash flows which they generate.

- The extension of domestic parcels operations on a European and global basis was a natural progression for postal operators to take advantage of the increased internationalization of goods flows.

- They recognized that they were in a good position to exploit the trend towards integrated, global supply chains by co-ordinating flows of goods, information and funds.

- E-commerce has become the major growth sector in the express and logistics industry. Post Offices are very well placed to offer fulfilment services and 'last mile' delivery.

Although the Dutch post office was first to acquire internationally, Deutsche Post implemented the most ambitious expansion plan. By buying Danzas, AEI, DHL, Exel, Airborne Express (since sold), and subsequently a multitude of in-fill companies, it constructed a global mail, express and logistics company. Other post offices have tried to follow suit on a more modest basis. Royal Mail acquired a European network, General Parcel, for in the region of €750 million, and La Poste (through subsidiary GeoPost) took a controlling interest in DPD.

Railways

The European railways sector has also become a factor in the logistics acquisition market. This is partly as a result of liberalization of rail markets, which has seen competition increase on a domestic and international level.

The management of Deutsche Bahn (German Railways) also had the ambition of arresting the long-term decline of rail as a modal choice by acquiring freight forwarders and logistics providers (which control a large proportion of cargo volumes). In this way, they believed, railways could leverage their sizeable resources to ensure that rail was not further marginalized. By doing this, railway companies would be able to acquire customers directly, thereby also increasing their level of value add (and hence improve margins). The risk of such a strategy was the alienation of existing client forwarders, which following such a move become de facto competitors.

In the execution of this strategy, Deutsche Bahn has been the most aggressive of the European rail operators. It made significant acquisitions both to expand the geographic scope of its operations throughout Europe through its DB Logistics division (including Brunner Railway Services in Switzerland; EWS in the UK; Transfesa in Spain; joint ventures in Sweden and Poland) as well as expanding its Schenker road/freight forwarding operation. The latter was transformed through the acquisition of global forwarder Bax Global.

However, Deutsche Bahn's ultimate plan of a listing of its shares on a stock exchange in a similar way to that of Deutsche Post ran into political problems. There was a fear amongst politicians and unions that by turning Deutsche Bahn into a fully commercial entity through an IPO, key interest groups would suffer. This highlighted the tensions between those who wanted full privatization and the welcome influx of foreign capital, and those who saw such a move as leading to the destruction of an important public service. Ultimately the latter forces won and the chief executive and architect of these plans, Hartmut Mehdorn, eventually left the company.

Not to be outdone, French railway operator SNCF has also carried out aggressive inorganic expansion in the logistics and express sectors. Already a major shareholder in French logistics company Geodis, in 2008 it acquired the remaining stake. The deal was a major part of its plan to create an international multimodal operator in the field of logistics and transportation. Following this, it also acquired IBM's internal global logistics operations, managing approximately €1 billion per year of IBM's logistics costs worldwide. These were then integrated into Geodis's existing operations to make it a global player.

Freight forwarders

Freight forwarders have a number of natural advantages in the present logistics environment. They have global operations and can manage complex goods flows through the information systems they have built. This has meant that they have been amongst the largest beneficiaries from the globalization trend.

Freight forwarders achieve considerable competitive advantage through scale, as the more volumes they control, the greater is their bargaining power with carriers. Therefore many acquisitions by freight forwarders have been made to build presence on certain traffic lanes. An example of this is CH Robinson's acquisition of Phoenix International which gave it an enhanced presence on the Asia-North America routes.

There are a number of other reasons why freight forwarders have been prominent in the acquisition market. For many years they have been under pressure from international parcels carriers which have succeeded in acquiring most of their high-margin small consignment business. Without being able to offer the client value-adding services, freight forwarders risk being marginalized. Therefore the more innovative companies have increased the number of services that they supply, and increased the depth of relationship which they have with their clients, from ad hoc to long term. This has been achieved not least through the acquisition of capabilities.

The very fact that forwarders already have in place global networks has also made them highly attractive to logistics players which have developed from a domestic or regional focus. There are numerous examples of this, but CEVA's takeover of EGL and Geodis's acquisition of TNT Freight Management (Wilson) and German forwarder Rohde & Liesenfeld are amongst the most prominent.

Parcels networks

The main global and European parcels operators have all been highly acquisitive over the last 20 years. The primary reason why many parcels operators have chosen acquisition over alliance is that it gives them a greater level of strategic control. In the parcels industry it is essential that there is consistency of products, pricing, service and quality on a regional and global basis. Hence Royal Mail and GeoPost both chose to buy existing franchise operations, General Parcel and DPD, rather than work in partnership with them. UPS, TNT and Deutsche Post DHL have also been highly acquisitive, and for Royal Mail and GeoPost the threat of network partners being bought by competitors was also a driving force.

UPS has been one of the most acquisitive of the parcels companies, investing billions of dollars in building an owned distribution network. It has also developed a substantial logistics presence in and outside of the United States. Its prime reason for this was that it wanted to take advantage of its relationships with many large shippers, as well as benefit from the fast growth of the logistics industry. This was especially the case in sectors such as service parts logistics or high tech logistics where it could integrate its own express operations with value-adding activities. The company also acquired freight-forwarding capacity through the purchase of Fritz Companies and Menlo Worldwide Forwarding.

The major integrators have focused their acquisition strategies both on Europe and developing markets. Although varying geographically, the main targets have been domestic express carriers.

In Europe two of the biggest acquisitions occurred in the UK: in 2006 FedEx bought the UK Express Company ANC for £120 million. The deal marked the US integrator's return to the domestic express markets in Europe after an absence of more than 10 years. In 2005 UPS acquired UK package delivery company Lynx Express Ltd, for £55.5 million.

The UK has seen consolidation of its own domestic express sector, which has historically been highly fragmented. This trend is likely to be ongoing, not only in the UK but also in other European countries.

UPS has also bought in Eastern Europe – Polish Messenger Service, Stolica SA. TNT, meanwhile, acquired in Spain TG+, a leading Spanish domestic distribution company. In 2012, UPS attempted to take over TNT, but this was thwarted by the European competition authorities.

Outside of Europe, the main acquisitions have occurred in China and India. In China:

- In 2005 UPS acquired its express operations from Sinotrans, its joint venture partner. The deal was valued around €100 million.

- In 2006 FedEx Corporation acquired DTW Group's 50 per cent share of the FedEx-DTW International Priority express joint venture and its domestic express network in China for US $400 million.

- In 2007 TNT completed the acquisition of Hoau, a leading freight and parcels delivery company in China. This was subsequently sold in 2013.

- DHL prefers to work through its joint venture partner, Sinotrans.

In India:

- In 2006 FedEx acquired Indian air freight company Prakash Air Freight Pvt. Ltd (PAFEX) for $30 million.

- DHL has progressively acquired stakes in Indian air express company Blue Dart since 2004.

- UPS has a joint venture with Indian operator Jetair.

In-house logistics companies

Many of the largest contract logistics players have grown out of former in-house operations. This includes Wincanton (Unigate) and Easydis (from French retailer Casino). The German market in particular has a number of huge in-house operations some of which have been 'corporatized', either remaining in the ownership of the parent company or becoming independent. The latter provides the greatest opportunity as it allows the company to tender for business amongst competitors of its former parent company without any clash of interest. Arvato (subsidiary of Bertelsmann) is one of the best known.

Airlines

Airlines have been one of the few industry segments to eschew mergers and acquisitions. One of the main reasons for this is their position in the supply chain relative to their main clients, the freight forwarders. It is estimated that forwarders control about 85 per cent of airlines' cargo revenues and attempts to develop value-added services or extend the level of functionality have been resisted. The reason for this is simple enough: an airline which starts to offer a door-to-door service to shippers comes into direct competition with the forwarding community. Whereas 'disintermediation' has worked in other parts of the industry (for example, low cost airlines sell direct to consumers via the web), no air cargo operator has yet decided that it is in their interests to alienate their existing client base.

A further problem which exists for many air cargo operations of flag-carrying airlines is that freight has a low priority within their company's overall strategies. Routes and frequencies are driven by passenger volumes, rather than belly-hold freight, even though the two markets need not be in complete synchronization. Freight capacity has in the past been often sold on a marginal cost basis, as a by-product of the passenger services.

Finally, regulation of the industry has not allowed the larger airlines to develop comprehensive owned global networks which would be able to service all the needs of shippers. In the past airlines have been forced into developing marketing alliances with other airlines as an alternative to organic growth or acquisition. This may be about to change, as the negotiation of a US/European 'open skies' agreement could be a catalyst to mergers such as that between KLM and Air France or BA and Iberia. One of the results of this could be coherent cargo strategies with the development of products which reach beyond the freight-forwarding community.

Shipping lines

The shipping industry is highly cyclical. Despite the sustained growth of volumes from China to Europe and the United States, the industry has been plagued with oversupply with intermittent plunges in rates and consequent problems of unprofitability.

The business of shipping is also highly capital intensive, and consequently many lines have sought to create economies of scale both in the form of larger ships but also with larger fleets. Although some lines, such as MSC, have successfully grown organically, others have bought market share through acquisition. This has been with the intent to rationalize activities, reduce costs and minimize financial risks through the scale this would, in theory, deliver.

The largest example of this in the past decade has been the purchase of Safmarine, Sea-Land and, in 2005, P&O Nedlloyd by Maersk. Despite this, the latter acquisition was largely regarded as a failure. The second and third largest companies continued to gain market share (MSC and CMA CGM respectively), whilst Maersk lost customers at the same time as failing to exploit any potential economies of scale.

The other major acquisition of the last few years was the purchase of CP Ships by Hapag-Lloyd in 2005. With this the company became one of the top five shipping companies in the world.

Many shipping lines were originally reticent in developing logistics services that would potentially bring them into conflict with forwarders. However, freight forwarders have less leverage over shipping lines than they do over air cargo carriers, as a much larger proportion of shippers (the manufacturers and retailers) book direct. This has allowed companies such as Maersk, NYK and APL to build logistics divisions which provide services such as consolidation at origin and distribution on a global basis.

The major shipping lines have a considerable interest in developing logistics organizations. They provide a key source of extra revenue with the potential for higher margins through value-added activities.

Road freight

Europe

One of the most obvious industry segments to develop both functionally and geographically has been road haulage. As providers of capacity, road haulage companies offer a largely commoditized product with little opportunity to add value without expanding its associated services.

The major problem for companies involved in road haulage, whether domestic or international, is that the market is highly fragmented with few barriers to entry or exit. The economies of scale are limited which allows small, low overhead owner-drivers to compete effectively with large fleeted companies. Information and communications technology, which for a brief period had become a differentiator, is, at a basic level, now widely available. On an international basis, low cost hauliers from Central and Eastern Europe, which enjoy lower fuel and labour costs, are more competitive than indigenous providers which are increasingly burdened with a range of social costs and regulations.

This market environment has prompted many of the larger logistics companies to migrate to a business model where there are higher barriers to market entry. UK companies have been at the fore in evolving into contract logistics providers where there is a requirement for:

- higher levels of capital to operate;
- more sophisticated IT capabilities;
- a higher degree of intellectual capital;
- wider geographic scope;
- higher brand equity.

Perhaps the best example of a company with its roots in the road haulage industry in Europe was Exel, which developed from the nationalized UK company, NFC. It transformed itself into a contract logistics player, with operations in Europe and the United States. Following its merger with Ocean Group, Exel became a full service logistics provider with a global network and the capability to integrate its forwarding and logistics activities for multinational clients, before eventually being bought by DHL.

Another way in which road hauliers have been able to differentiate themselves has been by developing less-than-truckload (LTL) (otherwise known as groupage) networks. This relies on a large capital investment to build presence on a European-wide basis, as well as the IT to support the flows of goods.

With a complex of depots, companies can construct a hub-and-spoke model ensuring frequent services, but at a lower cost. This model is hardly new, but it is now emerging as a key strategy employed by the large logistics companies to increase their grip on the road freight/trucking market.

European logistics company Kuehne + Nagel has indicated its plans to expand its already large road freight network by acquiring medium-sized road freight companies. Alongside companies such as DHL, France's GEFCO and Geodis, and Denmark's DSV, the big European logistics service providers seem to regard LTL as both an essential part of their wider service offering and as a growth opportunity in itself.

North America

North American (mainly US) trucking companies have focused largely on creating scale, and increasing functionality has been of secondary importance. There have been some spectacularly big acquisitions in recent years, driven in part by the entrance of UPS and FedEx into the market.

The truckload sector is highly fragmented, with more than 500,000 carriers operating in North America. The majority of these carriers are smaller operators, working with less than 20 trucks. Consolidation in the truckload sector will mean carriers are able to increase capacity and volume across their networks, as well as broadening their geographical presence. This is particularly attractive for regional LTL players looking to increase scale and move into national LTL markets.

The LTL sector is much more consolidated than the truckload sector, with less than 10 companies in North America accounting for more than two-thirds of the industry revenue. National carriers are driving consolidation by moving into the retail markets in search of additional growth and more opportunities for profitable growth. However, the lines between the long-haul market and the regional market are being blurred as regional carriers push into the national market.

The most notable acquisitions in recent years include:

- Con-way Inc's 2007 acquisition of Contract Freighters, Inc (CFI), a privately held North American truckload carrier in a transaction valued at $750 million.

- FedEx's 2006 acquisition of the LTL operations of Watkins Motor Lines for $780 million.

- The 2005 UPS acquisition of Overnite Corporation for approximately $1.25 billion.

- Also in 2005, Yellow Roadway Corporation (itself a merger of two giant trucking companies) acquired USF Corporation in a transaction valued at $1.37 billion.

CASE STUDY   Deutsche Post DHL: the emergence of a global powerhouse

---

Deutsche Post DHL (DP DHL) has its origins in the former German state mail, telecoms and post saving bank. In 1989, the German government decided to split these business functions and give them separate management structures. In 1995 legislation was passed which turned Deutsche Post from a government department into a private company. This enabled the management to work towards full privatization although in 2013 around 25 per cent of shares were still held by the German government's state holding bank, KfW. With revenues of €55 billion, the company is now one of the world's largest transportation and logistics groups.

The company's primary aim, led by CEO Klaus Zumwinkel, was to develop diverse revenue streams which would reduce its reliance on declining German mail volumes. As a result it became the main protagonist in the consolidation of the express and logistics industry throughout the 1990s and 2000s.

Deutsche Post's first step was to enter the air express parcels market by taking a strategic stake in DHL in the late 1990s. By 2002 it had obtained control and it began to develop DHL as its flagship brand. At the same time it acquired many other well-known names in the industry, including Danzas, AEI, ASG and Nedlloyd, building a global presence.

In 2005, Deutsche Post made a transformative bid for global contract logistics and freight forwarding group Exel, itself a merger of the Ocean Group and Tibbett & Britten. It paid €5.6 billion for the company, a move which led to market leadership in both of these additional sectors.

However, progress has not been without major challenges along the way. In 2003 DP DHL acquired the US domestic express service provider Airborne Inc, (at an acquisition cost of €983 million) which gave it a ground and air transport network in the United States, the world's largest express market. However, following integration, customer service and profitability deteriorated to such an extent that DHL was forced to pull out of the market in 2008, preferring instead to focus on its profitable international services. This also forced it to reappraise its domestic operations throughout the world, including the UK and France.

DP DHL is still heavily focused on the European market, with almost two-thirds of its revenues generated in this region. However, through its mix of freight forwarding, express, contract logistics and road freight operations it can claim to have a greater depth of service provision than any of its competitors. Its strategic ambitions are much more conservative than they were at the height of its aggressive acquisition programme – profitability has become critical to the group's goals. This is partly as a result of its disastrous foray into the US domestic parcels market and partly due to the global economic situation. However, it is very well placed to take advantage of the dynamic growth opportunities presented by the emerging markets in Asia, Africa and Latin America.

Logistics market development by geography

03

Influences on market characteristics

Despite growing globalization, logistics markets are still largely defined by national characteristics. A combination of government regulation and economics has been behind the development of transport provision. Some of the key industry drivers are discussed below.

Regulation

Up until relatively recently, most European countries operated a system of permits which acted as quantitative controls on the entry of new operators into the transport market.

In Europe, these were swept away during the 1980s and 90s by liberalization, but controls still exist in terms of quality, if not quantity. In fact there is growing evidence that the European Commission would like to use quality tests, such as the 'Financial Evidence' regulations (ie those which insist that operators have a certain amount of money in the bank to cover maintenance and upkeep of vehicles) to reduce the continuing fragmentation of the industry. This acts as a de facto intervention in the market by raising barriers to entry by the back door, so to speak.

In the United States, there were similarly high levels of regulation, most of which have been done away with, at least on a domestic basis. However, restrictions apply to the transport of goods from Mexico to the United States.

In many countries in the developing world, restrictions exist on foreign investment in the transport sector. For instance, the only way for a company to enter the Indian logistics market is through a joint venture with a local operator. Protectionism creates a sclerotic market in which new developments and practices are not able to develop. In these markets, logistics costs will remain high and efficiencies low.

Openness and trade

The openness of a country's economy is also important to the transport market. Belgium and the Netherlands, for example, have highly developed international road freight markets due in part to their geographical location on key transit routes, but also due to centuries' old tradition as important trading hubs.

Retail development

Consolidation of a country's retail sector is also very important. In the UK a relatively small number of very large contract logistics players have developed by doing business with a handful of giant supermarket chains. This contrasts with Italy or Spain, where a fragmented retail sector in which local stores predominate has meant that logistics companies have not developed to the same sort of scale.

Import/export balance

In some developed markets, such as Europe, the balance of logistics provision will be on secondary distribution (from warehouse to retailer or consumer) as relatively few consumer goods are manufactured in the region. However, in China the transport market is still largely focused on moving goods from factory to port – a largely commoditized activity. As consumer markets in China develop, so will the secondary distribution market with greater opportunities for logistics providers to add value.

Urbanization and population distribution

The level of urbanization in a country is also a major influence on the development of the logistics sector. Countries with dense urban communities can be better served by a range of more sophisticated contract logistics and express parcels providers than those with dispersed populations.

For example, in the UK the contract logistics industry developed around retailers' regionally centralized distribution requirements. One distribution centre could effectively serve the whole of a region, with transport assets being fully utilized on a daily basis. In other countries, where geographical distances are much greater between population centres, alternative strategies have to be employed, and there is a much greater emphasis on inter-regional trucking (such as in the United States). Logistics costs can consequently be considerably higher.

Geographic market profiles

The Western European logistics market

Logistics markets in Western Europe are highly competitive. Not only is there a wealth of global LSPs but there are also no shortage of medium to large national players with good logistics capabilities.

Germany

Despite a slow start due to the regulation of the market up until the mid-1990s, German logistics companies have become amongst the most highly developed and expansionist in the world. Consequently, German manufacturers and retailers have access to a sophisticated supply-side which facilitates their supply chain strategies. Up until the early to mid-1990s a comprehensive permit system was still in place which regulated not only the quality (which is normal in all markets throughout Europe) but also the quantity of road haulage capacity.

The existence of controls on the quantity and type of service that logistics companies could provide did not apply to the in-house operations of manufacturers and retailers. This meant that there were fewer compelling reasons for companies to outsource their logistics needs to the third party market and consequently it is only over the last 10 years that service providers have been able to increase their penetration of the in-house market.

The complexity of regulations and the tariff system which existed (fixing the rates that transport companies could charge for certain products, routes and mode of transport) led to the development of 'Spedition' companies. These were essentially domestic freight-forwarding operators which could manage freight movements throughout the complex German transport regime.

Despite the liberalization of the markets, the pace of change has still been slow. This is perhaps due to the conservatism of German logistics companies which tend to be owned by families or by banks rather than shareholders. Also retailers have not been as enthusiastic to utilize logistics providers in the same way as their UK counterparts. However, automotive manufacturers have been at the forefront of adopting leading edge supply chain techniques and working with companies such as Schenker, BLG and Rudolph Logistik to fulfil their requirements.

Outsourcing will become more important for industries still unfamiliar with this trend, eg healthcare, public authorities and the construction industry to name just a few.

Two of the leading companies in the market are Deutsche Post DHL and Deutsche Bahn Schenker. These companies have grown out of their original functions of mail and rail and, building on the monopolies which they enjoyed for many years in their home market, expanded geographically and vertically.

One characteristic of the German market is the number of partnerships which exist between the many mid-sized logistics companies. These alliances offer customers national delivery through a franchise system and a way in which they can compete with the two market leaders in road freight, Schenker and DHL. In recent years, European operators such as Kuehne + Nagel, DSV and Geodis have bought their way into the German road haulage market by acquiring membership of many of these alliances.

Germany has a distinct logistics market. An economy with a very large automotive sector and large chemical industry, logistics is more skewed towards industrial logistics than other major European economies. Germany has a strong supply of specialist logistics providers, particularly in areas such as chemicals. However, with strong grocery retailers such as Metro and Lidl, German LSPs are certainly exposed to large-scale grocery retailing.

Production in sectors such as automotive and chemicals is also dominated by large corporations, and their approach towards purchasing logistics services has a big impact on the sector. For example, VW, which is one of the largest purchasers of logistics in Germany, likes to do business with medium-sized German providers as well as larger LSPs. This has been beneficial for a mid-sized company such as Schnellecke Logistics, which not only has a substantial business across Germany but is expanding outside Europe. Similarly, companies such as Rudolph, BLG Logistics or Rhenus have expanded into value-adding logistics on the back of business from the likes of BMW and Daimler. This is all the more remarkable as two of the world's largest contract logistics providers, DP DHL and DB Schenker, are headquartered in Germany.

As a result of this, the German contract logistics market remains more fragmented than elsewhere in Europe, with medium-sized providers plentiful and often looking to grow.

France

Deregulation of the French transport market commenced in the late 1980s with the scrapping of a fixed price tariff system known as the Tarification Routière Obligatoire. This system placed controls on the price which transport providers could charge their clients, although in practice many large shippers were able to circumvent the regulations. A permit system was also in place which limited the number of transport companies that could operate in the market, although this had become largely redundant by the early 1990s.

The legacy of these regulations was a strong in-house logistics sector and this resulted in a slower conversion to the outsourcing concepts which at about the same time were being adopted in the UK. However, in recent years outsourcing has become a major trend in industry, creating a vibrant French third party logistics sector.

The French market was characterized by the number of strong regional players which were in existence. This was symptomatic of France's large geography which forced a number of alliances between medium-sized companies in order to provide manufacturers and retailers with national distribution. However, a number of major national players (eg Geodis, Norbert Dentressangle) have evolved to meet these needs through purely owned operations.

Another reason for the slower take-up of outsourcing in France has been the dynamics of the French retailing sector. In France the hypermarket model is widespread, where emphasis is placed on bulk purchases of goods at a discount from manufacturers, rather than the Just-in-Time (JIT) delivery of product directly to the shelves. Consequently, it is perceived by retailers that there is less to gain from taking over the distribution of goods from their suppliers. As a consequence of this, the shared user model is far more popular in France than dedicated distribution operations. However, there are signs that the major French retailers (such as Carrefour) are increasingly taking ownership of their supply chains.

Although the market is far more deregulated than it was, one piece of legislation to have a major impact on the transport market has been the Working Time Directive (WTD). The French government established this at 35 hours, far lower than the EC mandatory 48-hour working week. One of the effects that this has had on the industry has been the creation of more strategically located hubs throughout the country in order to reduce the duration of driver trips. The impact of the WTD has been an increase in social costs, which some analysts estimate to be 36 per cent of the cost of transport. Consequently the industry has become less competitive than its European neighbours, and far less competitive than Eastern European companies.

Another challenge for French hauliers is the rising cost of tolls, which they complain they have not been able to recover from clients in the present economic climate. The cost of using France's motorways has risen by about 25 per cent in three years.

There is the belief that the French market is being squeezed by lower-cost Spanish hauliers to the west and the operators moving into the market from Eastern Europe. As well as this, German and Dutch international operators are well-placed to offer both international and cabotage services. The development of manufacturing in Central and Eastern Europe is possibly one of the greatest challenges to the industry. This has led to the development of a network of suppliers throughout Europe, which are increasingly served by low-cost, lower-regulated operators based in Poland, Czech Republic etc. French hauliers have been the victims of this trend.

Several strategies for the French road transport market have been suggested:

- they should adopt the network models prevalent in the German market which has given small operators the necessary scale and access to resources (such as marketing and IT);
- further consolidation in the market, especially as part of wider air/sea/intermodal/3PL groups;
- specialization on market niches;
- expansion into Southern Europe/the Mediterranean.

The UK

The UK has the most mature logistics market in Europe, mainly due to the length of time that it has been deregulated. Since the early 1970s there have been no quantitative controls on the number of logistics companies operating in the market, which has led to a high degree of competition.

The early adoption by UK manufacturers and retailers of outsourcing their non-core activities has also helped to fuel the country's logistics sector and allowed a much faster rate of expansion than in other EU countries. At the same time, the grocery retailers have been at the forefront of introducing best practice in supply chain management, and they have encouraged logistics players to meet their sophisticated and ongoing needs.

As a consequence of this, the market has seen a high degree of development with contract logistics companies such as Exel (now DHL Supply Chain) and Wincanton at the forefront, differentiating their products from the smaller market entrants.

The market in the UK has matured over the past 5–10 years as large grocery chains have diversified into consumer durables, becoming the leading players in areas such as clothing or electronics. This was ideal for the big national players as they could expand volumes with existing customers, as those customers took market share from smaller retailers with less efficient logistics. Another feature of this growth is the role of globalized supply chains. A substantial proportion of cheaper consumer durables are sourced in China and consequently logistics provision has increasingly become orientated around goods moving through container ports. An example of the latter has been the growth of consolidation centres in large port-based distribution parks. Intermodal 'inland ports' have also benefitted from the trend.

It is probably safe to say that this growth has come to an end. Consumer expenditure in the UK has hit a ceiling for the moment and is unlikely to increase substantially for a number of years. Rather, the UK economy is showing distinct signs of structural change. This is very likely to mark a shift away from retail growth towards other sectors.

Although logistics sectors such as the automotive industry are quite healthy, a high proportion of production is of luxury vehicles rather than volume models. Sectors such as chemical production may also undergo a similar change with production of bulk-petrochemicals increasingly based in the Middle East whilst higher added value production grows in the UK. Similar trends are seen in other areas of engineering. Consequently the market for contract logistics may be as much about co-ordinating global production, of which the UK is an element in the supply chain, as simple export activities.

The UK has seen significant change in the structure of its logistics market. Two significant larger players, Christian Salvesen and TDG, have been bought by the French family business of Norbert Dentressangle. There are also signs that Kuehne + Nagel is continuing to reinforce its already strong presence in Britain through the recent acquisition of R H Freight, although this was largely targeted at the road transport sector. What is notable about the British market is the comparative power of large LSPs such as DHL, CEVA and Kuehne + Nagel.

Italy

The Italian road transport industry is characterized by extreme fragmentation with high levels of owner-drivers (the so-called *padroncini*) dominating the sector. Over 50 per cent of those employed in the industry work for companies with one to five staff. This compares with the UK and France, where the comparable figure is only 21 per cent.

Whereas the German and French logistics markets could be said to have been held back by over-regulation in the 1980s and early 1990s, the opposite could be said to be true for the Italian market. Low levels of regulation, as well as ease of entry and exit from the market, have made it more difficult for larger transport concerns to build scale and profitability in a market typified by wafer-thin margins. The owner-drivers can compete effectively with their larger counterparts, often with far lower overheads.

The 'own account' sector in Italy is still strong. However, it has been found that this has been a drag on the efficiency of goods movement through-out the country. Empty running by own account operators is around 40 per cent of vehicle trips, far greater than the corresponding level in the third party market. This has been identified as a major policy issue for the government.

Cabotage is also a concern for the industry. It has been estimated that the penetration of the domestic market by foreign hauliers – mainly from Eastern European origins – has risen from 1 per cent in 2004 to 5 per cent in 2009. To counter this growth, the industry believes that there should be more regulation to prevent the influx of foreign operators, as well as initiatives to restore business competitiveness and generate long-term profitability. One of the government's primary concerns is over the loss of taxation revenue caused by the loss of market share of Italian corporations.

Within the contract logistics sector, CEVA Logistics (formerly TNT Logistics) dominates the market. Partly the reason for this is the position of Fiat, CEVA's biggest single client worldwide, within Italian industry.

The lack of large Italian contract logistics players has made it difficult for other foreign-owned companies to develop scale in this sector through acquisition.

The largest single transport organization (taking into account express parcels) is DHL, which has acquired a number of large players in the express industry (such as Ascoli) and in addition has significant air, sea and road business.

Foreign investment in logistics operations has come despite the fact that the Italian economy is not particularly vibrant. As the requirements of shippers become more sophisticated, the larger logistics companies will increasingly gain a competitive advantage over their smaller rivals, driving higher levels of market growth.

Spain

The Spanish logistics market was highly regulated right up to the mid-1980s. The responsibility rested on new haulage companies to prove a requirement for their services to the local authorities prior to the award of an operating permit. From the 1990s onwards the market has been liberalized and regulation is currently in line with other developed European economies.

Spain has a highly fragmented road haulage sector, with a large number of small players offering non-specialist haulage and warehousing services. Due to the lack of resources of these smaller companies, the development of a more sophisticated contract logistics industry has been hindered. This has led to the influx of foreign companies supporting the logistics operations of multinational retailers and manufacturers which have recently entered the Spanish market. In many cases this has been by acquisition.

Madrid is the most important region for international goods flows; it is responsible for 60 per cent of international traffic and 33 per cent of domestic traffic. Catalonia (focused around Barcelona) is perhaps the most important for logistics activities, accounting for 25 per cent of all logistics properties. The road network in the region has produced two major transit routes for goods. The north–south route links France with the Mediterranean, while the east–west route connects Barcelona with the rest of Iberia.

The market is highly competitive, with foreign-owned companies struggling to make any headway. UK-based company Wincanton has withdrawn its operations, although others, such as Schenker and DHL, continue to push into what is a highly strategic market. Schenker has acquired TIR and Transfesa, two of Spain's largest operators.

The Spanish retail sector has been one of the driving forces behind the growth of the logistics industry. The retail sector has undergone a transformation, with the emergence of a number of major French groups such as Carrefour. The entrance of international retailers has changed a market which was previously dominated by family-owned micro-stores to one in which hypermarkets and supermarkets play a much more important role. Foreign logistics companies are leading the way in introducing best practice from more developed markets, such as the UK, to support these multinational retailers. The growth will also be reinforced by the trend towards outsourcing, which is being increasingly adopted by many major manufacturers and retailers.

The intermodal sector will play an important role in the development of the industry over the coming years. Ports, such as Barcelona, are investing heavily in intermodal operations as they seek to develop their European 'gateway' status. This will link them to other key Southern European countries as well as improving distribution around Spain. However, road freight will stay dominant in sectors outside of containerized freight.

The situation in Spain is similar to other European markets, if more extreme. Spain has also experienced strong consumer-led growth over the past decade. This provided the logistics market in Spain with a good opportunity to diversify from the automotive sector which had dominated its business from the 1980s. To complement this, Spain also experienced a construction boom, which affected the logistics sector. This trend has not only halted over the past two years, but the sector has experienced a considerable reversal.

The consumer industry is likely to continue to shrink and the construction sector is deeply depressed. The automotive sector in Spain is experiencing competition from Central Europe, with no plants opening over the past decade. Spain badly needs investment-led growth of the type seen in the 1980s with one source being a 'spillover' from German production, although this is a slow process. Consequently, the logistics market in Spain is in far from healthy shape.

Central & Eastern Europe contract logistics market

Central Europe has been a dynamic market for larger logistics companies. Although the region suffered from poor infrastructure and patchy services in the decade after the fall of the Berlin Wall, since 2000 the sector has grown enormously.

Key to the development of logistics in Central Europe has been the nature of economic growth in the region. This has been driven largely by external investment by manufacturing companies looking to exploit the region's competitive strengths. The automotive sector has been the leader in this trend, with German vehicle manufacturers the largest investors. The vehicle assembly plants that have been built are generally 'green field' sites with large capacity and a high level of productivity. Consequently the vehicle manufacturers generally look to larger LSPs to provide the level of logistics services demanded by such plants. Equally this applies to the component suppliers who have located in the region to support the assembly plants.

The impact on the region of this wave of investment was quite sudden. Previous to 2005 disposable income was too low to drive the retail sector. However, over recent years this has changed, and increasingly the consumer sector has been building a substantial logistics infrastructure in most of the countries of the region. The economies of the region do vary considerably, however. Poland accounts for around half of the economy of the region, whilst certain countries, such as Slovenia, have a GDP per head approaching that of Western Europe. Other countries have much smaller economies, such as Romania and Bulgaria.

The position of different LSPs in the region is heavily influenced by the nature of local and national economies. DB Schenker, for example, has a strong presence in the Czech Republic due to the size of VW Group operations in the country, although DHL Supply Chain has penetrated into much of this business in recent years. GEFCO is strong in Slovakia due to the presence of the Toyota Peugeot-Citroën joint venture in Kolin. Glovis has established a presence in Slovakia to serve its parent Hyundai-Kia's new plant in the country.

A feature of the Central European logistics market is that there are very few indigenous contract logistics providers but a large number of local road freight operators.

Poland

One of the more mature economies of Central Europe, Poland is also the largest. Although the automotive sector is not quite as large a proportion of its economy as in the Czech Republic and Slovakia, it still has significant plants, notably run by GM and Ford. Unsurprisingly, German companies are major investors in the country and are disproportionately represented in Poland's logistics market. Poland's successful economy is now triggering growth in areas such as retail. Transport infrastructure, however, remains a problem.

Czech Republic and Slovakia

The level of automotive logistics investment in both the Czech Republic and Slovakia has been substantial. Volkswagen is the largest investor, bringing with it extensive logistics operations. The German carmaker not only operates the two large Skoda facilities but also has engine and bodywork facilities. Consequently, many of the logistics providers who support VW Group's supply chain have a very strong presence in both countries. Schenker and Schnellecke are prominent amongst these.

Hungary

Hungary's economy may be less dominated by automotive production than some of its neighbours, yet the production at the VW–Audi Györ plant and the new Mercedes Benz Passenger Cars plant at Kecskemét will nevertheless dominate the logistics sector in the country. This is all the more the case as the economic crisis will depress consumer-driven sectors. Hungary is notable for having one of the few major Central European contract logistics providers in the form of Waberer's Optimum Solution.

North American logistics market

The North American logistics market is a fragmented one. Besides transportation services and warehousing and distribution services, numerous niche players offer specialized services such as reverse logistics, IT services and consulting. As the economy continues to show improvement, consolidation within the logistics market, particularly in the United States, is expected over the next two to three years. The US market, albeit a mature one, remains a focal point for North American logistics.

Trade continues to steadily improve as the North America region emerges from the 2009 recession. However, rising transportation rates and diesel prices, tight capacity, infrastructure and government regulations are affecting the industry.

Infrastructure is an issue for the region. Canada is seeking funding to improve roads and rail along the US–Canada border. The Mexican government has invested billions of dollars into improving its ports in anticipation of increasing Asian trade. Investments have also been made in Mexico's road and rail networks to connect the country with the United States. Due to the high debt the US government currently has, funding for many infrastructure projects is on hold.

The need to improve the highway systems is great, as many have seen little improvement since the 1950s. The eastern ports are in need of additional dredging in order to remain competitive. The Panama Canal expansion is expected to be completed in a couple of years and will allow much larger vessels to pass.

Trends in distribution centres are changing as many shippers are consolidating their requirements. The number of distribution centres is declining for the average shipper and now are being located in more strategic locations throughout the region. Multi-customer distribution centres are also being utilized to provide customers and providers additional cost savings.

USA

The transportation and logistics market in the United States is highly fragmented and consists of a variety of services, including third party logistics, intermodal, brokerage and pure-play truckers and railroads. The truckload sector is highly fragmented with more than 500,000 carriers. The majority of these carriers are smaller operators, working with less than 20 trucks. The less-than-truckload (LTL) sector is much more consolidated than the truckload sector, with less than 10 companies in North America accounting for more than two-thirds of the industry revenue. National carriers are driving consolidation by moving into the retail markets in search of additional growth and more opportunities for profitable growth.

Like its European counterparts, US market was highly regulated until 30 years ago. The Motor Carrier Act of 1935 stipulated that companies that wanted to haul freight across state lines on a for-hire basis had to obtain authority from the Interstate Commerce Commission (ICC). Prices were determined through a collective ratemaking process made legal by federal antitrust exemption. Carriers were able to file their own rates, although subject to challenge from regional bureaus. Therefore, most chose to go along with the conference pricing.

The principally deregulating Motor Carrier Act of 1980 did not eliminate all of the previous rules and most states imposed some economic regulation on trucking. The Act of 1980, however, made some changes. Interstate trucking companies should still obtain ICC operating authority but the application and review process was simpler. Ratemaking was still carried out through regional bureaus but independent rates could not be challenged, with the result that more carriers selected their own prices. Contract carriers were no longer restricted in how many customers they could serve.

Following deregulation, many carriers accelerated long-term expansion plans through adding terminals and equipment. Annual growth rates of 30–40 per cent were not uncommon and overcapacity forced rates down. Since deregulation, many thousands of carriers, including 74 of the 1980s' top 100, have gone out of business.

The sector has undergone major consolidation in the past five years, with both UPS and FedEx entering the market to round out their freight portfolio. FedEx is now market leader, following a disastrous period of acquisitions by the former leader Yellow Roadway. Other big players include Con-way and Schneider.

A major issue within the logistics sector as a whole is unionization versus non-unionization of transportation and logistics companies and its effects on operating costs. The principal union representing transportation workers is the International Brotherhood of Teamsters. After the deregulation of the motor carrier industry, those companies without union representation saw labour costs decline far more dramatically than those with union representation. The single largest employer of Teamsters' members is UPS, employing more than 200,000.

Outsourcing in the US market is not as far advanced as in parts of Europe, with a large proportion of business remaining in-house. The largest contract logistics player in the market is DHL Supply Chain, which was built on the back of Exel (in fact it is still branded as 'Exel') and Tibbett & Britten. UPS Supply Chain Solutions, Ryder, Menlo and CEVA are also well developed.

Recent shifts in domestic transport networks are starting to alter the locations of warehousing and distribution facilities. Long known as the world's leading importer, the US economy has found itself no longer able to sustain the amount of imports it had once been able to. Like the rest of the world, its trade patterns appear to have changed in this new global economy – a result of the 2009 economic decline. Many US ports recorded either only slight increases or actual declines in imports in 2011. Instead, exports were on the rise. In addition, as the Panama Canal widening moves to completion, east coast ports are expanding in anticipation of gaining market share from the possible shifts in trade that is expected.

As this shift continues the rise of intermodal transportation is on the upswing. This increase is due to a number of reasons, such as the rise in oil prices, the lower costs of intermodal transportation, a shift from exclusive use of trucking because of tight capacity and the more 'environmentally friendly' use of rail versus truck.

The 2009 recession was a severe blow to the industry, but from which it recovered well in 2010. Manufacturing picked up, consumer spend improved and demand from overseas increased. Capacity remained tight and rates increased across the board as transportation providers tried to recoup revenue lost during the recession as well as improve yields.

As confidence continues to rise over the recovery in the freight transport market, consolidation within the logistics industry is increasing. In 2010, deal volumes increased by 25 per cent and in 2011 by around 30 per cent. Many industry analysts believe the industry will experience an active consolidation period over the next two to three years with an emphasis on transportation services and non-asset-based providers.

Other trends affecting the US contract logistics industry include the rise in e-commerce activity. Retailers are adapting to the rise in e-commerce by dedicating more of their distribution centres to the service. Amazon is investing heavily in distribution centres right across the country.

Another growth opportunity for contract logistics providers is the healthcare sector. The growth of healthcare has resulted in many logistics providers offering specialized services devoted to this sector.

Canada

Canada has developed economically and technologically along with the United States, its neighbour to the south. In fact, the country enjoys a substantial trade surplus with the United States which absorbs over 70 per cent of Canadian exports. Canada, in turn, imports over 50 per cent of US exports annually.

The importance of Canada–US trade needs to be emphasized. With 90 per cent of Canadians living within 100 miles of the US border and 85 per cent of Canada's 20 largest cities located within 110 miles of the border, Canada–US trade is robust. Most of these imports include cars and automotive parts and energy products, including oil, gas, uranium and electric power. About 50 per cent of all merchandise trade consists of intermediate production inputs, and more than 33 per cent of cross-border shipments are intracompany transfers. Automotive parts, for example, frequently cross the border six or more times before entering the final assembly stage.

Growth in international trade has spurred the demand for logistics services. This can be seen in Canada's west coast container port traffic, which increased by 592 per cent between 1990 and 2010, while Canada's east coast port traffic grew by 83 per cent. Although the United States is Canada's major export partner, China is Canada's second largest import partner, behind the United States.

Due to the growth in international demand as well as consumer demand, investments in distribution facilities in Canada have increased greatly over the past five years. The main areas of distribution facility investment were in Ontario (32 per cent of total investment) followed by Alberta (25 per cent), Quebec (12 per cent) and British Columbia (10 per cent).

In the oil and gas extraction sector, storage and transportation of equipment represents a significant portion of investment. Heavy equipment is kept in fewer yards located in more active areas, while tools and spare parts for oil and gas extraction and production are stored in distribution centres near major exploration sites.

Mexico

Mexico's logistics industry is one of great potential that has yet to be fully realized. The prospect of near-shoring is promising for Mexico as manufacturers move facilities from China to Mexico to be closer to the US market. Since 1994, the country has been a participant in the NAFTA trade between the United States and Canada. In 10 years, trade between the three countries has increased by almost 50 per cent.

Fairly sophisticated cross-border logistics exists. The large-scale manu-facturers on the Mexican side of the US border utilize state-of-the-art logistics processes and technology to connect their factories with global suppliers and US customers.

Though much improved over the last 10 years, the country remains reliant on old and inefficient infrastructure. Fewer Mexican companies are using contract logistics providers than those in the United States and Europe; this difference is even more exaggerated among small and medium-sized companies. Those companies that are using logistics providers are focusing on more routine activities, such as customs clearance and freight bill auditing and payment. Mexican companies are also focused less on cost reduction than they are on improved flexibility and customer service.

According to a recent survey, warehousing is still a less mature market, with major differences in service quality between providers. In most cases, third parties are used only temporarily. Respondents of the survey noted they preferred in-house, rather than to outsource their warehousing and inventory management, for reasons of trust and security.

Asia Pacific logistics market

Increasing intra-Asian trade, along with a growing increase in imports not only for manufacturing inputs but also consumer products helped lead the world out of the 2009 recession. The growth of this region continues to increase as the world recovers from the economic upheaval.

Instead of specializing in producing certain types of final goods, Asian exporters increasingly have specialized in certain stages of production and have become vertically integrated with each other. For example, the iPad final assembly is in China; however, most of the components are actually manufactured in other Asian economies, including Korea, Japan and Taiwan. Growth of cross-border supply chains is growing and will continue to do so; however, China will continue to be the focal point of the Asian supply network. China now accounts, directly or indirectly, for about half of all imports of intermediate inputs within Asia. For many of its Asian partners, China has become the single most important destination of intermediate goods exports. For example, China accounts for 20–25 per cent of all capital goods exports from Japan and Korea, a fourfold increase on a decade ago.

Adequate infrastructure is needed to support this vertical integration amongst Asian countries. To do so, individual Asian governments have launched initiatives to improve the road, rail, port and airport networks. Although government-sponsored infrastructure improvements are under way, logistics providers such as DB Schenker are investing in the rail network to link Europe with Asia whereas TNT, and others, have invested in the road network to link Southeast Asia with China.

As vertical integration amongst the Asian countries continues to evolve, China is experiencing a shift in manufacturing locations. Historically, manufacturing was located in the eastern parts of the country. However, due to rising labour wages, manufacturing is shifting to the west of China in search of lower labour wages. Instead of moving westward, some manufacturers are opting to relocate to other Asian countries such as India, Vietnam or Thailand while others are choosing to move closer to the market(s) they are servicing such as the United States or Europe.

To sustain its growth, China recognizes the need for a strong domestic economy and as such it is now seeking to stimulate domestic consumption to spur this on. Higher levels of disposable income have led to increased demand for a variety of consumables. This has in turn placed higher performance demands on the overall supply chain, from manufacturers who have ramped up supply, to the 3PL operators who provide the service link to the retail outlets. The larger retailers, in particular those with multiple outlets, are now expecting higher levels of service from their manufacturing, such as daily deliveries and orders which may include a high percentage of case or split case picking.

Japan

Japan is considered Asia's logistics leader in terms of sophistication and transportation connectivity. However, Japan's logistics sector has been largely ignored by foreign investors in the past, their focus clearly on neighbouring China's huge and fast-growing market. In any case, economic stagnation, cultural barriers and the dominance of the Japanese conglomerates (*keiretsu*) have created a market which has proved largely impenetrable until recently.

To complicate matters, Japan's industry is refocusing on services, rather than manufacturing, and outsourcing has still not caught on to the same extent as in most other developed markets – the major manufacturers almost exclusively operate their own logistics subsidiaries. Japanese companies have also preferred to own rather than lease their warehouses or distribution facilities. However, this trend is changing, led by companies such as Nippon Express.

There are several reasons why prospects are good for global contract logistics players in Japan. Firstly, there are signs that the downturn in the market is finally acting as a spur for Japanese companies to sell off their logistics subsidiaries and open up to third parties. This will not only support balance sheets, but also introduce new thinking and efficiencies.

Secondly, Japanese companies, as with many global manufacturers, are shifting their production abroad – mainly to China. The increased internationalization of the product flows naturally suits global logistics companies which have significant capabilities in these key markets. This is an area in which domestic Japanese logistics companies are not as strong.

In this regard, DHL Supply Chain stands out. It was an early entrant into the market through Exel's earlier acquisition of Fujitsu Logistics in 2004. The company is organized along regional lines, with strong co-operation between the Japanese and Chinese businesses.

While the recent economic downturn is credited with spurring many Japanese companies to rethink their relationship with their logistics providers, the March 2011 earthquake and tsunami will result in many rethinking their overall supply chain strategy. The disruptions from Japan are resulting in many companies realizing that their supply chain risk profile is not driven only by the direct supplier network, but their suppliers' suppliers and perhaps even the suppliers of their suppliers' suppliers.

China

Due to its huge growth China occupies a special position amongst national logistics markets. Yet as many companies have found out, this is far from an unalloyed benefit, for the Chinese market may well be described as 'large but difficult'.

The Chinese economy is far from being a straightforward free market. It can be divided into three parts: the state, the 'state owned enterprises' (SOEs) and the private economy. This structure has a huge impact on the nature of logistics provision, with much of the SOE sector resistant to the concept of outsourcing, especially to non-Chinese companies.

The ironic aspect of this is that private sector growth in China has been hugely dependent on Western logistics operations. Around 60 per cent of the Chinese economy is based around the Pearl River Delta, which owes its origins to its proximity to Hong Kong port. The profile of the private sector and its appetite for contract logistics is quite different to that of the SOE sector. A great deal of the Chinese-owned business is export orientated, producing consumer goods such as furniture, clothing and consumer electronics, often as part of a wider supply chain.

This results in complex interfaces with contract logistics providers. Chinese suppliers will frequently feed into the supply chains of large global original equipment manufacturers (OEMs) or retailers, run by global LSPs. Yet providers still do not form a substantial market for contract logistics. This is in part due to the position that Chinese suppliers play in the global supply chain. However, it must be seen as a major opportunity for growth in the global contract logistics market. At present, the services that are bought are a mixture of road freight, port services and sea freight, frequently co-ordinated through a forwarder. However, it would be a logical evolution of these supply chains for them to be co-ordinated and developed with contract logistics input.

The situation of global companies operating in China is also complex. Their need to support operations is becoming more complex as the nature of investment changes. Up until very recently the bulk of non-Chinese investors were located in the Pearl River Delta – especially Shenzhen – and their supply chain very much resembled that of Chinese suppliers. However, this is changing. Investors such as retailers are increasing, as well as producers of consumer durables selling into Chinese markets.

This requires new types of logistics provision, but these investors often struggle to find what they need. Non-Chinese contract logistics companies have struggled to establish operations in much of China, with local regulatory authorities discouraging competition to local companies. Consequently, major investors increasingly rely on internal management structures to purchase and plan individual logistics functions. In short, they have in-sourced much of what is outsourced in other markets.

This enables them to buy individual services, such as transport or warehousing, from local companies. There are examples of more extensive relationships, which might be called contract logistics; however, it is difficult to tell what the exact nature of the relationship is. One example is the German retailer Metro, which has agreed to use Shuanghui Logistics to support its frozen food operations. Shuanghui Logistics is owned by the food processing company Henan Luohe Shuanghui Industry Group, which is owned by the local government in Henan province. It is presumed that Shuanghui will be using its existing frozen food infrastructure to support its own food distribution activities.

At present even the pioneering fast-moving consumer goods companies are focused on the big eastern urban conurbations. As the cities in the western interior of China become more prosperous these companies are facing the need to support sales in these locations. The problem they will have is that the logistics provision is even weaker here than in the eastern cities, which at least had the platform of port activities on which to build. With the reluctance of local authorities to let non-local logistics service providers gain large market-shares, it appears likely that China will emerge into a patchwork of smaller and medium-sized contract logistics providers based on locality and relationships with local political authorities and business interests.

That said, the Australian-based Toll Group is in the process of constructing a physical network throughout China, supporting both Western FMCG companies such as Colgate-Palmolive as well as Chinese competitors. The future of truly private contract logistics LSPs with a pan-Chinese presence, either Chinese or non-Chinese owned, is hard to ascertain. There are certainly important contract logistics providers who are capable of providing the most sophisticated services, but their ability to reach across China may well be constrained.

The situation in the automotive sector is not so different. Almost all global vehicle manufacturer operations in China are joint ventures. These operations have traditionally had complex supply chains, with substantial quantities of components being imported. This has made substantial demands on logistics provision, with freight forwarders being used to co-ordinate the flow of components. Companies such as Schenker or DHL, who have large forwarding businesses, are able to interface these with contract logistics operations in vehicle manufacturers.

These contract logistics operations are different to those found in the West as assembly plants schedule environments tend to be less 'JIT' with components consolidated at forwarders' consolidation centres near major ports. This situation is changing as more components are produced in China, although it is reasonable to say that large Western LSPs have a 'foot in the door' for supporting these plants. However, the situation is hugely complicated by the relationship with the Chinese joint venture partners. These companies – who usually have their own car production assembly operations as well – are junior partners in terms of engineering and production management, but are often responsible for logistics provision. They will seek to impose their own in-house or related logistics companies on the joint venture. This is not always as bad as it sounds. A few such logistics service providers are sophisticated companies capable of supporting large-scale car production activities. A good example is Anji-CEVA (formerly known as Anji-TNT), which is a joint venture between the SOE Shanghai Automotive Industry Corporation (SAIC) and CEVA. Yet, even here such a company is largely concerned with providing services to SAIC companies, not other Chinese vehicle manufacturers (VMs).

India

As Asia's third largest economy, India is witnessing a boom in economic and trade activity. Unfortunately, the growth rate has outpaced the country's infrastructure. Due to the lack of modern infrastructure, India's logistics costs are approximately 13 per cent of GDP compared to 9 per cent for the United States and 8 per cent in Germany. Warehousing, inventory costs and process ordering combined make up almost 60 per cent of Indian logistics costs.

The growth in external trade and the growth across major industry segments such as automotive, pharmaceutical, fast-moving consumer goods (FMCG) and the emergence of organized retail have favourably impacted the growth of the warehousing industry. At present, 50 per cent of the warehousing industry is controlled by small, unorganized companies and as such, these facilities serve mainly as storage facilities. Those warehouse operators that do provide value-added services charge a premium for such services as reverse logistics, kitting, labelling etc. Another complication for the warehousing industry is the fact that India's tax system is complex. To avoid multiple taxation, companies typically have warehousing operations in every state. The result is a large number of small warehouses across the country that lack the latest warehousing processes and technologies and do not offer economies of scale.

Until a few years ago, Indian firms outsourced only transportation and basic warehousing. That has changed in the last few years, particularly after the economic slowdown. Customers from retail, apparel, IT and telecom sectors are outsourcing quality checks, packing, labelling, store-ready delivery, parts of inventory management and billing function. Currently, the average annual growth rate of value-added services is 30 per cent while the logistics sector growth in general is 8 to 10 per cent.

However, providers of warehousing services are in need of capital and know-how from investors and operators. As a result, several government plans are in place to expand and modernize the industry in India. For example, as part of rail infrastructure improvements, India Railways has proposed the development of freight logistics parks at six locations between Delhi and Mumbai. The parks will be operated as joint ventures with India Railways and the respective state governments.

Local logistics providers are expanding operations as well as international rivals. Safexpress has more than 5 million sq ft of warehousing space across the country and is planning to set up 32 logistics parks and add another 5 million sq ft in the next two years. This will be helped by the phasing out of the central sales tax which has created high levels of inefficiency.

South America

South America has enjoyed an unprecedented increase in international trade due to demand for commodities such as minerals, oil, steel and agricultural goods. Demand for these goods is driven primarily by Asia, particularly China, whose need for these manufacturing inputs has prompted many Chinese companies to invest in not only South American companies but also the region's infrastructure in order to gain access to the commodities more easily.

Infrastructure remains a major issue for the region as development projects have not been able to keep pace with the increase in trade. Congestion at ports and airports, lack of paved roads and outdated rail systems have caused delays in the transport of goods and commodities to global markets. However, the last few years have seen major investments in the transportation infrastructure of most South American countries, particularly in Argentina, Brazil, Chile and Peru. In particular, demand for South American raw materials, agriculture and oil products have sparked much of the investment.

Diversification into other industries is greatly needed in this region as commodity prices for raw materials tend to fluctuate wildly on the global market. To maintain a more stable economy, South American countries such as Brazil, Argentina and Chile are successfully expanding their economies into such industries as pharmaceuticals, winemaking, automobile and aerospace and apparel manufacturing.

Intra-South American volumes are increasing as road and rail networks connecting east to west South America are created. Brazil is the largest country, economically and geographically within the region, and 26 per cent of its total trade is with other South American countries. For landlocked countries such as Bolivia and Paraguay, more than half of their trade is intra-South America.

As the economies of Argentina, Brazil and other countries in the region expand, increases in trade have provided many new opportunities for global and regional 3PLs, ocean carriers and other transport operators. Intermodal connections between the key southern Brazilian cities of São Paulo, Rio de Janeiro and Belo Horizonte have improved significantly in the last three to four years. Major logistics providers such as Schenker, Expeditors, Panalpina and Kuehne + Nagel have increased their investments in warehousing and related logistics services in Brazil and they expect further heavy investment in the country's logistical infrastructure over the next few years.

The region was not as affected by the 2009 recession as other regions due to its isolation from the global financial banking system. However, it was indirectly impacted by the weakness in key export markets such as the United States. China, whose economy continued to grow throughout, is becoming an important trade partner with the region. China is now Brazil's major trading partner, surpassing the United States.

Brazil

Brazil is the most important market in South America by a considerable margin. The country is a significant trade partner, not only globally, but also regionally and is a global producer of aircraft, consumer goods, steel, vehicles, rubber and paper. Along with local providers, global logistics providers such as DHL, Kuehne + Nagel, Panalpina, Expeditors, CEVA and UPS have all established operations to support Brazil's growing manufacturing and agricultural activities.

As with the rest of South America, Brazil's infrastructure has not kept up with the growth the country has experienced in the past few years. The government has introduced plans for infrastructure improvements; private companies have invested in Brazil's infrastructure and logistics providers are investing in the country's infrastructure. Still, the World Economic Forum recently described Brazil's infrastructure as 'appalling'.

Brazil is facing mounting pressure to improve and expand the country's infrastructure. Based on the World Economic Forum's report, Brazil's road infrastructure is lacking and maritime shipping suffers from insufficient capacity. Brazil's road network carries over 61 per cent of domestic freight whereas 70 per cent of the country's exports are transported via ocean vessels.

Brazil is a global top 10 producer of vehicles and parts. In terms of logistics suppliers, CEVA is the leader with a presence in all areas of the market across the continent. It even has a strong presence in the finished vehicle logistics market. However, just as strong in terms of inbound logistics is DHL Supply Chain. GEFCO has also developed its presence in the region, in part to support the operations of its parent PSA. Medium-sized US LSPs also have a useful presence in South America. Typical of this is a company such as Crowley Logistics, a Florida-based maritime and land transport LSP that provides support to vehicle manufacturers with supply chains in the United States but production facilities in South America (eg Ford).

With an annual production of 650 million pairs of shoes, Brazil is the third largest producer of footwear in the world after China and India. Brazilian shoe production is concentrated in the areas of Vale dos Sinos, which accounts for 80 per cent of all shoe production. Benefiting from this specialization, DHL Supply Chain manages a distribution centre on behalf of Nike in Louveira, São Paulo. The company provides receiving, storage, order picking, distribution and reverse logistics for three Nike units: footwear, apparel and equipment. Other logistics providers that provide services to the footwear and retail industry include Damco, CEVA and GEFCO.

Middle East

Although it might be perceived as an emerging market, the Middle East in terms of logistics is quite different from most others. Middle Eastern economies vary substantially, from Egypt, with its large population and growing economy based on tourism and manufacturing, to the oil and gas-driven economies of the Gulf. In terms of contract logistics, however, it is the latter that have made the running.

The dominant industry in the region is obviously oil and gas. Logistics provision in the oil and gas sector is not usually described as contract logistics, as the oil companies involved generally own much of their own logistics infrastructure, such as oil storage and terminals. To a lesser extent this also applies to areas of oil and gas storage. However, an important market for outsourced logistics companies is that of oil field maintenance. This mix of air transport and inventory management is largely dominated by the leading global LSPs who are often linked in to global oil and oil field services companies worldwide. That said, there is substantial activity in this area by local contract logistics players as well, particularly serving state-owned oil companies.

Another aspect of the Middle Eastern economies over the past decade is their programmes of diversification. Typified by the Emirate of Dubai, Gulf States in particular have invested in areas such as airlines, tourism and ports. The latter in particular has had a direct impact on the logistics sector. By building a large complex of container ports as well as substantial air freight facilities, Dubai has sought to position itself as the logistics provider for a huge area of the Middle East, Central and Southern Asia. It has been partially successful with the Port of Dubai acting as an important transshipment point for India. This has also meant that contract logistics providers, both global and Middle Eastern-based, have established Dubai as an important centre of operations.

The sectors served by Dubai-based logistics operations tend to be in the area of consumer durables. Electronic products in particular are suitable for strategic inventory holding in Dubai, but increasingly pharmaceutical logistics is attracted to the mix of good quality temperature-controlled warehousing and intensive air freight services. Tourism and hotel support logistics is also important.

Africa

The African logistics sector is more a collection of national markets than other, more integrated regions. Despite continuing severe infrastructure issues, Africa's growth has continued to be helped by the strength of its biggest trading partner, China, although logistics costs in Africa remain high, constraining the development of the sector. Corruption is rife in many parts of the continent, and this not only creates delays but adds to the cost of moving goods. Other problems include labour unrest and a major skills shortage.

However, the opportunities are clear. Africa is a resource-rich continent, and the growth of developing countries, such as the BRIC group, has led to huge demand for these resources. Despite this, the logistics sector will only take off when African industry moves up the value chain and manufacturing becomes more important. This may be a little way off, as although labour costs in Asia are reducing manufacturing's competitiveness in China and elsewhere, there is little sign that Africa is able to fill the void.

South Africa is increasingly being viewed as an important emerging market, with large investment opportunities. South Africa's automotive industry has been growing quickly, with vehicle manufacturers such as BMW, Ford, Volkswagen, DaimlerChrysler and Toyota basing production plants in the country. Manufacturers have established plants in South Africa to take advantage of low production costs, coupled with access to new markets as a result of trade agreements with the European Union and the Southern African Development Community free trade area. Opportunities also lie in the production of materials (automotive steel and components).

South Africa is also becoming increasingly important as a location for clinical trials, although there are longer regulatory timelines involved in setting up a trial in this country than in the developed world. However, compared with other 'emerging' markets, such as Eastern Europe and India, timelines are similar and costs are increasingly competitive.

There are significant opportunities for growth in the South African temperature-controlled logistics sector, but the market is not free of challenges. As the South African middle class expands, there has been increased demand for frozen foods. There has also been a growing trend towards using third party logistics providers. However, most retailers operate their own distribution centres. In addition, land to build is scarce causing the cost of land to almost double since 2007. Building costs are also escalating rapidly.

Nigeria is the second largest market in Africa. The principle interest which Nigeria holds for foreign logistics companies stems from its major oil production operations. The country is a top 10 player as far as production and reserves are concerned, and most of the major oil multinationals are active within the market, the largest being Shell.

By making Nigeria more investor and importer friendly, the authorities hope to make the country a hub for the west coast of Africa. Establishing a free zone makes relations with customs easier and more formal, although corruption in this market, and in fact throughout the whole region, is endemic.

The emergence of logistics clusters

04

Where to locate distribution centres?

'Primary' supply chain attributes

Manufacturers and retailers spend many millions on restructuring their logistics systems to ensure that customer expectations are met whilst inventory and transportation costs are minimized. This is a fine balance but getting it wrong has obvious implications in terms of efficiency and sales. Every company's distribution strategy is different but in the process of deciding where to locate distribution hub or hubs, a number of primary supply chain attributes first needs to be assessed.

Location in supply chain

The relative position of a distribution node in the supply chain has a very important influence on its geographic location. If its function is to carry out primary logistics activities, eg feeding vendor-managed inventory into a large manufacturing site, the overarching need will be to locate the hub near to its customer. If, however, the hub is designed for secondary logistics purposes, eg to distribute finished goods to a mass consumer market, then its location will be more governed by the need for geographic centrality.

Customer distribution profile

Leading on from this latter point, the customer distribution profile is obviously of prime importance to the location of a hub. This may mean geographic centrality, although this is not always the case. If the customer distribution profile is global (eg a medical technology spare parts operation) then the 'connectedness' of an airport may be the overwhelming requirement, more than its physical location.

Type of product which is being shipped

This is important, both from the perspective of a product's physical attributes as well as intrinsic value. If small packages are being shipped, location next to a parcels hub or airport will be important. For higher volume/lower value goods, location at a road interchange or proximity to a seaport may be more important.

Customer service levels required

In sectors where suppliers have to offer their customers a very high level of service (such as in the after sales market), achieving deliveries in small time windows will have a major effect on the structure of a distribution network. This may require a network of close-to-customer forward/field stock locations (FSLs), replenished from national or regional distribution centres.

'Secondary' supply chain attributes

Once these 'primary' supply chain attributes have been identified, a system of subsidiary factors can then be prioritized and 'weighted' in importance.

Air links

Where volumes include air cargo, proximity to an airport is obviously important. However, not any airport will do, as the level of 'connectedness' is essential. According to research undertaken by Chicago's Northwestern University, Paris, London, Frankfurt and Amsterdam are the four most connected cities in the world, with the highest ranked US city being Chicago, followed by New York, Atlanta, Dallas and Houston. In Asia, Tokyo, Beijing, Bangkok and Hong Kong are the best connected. As well as the number of distinct routes, frequency of flights has to be taken into account, as well as other potential environmental factors such as night-flying bans.

For high value-density shipments, the need for proximity to an international air express hub has led spare parts operations, retailers, high tech companies etc to cluster around airports such as Memphis (FedEx), Louisville (UPS) and Wilmington, Ohio (DHL) in the US and in Europe at Paris (FedEx), Cologne (UPS) and Brussels (DHL). In Asia Pacific, DHL has a major hub in Hong Kong; Shanghai is growing in importance through UPS's investment, and FedEx has its main hub in Guangzhou, southern China.

Shipping links

Similar issues of 'connectedness' exist for sea freight. As well as the number of routes available from a sea port, fleet deployment (number of ships), container carrying capacity (number of 20ft equivalent units (TEUs)) and number of shipping lines are important factors. At country level China, Hong Kong and Singapore have the highest level of connectivity, according to the UN Conference on Trade and Development (UNCTAD). These countries are followed by the United States, the United Kingdom and the Netherlands.

At port level, Shanghai, Hong Kong, Singapore, Los Angeles, Rotterdam, Antwerp and Hamburg offer the most choices for shippers and have consequently attracted substantial investment in distribution centres.

Good port-to-port links are just part of the equation. Efficiency in loading/offloading and congestion in and around the ports have become major factors in recent years, given the increase in global shipping volumes. This has had a major impact on routing decisions with some shippers bypassing west coast ports of the US and opting to distribute from hubs based near to ports such as New York or Charleston.

Competition for space in and around ports has led to the development of 'inland ports'. This has resulted in the growth on the 'Inland Empire' in California and intermodal ports such as Duisport in Germany.

Road links

For most manufacturers or retailers, road links are the most important modal factor in the location of a distribution hub, influencing access and time to market. In Europe this has led to the development of hubs around towns such as Venlo, Eindhoven or Roermond in the Netherlands, all of which are on key arterial routes between the manufacturing and consumer centres of Germany, France, the Netherlands and Belgium, the main ports of Rotterdam and Antwerp, and the airports of Amsterdam, Brussels and Cologne, to name but a few.

In Western Europe, the quality of road infrastructure is generally very good, which makes the decision on location reasonably easy, with plenty of options available. Regions competing for distribution hubs generally have to stress other advantages. Companies could base their logistics hubs as easily across the border in Germany as in Venlo – in this case it is a range of other non-modal factors which are more important, such as labour laws and costs. However, elsewhere in the world this is not the case. Few companies choose to site their distribution hubs outside of the main metropolitan areas in China for example, as road networks are still relatively undeveloped.

Non-modal factors

Generally, where there is little to choose between locations on the basis of transportation, decisions will be made through a combination of the following factors:

Cost of rental, land and build costs

The costs of renting, buying and building distribution warehousing varies considerably even over relatively short distances. For instance, in Europe rental at Heathrow Airport in London is highest, many times that of regions such as Limburg, the Netherlands or even of Frankfurt Airport, Germany. Building costs are highest at Vienna, Austria and cheapest in Marseille, France. Land costs, meanwhile, are most expensive in Heathrow and cheapest in Antwerp, Belgium.

Labour

Labour is an increasingly important factor in the location of a distribution centre. Legislation in some countries has made the workforce significantly less flexible than in others. As several hundred staff may be employed in any one centre it is essential to ensure the ability to take on and lay off staff during seasonal and cyclical peaks and troughs.

Labour availability is also important. Where there is full employment, the costs required to staff an operation rise considerably – and in some cases it is impossible to recruit good quality staff. Warehousing and hub employment remains unattractive to many people and therefore companies often have to resort to either higher wages or other benefits such as training and qualifications. This is the route which UPS took with the local government authorities in Louisville to overcome staffing shortages at its Worldport hub. Workers are paid to take a degree-level course and are rewarded for academic success and loyalty to the company. This has been very successful in ensuring the retention of staff, as well as motivation.

Other

Other factors involved in the location of distribution centres include the flexibility and efficiency of customs regimes (an important competitive advantage for the Netherlands) as well as the availability and quality of a large number and range of logistics service providers.

Centralization of distribution in Europe

The characteristics of European distribution structures, and how they operate, depends largely on the industry sector, the geographic markets that those industries serve, the product type and the location of manufacturing facilities. Generally, over the last decade or so there has been a move towards centralized distribution of products in Europe, due to the removal of customs barriers and the improvement of transport infrastructure across Europe.

Most distribution structures around the world follow similar patterns and normally fall into one or more of the following distribution centre functions:

- Global distribution centre: often located close to the worldwide manufacturing site and serves to distribute goods to the different worldwide geographic regions.

- European distribution centre (EDC): serving as a central storage of goods for the European, Middle-East and Africa (EMEA) regions and takes care of replenishment of the different regional distribution centres.

- Regional distribution centre, serving as a main distribution centre for a specific region within EMEA, for example the UK/Ireland region or the Nordic region.

- Country/local distribution centre, serving final distribution to customers.

These functions are generic and every company and industry sector will adapt these structures to fit their business. The amount of adaptation depends on the product type, historical development, availability of investment and strategic intent. In the fresh food industry, for example, global or European distribution centres are unusual due to the perishable nature of their products. The product type therefore dictates a local distribution structure. This contrasts with the high tech spare parts industry, where one can see all of the above distribution structures, due to the fact that spare parts need to be delivered within a few hours and are expensive, requiring a centralized distribution structure combined with local delivery points.

The industry trend towards European distribution centres has been driven by large-scale changes in the European transport, supply chain and logistics sector. Over the last decade or so, many barriers to cross-border transactions between countries within the European Union have been removed. Companies therefore have been able to centralize European supply chain structures leading to large cost savings.

Companies such as Deutsche Post and Schenker have built, through acquisition, European and global structures allowing them to service the pan-European and global supply chain requirements of their largest customers. However, this is only a relatively recent development, and many retailers and manufacturers are still operating 'national' supply chain structures (ie within country borders) as part of an overall global strategy. This is evidenced by the fact that logistics companies are still winning national, rather than multinational, logistics contracts. In spite of this, many larger multinationals have moved to a pan-European structure and have benefited from large supply chain cost-savings as a result.

The implication of these trends has meant fundamental changes in the use of warehousing and distribution property. Clearly, a move to a centralized European structure means less demand for smaller, national distribution centres and an increased demand for larger, central pan-European and regional distribution centres.

Several European countries possess many of the key attributes which make them good locations for distribution facilities. The most popular are Belgium, Germany and the Netherlands:

- Belgium benefits from its proximity to seaports (such as Antwerp) and airports (Brussels), its transport infrastructure and the incentives it offers to investing companies.

- Germany benefits from being the largest economy in Europe, its proximity to rail hubs and its infrastructure.

- The Netherlands benefits from its proximity to seaports (Rotterdam) and airports (Amsterdam Schiphol), its transport infrastructure, the incentives offered to investing companies, the multilingualism of its nationals and the positive business environment (including flexible customs regime).

Slightly less attractive are Denmark, France, Ireland and the United Kingdom.

For many manufacturers and retailers, the expansion of the European Union has required a new pan-European distribution strategy. With 10 of the EU's most recent members located in Central Europe, many European companies are looking to extend the reach of their supply chains in an eastward direction. The focus of these companies' efforts has been concentrated in Poland, the Czech Republic, Slovakia and Hungary. Retailers

FIGURE 4.1   Preferred/future European distribution centre locations

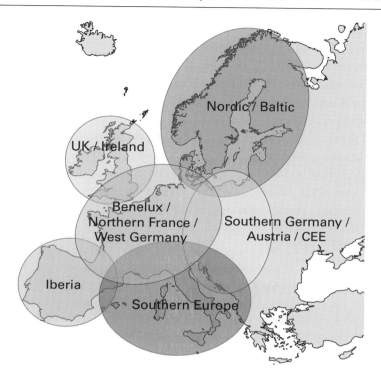

FIGURE 4.2   Location of European distribution centres

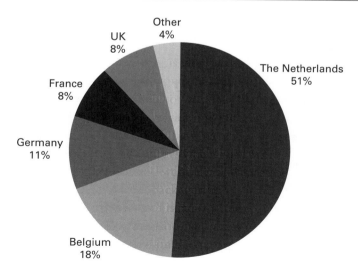

SOURCE: HIDC

such as Carrefour, Auchan and Tesco have partnered with logistics providers to extend relationships into Eastern Europe; European manufacturers such as Volkswagen, Volvo, Fiat and Unilever have relocated part or all of their production facilities to the region.

Clearly, the accession of Central and Eastern European countries into the European Union has had an impact on European distribution. These countries are attracting many Western companies for location of production and/or distribution facilities due to their relatively less expensive land and labour costs. This, in turn, is changing distribution structures. The infrastructure does not currently exist to serve all these new markets from a central distribution location in Benelux, where most European distribution centres are based. Therefore, as distribution throughout the region becomes centralized, locations in the more developed Eastern European countries such as Poland or Hungary have been favoured as well as in Eastern Germany.

Future locations for strong demand

For pan-European distribution, the strongest locations for European distribution centres will continue to be the Netherlands, Germany, France and Belgium, for the short term at least. Germany is likely to experience significant growth in EDCs, due to the accession of Central and Eastern European countries. Existing structures with European Distribution Centres located in Benelux or France can be enhanced in the short to medium term with additional 'satellite' regional distribution centres strategically located in Northern Europe (Nordics), the UK & Ireland, Southern Europe, Eastern Europe and Italy/Greece.

On a national level, a general trend can be observed in many European countries, where new-build warehousing and distribution property is being sited outside of main capital cities, in locations with good transport links, availability of labour and less expensive land, rental and lease costs. Examples of these include:

- in the south and east of Paris and Lyon;
- east of Madrid in San Fernando de Henares, south of Madrid and Tarragona;
- the Rhine-Neckar area or North Hessen in Germany;
- Wroclaw, Silesia, Poznan and Lodz in Poland;
- Brno, Plzen and Ostrava in the Czech Republic;

- Gyal and Győr in Hungary;

- Transilvania, Ploiesti and Banat in Romania;

- Daventry, Kettering, Stoke, M1 corridor above Northampton in the UK (Nottinghamshire, Leicestershire and Derbyshire);

- Kempen, Limburg, Liège and Hainaut in Belgium;

- for the Netherlands, the following areas will be active: Coenhaven, Vlothaven in Amsterdam, Spaanse Polder in Rotterdam, De Hurk/Ekkersrijt and De Kade in Eindhoven, Lage Weide in Utrecht and Trade Port in Venlo;

- Piacenza, Novara and Chieti in Italy.

Of course, ports are key strategic locations for warehousing and distribution property: Rotterdam, Le Havre, Barcelona, Hamburg, Marseille and Antwerp will see further expansion of warehousing space. Airports too will continue to be popular locations.

FIGURE 4.3   European strategic distribution locations

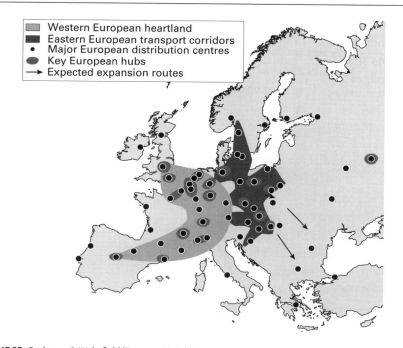

SOURCE: Cushman & Wakefield/Transport Intelligence

Centralization of distribution in the United States

Geographically, distribution space in the United States is divided between coastal areas and 'inland ports'. Traditionally, ports in California, Seattle, Florida and the east coast around New York and New Jersey have been a magnet for warehousing and distribution space. However, a lack of space around the ports of Los Angeles and Long Beach has seen the growth and development of the Inland Empire, situated slightly further in from the coast.

The saturation of coastal space has also seen the development of 'inland ports' in locations such as Chicago, Atlanta and Dallas. Other locations include Kansas City, Memphis, Columbus, Harrisburg and Front Royal, Virginia. Goods arriving at ports such as Jacksonville, Savannah and Charleston on the east coast are transported to distribution centres in Atlanta. Here goods are stored, ready for dispersal throughout the east of America.

These 'inland ports' have also seen an increase in activity due to the increasing level of goods that are arriving from Asia Pacific and in particular China. The volume of goods arriving on the west coast has increased dramatically in the last 10 years. These goods are transported from west coast ports via rail to Chicago and Atlanta for distribution to the east of America. Dallas likewise acts as a distribution hub, located between the west and east coast of the country.

Dallas, and Texas as a whole, has also increased in significance as a distribution hub due to its location on the border with Mexico. US manufacturers are increasingly using warehousing space in northern Mexico where costs are cheaper. As a result, warehouses are also needed on the American side of the border from where goods can then be distributed to the rest of the country.

As ports become more congested companies are delaying breaking containers until trains can carry them much further inland to locations such as Texas. Companies are also starting to use deep-water ports in Mexico, as an alternative to the ports of Los Angeles and Long Beach, which has increased the importance of movement between Mexico and Texas.

Business-related taxes play an important role in determining where to locate a logistics hub. Sales and use tax, the cost for unemployment insurance for employees, corporate income tax, personal property, inventory, and fuel tax rates are all important factors.

There have been major changes in distribution patterns in the retailing sector. The past decade has seen Walmart consolidate its national presence across the United States. Walmart now has a well-established infrastructure of distribution centres across the United States. This is characterized by centralized distribution centres around the centres of gravity of major markets.

The continuing change in this market subsegment – which also applies to major home products company Home Depot – is the reorientation of its supply chain to sourcing from China. This has had the effect of major retailers relocating their warehousing to adapt to the new supply chain geography. Up until recently product was generally delivered to regional distribution centres, usually multimodally. However, such is the volume of product entering the United States that specific facilities have been created to consolidate and store inventory before it is fed out to the distribution system across the country. Obviously, these have tended to be located on the US west coast, particularly around Los Angeles. However, there are important new locations. For example, the port of Tacoma, which has grown on trans-pacific volumes, has seen the furniture retailer IKEA open an 800,000 sq ft development.

More extreme is the growth of facilities on the east coast. Notable is the development of a 900,000 sq ft facility by Walmart at Jacksonville port on the Atlantic coast of Florida. The logic behind such development is the ability to bypass congested ports and rail capacity coming out of the west coast.

FIGURE 4.4   The United States – main distribution centre hubs

In terms of developments further down the supply chain there have been several contradictory developments. On the one hand the continued move to big box retailing had led to a consolidation of logistics infrastructure. However, there is a marked shift towards less commoditized retailing emerging over the past two years both in non-food and food retailing smaller shops.

Another clear trend in US retailing is the move towards internet retailing activities. Probably the most high-profile brand in this area is the e-retailer Amazon that has diversified in other product areas. Its market penetration is strong across the United States and it has constructed an established network of large facilities.

Key hub locations in the United States

Atlanta

Due to Atlanta's geographic location, the area is a popular location for warehousing and distribution facilities, particularly for logistics and transportation providers as well as retailers. The growing automotive industry in not only Georgia, but the surrounding states – South Carolina, Tennessee and Alabama – is also spurring growth.

The region serves as a major transportation hub. Close proximity to major interstates allows truck companies to reach 80 per cent of the United States within two days.

Atlanta also benefits from Atlanta Hartsfield-Jackson International Airport which is the eleventh largest air cargo in the United States, as well as the Port of Savannah which, located a few hours to the south, is the second busiest US port for containerized export tonnage.

Chicago

Chicago is a major transportation hub, in which all modes of travel and freight movement intersect. Five federal highways and six of America's major railroads pass through the city. The region also has a port and offers air freight services via the Chicago O'Hare International Airport and Midway International Airport.

The state of Illinois has the second largest rail system in the United States, with almost 10,000 route miles of track and 39 freight rail companies. As a result, Chicago is not only a major hub for the nation's rail system, but is also one of the largest intermodal systems in the country. Congestion is a major problem for the road network within the Chicago area.

Louisville, Kentucky

Louisville is the home to UPS's Worldport, the global headquarters for UPS Airlines, located at Louisville International Airport. One of the area's largest employers, UPS also has numerous warehousing and distribution facilities in the area including two temperature-controlled centres. In total, UPS has approximately 70 customers that utilize its facilities, mostly in the high tech and healthcare industries.

Canadian Pacific, Norfolk Southern and CSX operate in Louisville. CSX recently built an intermodal hub which connects the city with its north-east Ohio intermodal network. Besides its rail connections, Louisville also is accessible via three major interstate highways – I-65, I-64 and I-71 as well as two inland ports on the Ohio River that connects with the US inland waterway system.

Memphis, Tennessee

Memphis is called a 'quad-modal' hub – that is, goods may be transported by river, road, rail or air from this city. Memphis sits on two major national interstates – I-40, which links it to California to the west and North Carolina to the east and I-55, which links the city to New Orleans to the south and Chicago to the north.

The Memphis International Airport is the largest cargo airport in the United States. FedEx, headquartered in Memphis, utilizes the airport as its primary hub. UPS also considers the airport as an important air hub for its operations.

Los Angeles, California

Los Angeles is a major location for warehousing and distribution centres due to its position as a major west coast port. Located to the south of Los Angeles, the Riverside-San Bernardino-Ontario area is one which is collectively known as the 'Inland Empire'. Due to a large supply of vacant land and a transport network where many highways and railroads intersect, the Inland Empire has become a major shipping hub.

The LA/Ontario International Airport is a major west coast air and truck hub for UPS whilst Los Angeles International Airport serves as a major west coast hub for FedEx.

The ports of Los Angeles and Long Beach handle about 40 per cent of the nation's Asian imports. Both Union Pacific and BNSF railroad companies provide direct rail access for the ports.

Centralization of distribution in China

As a region that is responsible for over 35 per cent of total global exports, Asia's airports and seaports are consistently ranked as some of the largest in the world for tonnage carried. In fact, the top eight largest global ports are located in this region. Many Asian countries are expanding these ports as well as building new ones to accommodate growing trade. In addition, four Asian airports are ranked in the top 10 largest global cargo airports – Hong Kong, Shanghai, Incheon and Tokyo.

As trade continues to increase throughout the region, Asian countries are investing in much needed infrastructure projects within their borders. As individual countries improve their networks, the need to link these countries is also increasing. Intra-regional trade and the need to efficiently transport goods to outside markets are the primary reasons for the need of a combined network. As such, international organizations, China, the ASEAN economic community and logistics providers are pushing to improve links throughout the region.

For years, the United Nations Economic and Social Commission for Asia and the Pacific (UNESCAP) have worked with Asian countries to develop the Asian Highway. Conceived in 1959, it did not receive much traction until about 10 years ago. Since then, 23 Asian countries have signed the Asian Highway agreement and are working towards completing a 141,204 km network that will integrate the region.

Logistics providers are also connecting countries via road and rail service offerings. Perhaps one of the best known offerings is TNT's Asia Road Network. Established in 2005, the network is modelled after TNT's European Road Network and is wholly managed by TNT. The network stretches across 127 cities in seven countries across Southeast Asia and China for a distance of more than 7,650 km.

Agility's integrated trucking network provides shippers with an option to truck directly to several major cities in Southeast Asia and China as well as direct connections to major airports and ports in the regions. According to the company, the service provides shippers with a cost-effective alternative to air freight with savings of 30 per cent to 40 per cent.

Countries within the Asia Pacific region have varying levels of intermodal infrastructure, and face different geophysical and institutional challenges in upgrading existing infrastructure, or in the creation of new intermodal terminals. The Asia Pacific countries are at differing stages in devising solutions for removing inefficiencies and competition between companies operating different modes. The respective governments and industry groups, however, recognize the benefits attained by establishing intermodal freight systems to deliver improved economic performance.

However, compared with the integration of markets in the EU, progress towards market integration is at a very early stage and consequently the vast majority of secondary distribution throughout the region occurs on a national, rather than intra-regional basis. Rationalization of tariffs, customs clearance and duty procedures have yet to allow the development of region-wide distribution centres to anywhere near the same extent as in Europe.

Key distribution hub locations in China

Since the mid-2000s, the significant demand and growth potential of Chinese distribution markets has been driven by a number of key factors including:

- World Trade Organization related policy changes;
- a strengthening manufacturing sector;
- growth in export markets;
- 'Open Skies' aviation agreements;
- expanding domestic markets and investment.

FIGURE 4.5   China – main distribution centre hubs

Tax incentives and aggressive infrastructure development have been used to attract foreign investors to the Chinese market in development zones specified by the authorities, in either free trade zones or bonded logistics parks.

Geographically, distribution centres in China have been based in three regions: the Pearl River Delta (south), the Yangtze River Delta (east) and the Beijing Tianjin area (north-east). These areas are identified within the Chinese market as the primary hubs; secondary and emerging hubs are also identified. Secondary hubs are those that are beginning to attract an increase in attention from international operators, and emerging centres are those that have strategically important locations.

Chinese infrastructure is receiving significant investment to support the rapid growth of the economy. Ports have played a vital role in the development of the logistics industry and will continue to develop with China's global manufacturing role. Excluding Hong Kong, Shanghai and Shenzhen rank amongst the largest ports in the country.

In terms of air transport Hong Kong remains the most important link, primarily due to the large number of destinations served, the modern facilities and the efficiency of the operation. Shanghai, Beijing and Guangzhou are the three major air cargo hubs situated on mainland China. China is in the process of constructing a further 40 new airports across the country although air cargo growth is expected to focus on these four key hubs.

Inland waterway operations are centred on the Yangtze River, although use of this mode is restricted by low bridges. Rail and road networks are experiencing significant investment. Road is to be expanded from 41,000 km to 85,000 km by 2020 and rail from just over 70,000 km to nearer 100,000 km in the same period. Both networks are planned to expand into western China, although it could take up to a few decades to make an impact within the region.

The distribution market is forecast to see consolidation and a move towards outsourcing. This in turn will create high demand for warehouses of higher standards and increased use of technology within the facilities. The use of warehousing is expected to incorporate value-adding activities, a move away from traditional storage uses.

The locations of warehouses are focused in the three regions of the Yangtze and Pearl River Delta's and Bohai Bay (Beijing and Tianjin), with only 15 per cent of facilities located outside those. Shanghai boasts over one-third of China's warehousing capacity.

FIGURE 4.6   Chinese warehouse locations by region

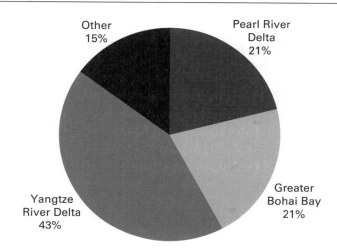

SOURCE: Jones Lang La Salle

05 International freight forwarding

The structure of the freight-forwarding industry

A market definition

Freight forwarders play an important role in facilitating international trade, fulfilling a number of distinct functions. In basic terms they act on behalf of exporters to buy and manage transportation services. These usually include air or sea freight, as well as the land transportation required to move the goods from the shipper to the port.

In its purest definition a freight forwarder owns no assets of its own, rather managing the transport and warehousing assets of others. However, in reality many freight forwarders are also involved in what could be termed 'integrated logistics'. One of the main reasons for this is that it enables companies to move from the commoditized buying and selling of carrier capacity to offering value-added services, increasing what is traditionally a low-margin business.

Clecat, the European forwarders' association, provides a comprehensive definition of the current forwarding industry. It states that 'Freight Forwarding and Logistics Services' include services of any kind relating to the carriage (performed by single mode or multimodal transport means), consolidation, storage, handling, packing or distribution of goods, as well as related ancillary and advisory services. The latter includes customs and fiscal matters, declaring goods for official purposes, procuring insurance and collecting or procuring payment or documents. Freight Forwarding Services also include logistical services with modern information and communication technology in connection with the carriage, handling or storage, and de facto total supply chain management. These services can be tailored to meet the flexible application of the services provided.

This definition draws little distinction between freight forwarders and global logistics providers, and indeed at the top end of the market this could well be the case. Companies such as Schenker, Kuehne + Nagel and DHL often combine logistics with freight-forwarding services for global key accounts. For smaller customers there is no such crossover, with a more traditional approach to freight forwarding being adopted.

Customs brokerage

As well as buying and selling capacity from carriers, freight forwarders also play an important role in liaising with various customs authorities, acting on behalf of the exporter or importer. This is often referred to as 'customs brokerage' and includes the preparation of the requisite trade documentation as well as the payment of customs duties on behalf of the shipper. This calls for a knowledge of trade regulations, quotas and tariffs.

A customs broker will often also undertake bonded warehousing, which allows a shipper to defer payments of duties and taxes until a later stage in the sales process. For instance, it will be able to store imported goods until they are sold, at which time the duties become payable. This helps the shippers' cash flows.

Non-vessel owning common carriers (NVOCCs)

A specific type of operation exists in the sea freight sector known as non-vessel owning common carrier (NVOCC). This is not only a term to describe a specific business function in the freight-forwarding industry, but in some markets, mainly the United States, it also carries legal weight. In functional terms, an NVOCC buys space from a shipping line and then retails this space, usually to other freight forwarders, on a less than container load basis (LCL). This provides a service to forwarders which do not have the necessary volumes to book a full container load directly with the shipping line. In many ways this is a similar service to that provided by air freight wholesalers. NVOCCs buy the bulk space by entering into service contracts with ocean carriers that require the shipment of a minimum quantity of cargo throughout the year or the payment of damages.

The status of NVOCC is highly ambiguous, given that in function it resembles another form of freight forwarding, yet legally (in the United States for instance) it carries with it the specific responsibilities of carrier status. In maritime law, although an NVOCC accepts a 'carrier's entrustment' it is also charged with taking delivery and delivering cargo in the name of carriers, two contradictory principles. To complicate matters further it publishes tariffs and schedules in the same way as a carrier.

The ambiguity comes about as in maritime law the definition of 'carrier' does not depend on the criterion of 'having vessels' or 'not having vessels', but whether interested parties have a contractual relationship of transportation, and whether the party providing transportation service is liable for the transportation in accordance with the contract or law. From the perspective of global transportation practice, the NVOCC concept is only uniquely found in US legislature, at odds with prevailing international transportation practice.

The status and definition of the NVOCC has been called into focus by attempts by China to create a regulated market. The authorities could either follow the US example, and create a layer of regulation and administration dealing separately with freight forwarders and NVOCCs, or adopt the internationally accepted pragmatic view that NVOCCs are a type of freight forwarder and should be dealt with as such. This latter approach would prevent confusion for new market entrants as to whether they should register as freight forwarders or NVOCCs.

Size is an important competitive advantage for NVOCCs. It gives them economies of scale in infrastructure, a wider range of routes and ability to obtain better load ratios for their containers. With these advantages, its current market position seems defensible and there is an opportunity to develop in the 50 per cent of the market served by forwarders using in-house provision and also to improve import market penetration.

Air freight wholesalers

Although the major freight forwarders are able to buy and fill belly-hold space direct from the airlines on certain key routes, many smaller forwarders do not have the necessary volumes. Instead a group of companies known as 'wholesalers' buy capacity, which they then sell on in smaller packages to freight forwarders. A wholesaler will act as a consolidator in much the same way as a NVOCC operates in the sea freight business. Wholesalers providing a 'scheduled' service are able to command competitive rates on behalf of their clients as they book regular space with the airline.

Modal choice by shippers

The decision by a shipper to use either air or sea freight is driven by four main factors:

- The value of the goods
  If the transportation element of the final cost of the goods is small, say in the case of high tech shipments, shippers can afford to send the goods by higher cost modes, such as air.

- The time sensitivity involved
  Although the goods themselves may not have an innate high value, such as a spare part for a production line or a ship, the consequential loss which could be incurred by longer shipping times may itself be a factor in the choice of mode. This works equally well for documents and goods with short product life cycles where there is a critical need to get to market.

- The weight of the shipment
  The cost of transporting heavier weights usually precludes the use of air, either through cost, or through the constraints placed upon air freight consignments by the size of capacity.

- Product attribute
  Some consignments, such as some classes of dangerous goods, are not allowed to travel by air. This leaves a shipper with sea freight as its only option.

TABLE 5.1 Key factors in modal choice

Merchandise attributes	Air freight	Sea freight
High value	Y	N
Time sensitivity	Y	N
Quick response	Y	N
Short product life cycle	Y	N
High value: density ratio	Y	N
Dangerous goods	N	Y

Although individual circumstances often drive the modal choice, it has been suggested as a rule of thumb that a shipper will send goods by air only if the costs are less than 15–20 per cent of total value.

Fashion goods can fall into either category, largely due to the needs of the shipper at the time. Most retailers will attempt to forecast needs far enough ahead to use lower cost ocean freight to move goods. However, if sales are stronger than predicted, air freight can be used to replenish stocks, albeit at a lower margin.

Fragmentation and consolidation

Freight forwarding is a highly fragmented market, characterized by small to very small companies. Low barriers to market entry allowed very small enterprises to enter the market and compete effectively with the major players, depressing margins.

This is despite the development of a small number of large companies which have sought to differentiate their products through intellectual capital and IT systems that provide visibility and co-ordination between the forwarder and the physical asset operators.

Larger companies can in theory also enjoy a competitive advantage through their scale. By being able to leverage their volumes on certain routes they can demand lower rates from carriers which they are then able to pass on to customers. However, this advantage should not be overemphasized, as smaller freight forwarders are able to use NVOCCs who consolidate volumes from different sources to achieve the same effect.

In order to gauge an idea of the level of fragmentation in the freight-forwarding market, the Herfindahl-Hirschman Index (HHI) can be utilized. The HHI methodology applies a weighted system to market share data in order to determine the dominance of leading players. Using a scale of zero to 10,000, a value of below 1,000 indicates an 'unconcentrated' market, while a value of between 1,000 and 1,800 indicates a 'moderately concentrated' market. If the number is above 1,800, the market is said to be 'highly concentrated'.

Using this technique, the freight-forwarding market was found to have an index value of 255 in 2011. This indicates a fragmented market with high levels of competition. While a very gradual upward trend in the index was seen between 2007 and 2010 (implying that larger players were gaining market share), the index fell back slightly in 2011.

This would seem to suggest that there is little evidence of increasing consolidation in the sector. Applying the Herfindahl-Hirschman Index methodology shows that there has been remarkably little change in the structure of the freight-forwarding business, either in sea or in air freight.

This is perhaps a little surprising, bearing in mind the acquisitive role of large forwarders such as DHL, yet it only serves to highlight that despite their clear position as the biggest forwarder in air freight, they hold a very modest overall proportion of the market.

FIGURE 5.1   The freight-forwarding Herfindahl-Hirschman Index

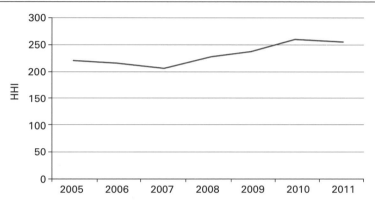

SOURCE: Transport Intelligence

The restructuring of the freight-forwarding sector

The last few years have seen considerable mergers and acquisition activity as all the major logistics companies have sought to increase their presence in the global forwarding market.

The highlights of this trend are:

● the purchase of Exel by Deutsche Post. Exel itself was the product of a merger between contract logistics company Exel and forwarder Ocean Group (including MSAS). Deutsche Post had already acquired a number of other large forwarders, notably Danzas, AEI and ASG;

● Deutsche Bahn's acquisition of German forwarder Schenker and US forwarder Bax Global;

● UPS's acquisition of two US forwarders, Fritz and Menlo (formerly Emery);

● CEVA's acquisition of EGL.

The reasons behind these different purchases vary to a degree by company, but have a unifying logic in reflecting the trends in the market for freight forwarding. For example DP DHL created out of its acquisition of both Exel and Danzas a logistics division that combines the ability to move large volumes of freight both by sea and by air, using its forwarding capability, with the road transport and warehousing capabilities of its contract logistics business. This is also the case with Kuehne + Nagel, which has aggressively built up its contract logistics/road freight network in order to complement its freight-forwarding business.

Essentially, what these companies are trying to do is increase market share by offering more integrated services and improve margins by offering more sophisticated services.

There is another aspect to the strategic trends in the freight forwarders' market. As in the case of UPS, a number of express parcel companies are trying to claim part of the business that has traditionally been undertaken by freight forwarders. This is particularly the case in air freight services for the electronics business, but is also seen in other sectors.

Integrators v freight forwarders

Air freight forwarders have seen their market share eroded over the last three decades by the emergence of the four major integrated express operators: DHL, UPS, TNT and FedEx. Their development has been aided by current supply chain management requirements; namely fast, reliable movement of goods underpinned by information technology. Originally, forwarders in Europe believed that integrators would provide little threat within the context of a complex multi-country trading environment, and would therefore largely be constrained to the United States. However, this proved not to be the case, and the integrators proved extremely able to compete in Europe even before the advent of the Single European Market in the early 1990s, which did away with customs barriers.

One of the main problems for the freight forwarders was that as their 'asset-light' business model relied upon contracting with carriers they lacked the control which integrators could exert over their own vehicles and aircraft. This gave them considerable advantages:

- The integrators were able to introduce track and trace technology at an early stage.

- They guaranteed capacity on their own aircraft, whereas forwarders' consignments were often 'bumped' (not flown) if a carrier had overbooked.
- Quality control could be ensured.

The hub-and-spoke networks which were operated by integrators allowed them to offer daily services, rather than less frequent consolidations ('consols') on a point to point basis.

As has been mentioned, the integrators' use of their own aircraft meant that they were not dependent on belly-hold freight capacity supplied by the main airlines. Air freight until recently was never given particularly high priority by the main air carriers, which would base their network strategies on passenger demands rather than on freight, which was seen as a by-product. Although this sometimes benefited forwarders as freight was priced on a marginal cost basis, it also meant that there was no long-term or consistent freight strategy in place. Speed and reliability can suffer where freight is subordinate to passenger requirements.

The result of competition from international express carriers led to the loss of the highly lucrative parcels for freight forwarders. Since then they have been forced to focus on heavy weight goods; on consignments which do not fit the integrators' need for high levels of standardization, eg dangerous goods or on price.

However, in recent years the major forwarders, in conjunction with the largest air carriers (such as Lufthansa, Air France), have fought back against the integrators. The airlines have introduced guaranteed time-definite services which have allowed their clients, the forwarders, in turn to provide their clients with a more reliable service. Advances in technology have allowed forwarders to increase the level of visibility with which they can provide the shipper irrespective of who owns the transport and logistics assets. This has reduced the competitive advantage of the integrators.

'Disintermediation'

The term 'disintermediation' was coined in the 1990s to describe the process of removing third parties from the client–supplier relationship and applies to a range of different industries. Specifically related to the air freight sector, the term applies to the potential removal of freight forwarders from the relationship between shipper (manufacturer or retailer) and the carrier.

The concept has attracted much discussion over the last decade, although there is no sign that it will be adopted. This is in stark contrast with the air passenger industry, where many travel agents have been marginalized, especially in the low cost, short haul sector. Airlines such as EasyJet and Ryanair in Europe have adopted a 'direct' sales approach through telephone or internet sales, thus eradicating sales commission.

When one airline, KLM, was rumoured to be developing a direct sales approach with some major shippers (such as Philips) it attracted widespread criticism from freight forwarders, its existing clients. Afraid of alienating its client base, it backtracked, and there has been little sign that other airlines would develop a similar approach.

The power of the freight forwarders in the airline industry contrasts with the situation in the sea freight sector. Here shippers are accustomed to going direct to the major shipping lines.

Freight-forwarding market dynamics

Essentially, a freight forwarder acts as an intermediary in the market between shipper and carrier. Their business model depends on their ability to buy capacity and sell it at a profit. This means that the fortunes of the freight-forwarding sector are directly affected by supply issues in the shipping and air transport industries as well as underlying demand from shippers.

The freight-forwarding market is countercyclical, which means that in times of economic downturn it is able to enhance profits, even though total revenues weaken. This is because as volumes weaken in a recession, the carriers (either shipping lines or airlines) have excess capacity, which allows the freight forwarders to drive down rates, whilst passing on only a proportion of these savings to the shipper.

As the economy picks up, carrier capacity starts to tighten and rates subsequently harden. Although the forwarder finds it difficult to pass on all these rate rises to its clients, its profits in absolute terms increase due to increased volumes.

Of course, there are times when this supply/demand pattern becomes asynchronous, especially in the air cargo sector. Supply is not just influenced by the demand for cargo as a large proportion of goods travel in the belly-holds of schedule passenger flights. This means that supply can be affected by socio-political events (such as the SARS virus or terrorism) which reduce movements of passengers, rather than by the economic cycle.

In sea freight the dynamics are slightly different, although the fundamentals are the same. In theory, capacity takes longer to bring on stream, due to the time it takes to build ships. Therefore, for long periods of the economic cycle there is often undersupply, due to shipping lines' inability to accurately predict demand, followed by oversupply when a large amount of extra capacity is introduced. Due to the time lag, this often occurs after the peak in demand, flooding the market and resulting in a collapse in rates. Of course, in reality it is often more difficult to work out patterns of supply and demand (see Figure 5.2 below).

The air cargo sector is also highly cyclical but even more volatile than shipping. It relies on the shipment of high value goods such as high technology and luxury items, which are dependent on the global economy. When there is a downturn in the economy, investment in new technology and sales in prestige goods are cut, with a significant impact on volumes.

Figure 5.2 provides an illustration of the relationship between carriers and freight forwarders throughout the economic cycle. It tracks demand, supply and the impact on forwarders' gross margins. This latter metric is most important for forwarders as it strips out the amount paid to carriers and is a better indicator of their performance.

FIGURE 5.2   Theoretical countercyclicality in the freight-forwarding sector – Scenario 1

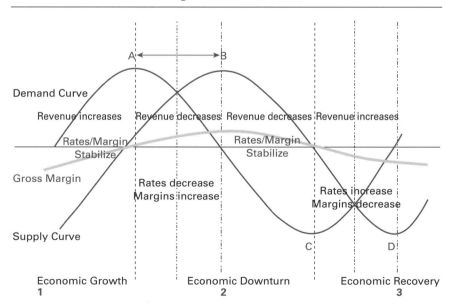

Gross Margin = gross profit/net revenue

Net Revenue is invoiced turnover (but not including duties and taxes)

Gross Profit is net revenue less fees paid to carriers

Gross Profit is sometimes referred to, confusingly, as 'Net Net Revenue' as it is invoiced turnover less duties and taxes, less carrier costs.

During a period of economic growth (1), demand and supply increase. In this particular 'normal' scenario, capacity and volumes are assumed to be growing at a similar pace, which means that rates and margins are stable.

However, as economic growth starts to slow (as the cycle enters its second phase at point A), supply continues to increase. The reason for this (as outlined above) is that the carriers do not have access to 'perfect' market intelligence. Therefore, their decision making as regards whether to bring on or take out capacity, lags the actual market situation. The effect of this for forwarders is that gross margins start to increase, although revenue growth slows as volumes and rates drop. This part of the cycle demonstrates forwarders' 'countercyclical' business model which is one of the sector's key strengths.

At point B shipping/airlines have realized that they need to adjust their capacity and supply declines. Rates and forwarders' margin start to stabilize.

At point C, the economy has reached the bottom of its cycle and demand once again picks up. However, due to the lagging effect, supply continues to be taken out of the market, meaning that rates harden and forwarders' margins drop. The latter bottom out at point D, when supply (capacity) is brought back into the market. During this time forwarders still benefit from rising volumes.

It should be noted that the closer point A is to point B, the lower the amplitude of change in forwarders' gross margins (in other words the flatter the curve will be).

Another scenario is shown in Figure 5.3.

Here, the capacity and demand curves are further out of alignment. Supply (point X) peaks higher and later than the peak in demand. This creates a period of time (between points A and B) during which volumes are still rising, but are being outstripped by supply. This means that rates are falling, forwarders' gross margins are rising and so are their revenues. It could be termed a 'golden scenario' for forwarders.

Note, the peak of forwarders' gross margin occurs at X1, relating to the peak in supply (rather than that of demand).

FIGURE 5.3   Theoretical countercyclicality in the freight-
forwarding sector – Scenario 2

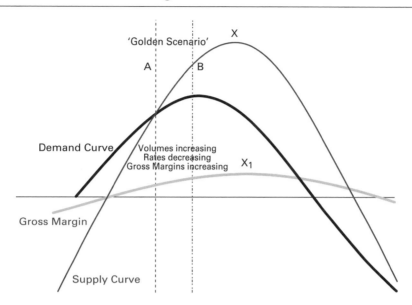

Market data supporting the countercyclicality model

Testing this theoretical model is more difficult, not least due to the difficulty in finding reliable and accurate market data. However, evidence does exist to support this hypothesis of countercyclicality.

The Demand Curve in the chart below is generated using estimates of annual container throughput (TEU) growth. The Supply Curve is generated

FIGURE 5.4   Demand, supply and gross margin in the sea freight
sector (Y-o-Y growth)

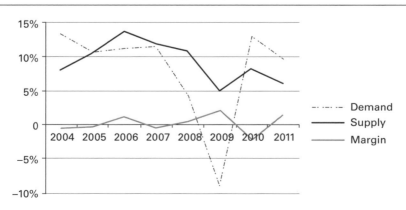

by using estimates of available slot capacity growth (TEU). The Gross Margin figures (year on year change in terms of percentage points) are sourced from global forwarder Kuehne + Nagel, one of the few to publish financial data for this entire period.

The first observation which can be made is that Demand, in terms of container throughput, follows economic development patterns, with growth slowing throughout the 2000s before going into reverse in 2008 and 2009 when the global recession took hold. It also shows clearly the 'V' shaped recovery which took place in 2010 and the dip in 2011 as the market growth moderated.

Supply actually tracks demand more closely than the theoretical model would suggest. However, it is the data from 2008 onwards which best illustrates the lagging countercyclicality of the sector.

As demand falls heavily in 2008 and 2009, after years of growth, shipping lines are not able or unwilling to remove capacity from the market. As a result, rates fall, and as already detailed, forwarders' margins rise. In 2010, demand recovers, but shipping lines are still wary of introducing more capacity as they have made major losses in the years prior. This results in soaring rates and falling forwarder margins. In 2011, the pattern is not so clear. It is true that growth in demand can be seen to drop but hardly sufficiently, it might be thought, to result in the extraordinarily low rates that were evident in the market. However, the falling rates which were observed had a highly positive effect on forwarders' gross margins.

In 2012–13 demand growth is once again likely to moderate, and shipping lines have taken capacity out of the market by scrappage, slow steaming, putting off new builds and forming alliances. Rates have soared; consequently expect forwarders' margins to decrease.

Future forwarding sector performance

As we have seen, forwarders' gross profits are directly influenced by the gap between demand and available capacity in the market place. Hence, to some extent, it is therefore possible to predict future gross profit margins by using estimates of future 'gap ratio'.

However, estimating the 'gap ratio' is not as straightforward as might be thought, as future capacity is not only a derivative of how many ships are being built, but of those which are being taken out of service, and the impacts of slow-steaming (ie in effect making the shipping industry less efficient, not more). In the air cargo industry the situation is even more opaque, given the higher levels of fragmentation and the diverse capacity strategies employed by all-freighter or scheduled 'flag-carrying' airlines.

To show this relationship between gap ratio and gross margins more clearly, Figure 5.5 tracks three different sets of metrics: the historic gap ratio between total available capacity in the container shipping sector (supply) and the total number of containers shipped (demand). This is indicated by the axis on the right-hand side as a percentage.

The second metric is gross margin (also indicated on the right-hand axis). To obtain sufficient historical data back to 2004 the figures used are those of Kuehne + Nagel.

The third metric is average shipping rates between Asia and Europe throughout the period in question. For this the left-hand axis is used.

FIGURE 5.5 The relationship between rates, gap ratio and gross margin

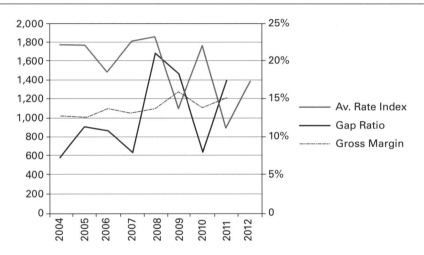

The period 2008–09 shows in sharp relief what would be expected in a downturn. As volumes slumped at about the time that capacity was reaching a peak in the market, the gap ratio soared, average rates fell violently, and forwarders' gross margins peaked. In 2011, the economic slowdown caused demand to fall again, and the gap ratio went back up again, leading to an increase once again in gross margins.

Overall, it can be seen that gross margins have generally improved over the past eight years, whilst rates have generally declined. During this time, gap ratios have been highly volatile.

However, as can be seen, there is a reasonable inverse correlation between change in gap ratio and rate index (−0.47). As well as this, there is a strong positive correlation between gap ratio and gross margin (0.65). The strongest inverse correlation is between rate increase and gross margin increase (–0.85).

Figure 5.6 shows two forwarders' margins – Kuehne + Nagel (line (1)) and Panalpina (line (2)).

It can be seen that the gross margin does not change by the same magnitude as either gap ratio or rates, both of which are much more volatile. Instead, it moves within a band of +/–three percentage points showing that forwarders are not able to 'profiteer' in times of weak demand/high capacity, but nor are they too badly affected when shipping rates soar.

FIGURE 5.6   Y-o-Y percentage point change in sea freight rates, gap ratio and selected gross margins

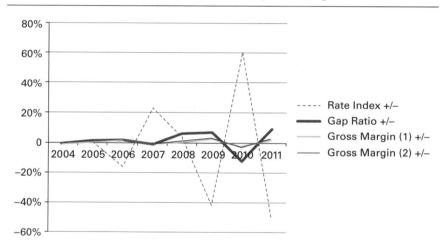

Further research has shown that in terms of countercyclicality and profitability, the air cargo sector performs in the same way to the sea freight sector.

Freight forwarders' profitability

As has been mentioned, freight forwarders are remarkably resilient in terms of profitability. Although margins have fallen slightly over the past six years, they have remained roughly around the 5 per cent level. This is despite the volatility in revenues which can be seen over the same period. Figure 5.7 tracks the profitability and net revenues of the largest, listed freight forwarders.

However, there is a considerable range in the profitability of the leading freight forwarders. Expeditors achieve operating profit margins of around

FIGURE 5.7 Freight-forwarding sector revenue index and operating margins

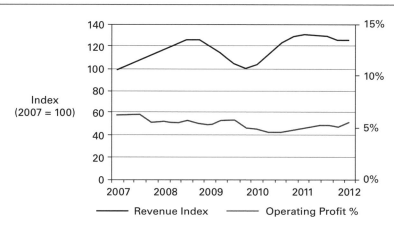

10 per cent, whereas at the other end of the scale a number of companies operate at margins between 2 and 4 per cent. The average operating margin of the companies included in this survey is 4 per cent, which has come down from 5.4 per cent in 2009.

Figure 5.8 plots forwarders' operating margin against their revenues. It is assumed that most companies would prefer to be in the top-right quartile – very large and highly profitable.

FIGURE 5.8 Selected freight forwarders: analysis of size and profitability

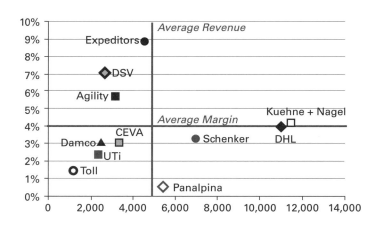

It is difficult to identify one single reason for the diverse range of profitability, given the companies all perform similar functions in the same markets. Some suggestions, however, are listed below:

- Management and staff. Freight forwarding relies heavily on the ability of staff to buy and sell effectively. It needs experienced and high quality personnel who are motivated and well managed.

- Buying power. Buying power in the industry is important. A freight forwarder with large volumes can buy better rates from a shipping/airline. However, the freight forwarder then has a choice. It can either benefit itself from the lower rates by not passing them on fully to shippers. Or it can use these lower rates to grab market share, by operating at lower margins.

- Overheads. Some companies will be better at operating with lower overheads than others – and this will include offices and IT. In many respects this comes back to the quality of the management making decisions on investment.

Contract logistics

Emergence of a global industry

The emergence of the contract logistics industry is driven by the level of development in an economy or, more specifically, the sophistication of its supply chains. As the world's economy continues to evolve through the development of global supply chains, the spread of contract logistics is being accelerated.

'Outsourcing' has traditionally been perceived as the driver of the contract logistics sector. Large corporations have focused on 'core competences' and in many cases this has not included logistics. Many large retailers and manufacturers have sought to rid themselves of transport and warehousing assets, although to begin with (and still the case for some companies) many have been unwilling to lose control of the management of their logistics. This outsourcing trend has been complemented by the need to manage global supply chains, resulting in a new structure to the logistics industry. Many logistics service providers' clients now look to them to provide management capabilities as well as transport and warehousing assets.

Globalization of industry has inevitably led to a globalized contract logistics market. Supply chains for many product types now stretch across the world driven by the dynamic of different value-adding processes taking place in a diverse range of countries. This has had an enormous impact on logistics.

Company logistics systems are not only now more important strategically, but the nature of activities has also changed. The geographic reach of supply chains demands logistics concerned as much with co-ordination as access to physical resources. Issues such as inventory management have become more complex, with product spread across world trading routes.

One of the salient characteristics of the larger LSPs in the sector has been their attempt to integrate freight forwarding into their business model. This is not new, with companies such as the former Exel combining the two types

of business in the late 1990s in order to serve customers in emerging production locations. Nonetheless, this trend has accelerated, with most major
contract logistics companies having a freight-forwarding business as well.

The origins of the contract logistics sector are quite parochial. Owing a
good deal to specific market conditions in the UK in the late 1970s and early
1980s it grew, in part, out of the wish of grocery retailers and fast-moving
consumer goods producers to improve return on capital.

However, it has since undergone a transformation. Although grocery retailing has remained important to the sector, a major driver of the business in the
1990s was the automotive sector in both Europe and North America. Yet
this remained largely based on national industries. Large German car manufacturers approached the business of buying logistics services in a different
manner than, say, Ford based in the UK. France was different again.

Towards the end of the 1990s this structure began to change, driven by
the changes in supply chain management. Increasing numbers of original
equipment manufacturers in the automotive, electronics and also consumer
goods sectors began to open plants in new production locations in Asia-Pacific
and Central Europe. Faced with underdeveloped transport markets they
approached the existing 'third party' logistics companies to help them with
logistics in these new locations. This started the trend towards a globalized
contract logistics market.

Over the past few years the market for contract logistics has spread aggressively into parts of the world where previously it had been absent and these
new markets are the major driver of growth for the contract logistics market.

The automotive logistics market is a good example of the change. Ford,
for example, has developed its production facilities in areas such as South
America, Turkey or Southeast Asia over the past 10 years. Although it has
had assembly plants in countries such as Brazil for several decades, it has
sought to improve the logistics operations in these plants by adopting the
types of systems it has developed in its European and North American
operations.

Key to doing this was bringing the LSPs it was using in Europe and North
America into South America. So, when Ford opened its new Brazilian plant
at Camacari, Bahia in Brazil it brought in Exel (now DHL Supply Chain) to
manage the plant's logistics. It is notable that this is an unusually comprehensive and close relationship. This illustrates that large customers such as
Ford are more reliant on big LSPs in locations such as Brazil than they are
in Western Europe and North America.

This trend has accelerated in the past decade and is very likely to continue
to do so. The automotive sector may be a pioneer in terms of entering new

markets, but it is being closely followed by other sectors. The consumer goods sector regards emerging markets as being key to their present and future growth. However, the logistics infrastructure in many of these markets is poor.

Consequently, big manufacturers are receptive to global LSPs entering markets in the Middle East, the Indian subcontinent, parts of Southeast Asia and to a lesser degree China, in order to support their businesses in the regions. This is particularly the case if LSPs construct physical infrastructure, notably warehousing, which is often in short supply. Other sectors are developing almost as rapidly, with electronic goods being a prominent sector.

The nature of this type of emerging market growth favours the bigger LSPs. They have the resources required both to establish a presence in these markets and they offer the depth and breadth of service that the big customers in these markets require.

The benefit of this market development for big LSPs is substantial. Not only are they offered the potential for much deeper – and therefore more profitable – relationships with customers, but they also have less competition. Markets in Western Europe and North America are highly competitive with the bigger LSPs often under pressure from mid-sized LSPs operating within their domestic economy. This pressure is markedly less in many emerging markets.

There is a tendency for some mid-sized LSPs to 'piggyback' into new markets on the back of big customers. An example of this is the German LSP Schnellecke, which has expanded into China on the back of Volkswagen's business. This is possible when the client is willing to provide sufficient assurance of a contract to support the development of physical infrastructure.

Selecting the right logistics service provider

Supply chain services have been outsourced for some time, with contract distribution developed throughout the UK in the 1970s and 80s and retailers leading the way. Initial outsourcing was designed primarily to consolidate deliveries.

Choosing the right outsourced logistics provider is one of the most critical steps which a manufacturer or retailer can take. It is now accepted that competitive advantage is achieved by having the best supply chain rather than just the best product, and the consequences of getting it wrong can be catastrophic. Although the wider public only usually gets to hear about the success stories, there have been some well-documented supply chain disasters which have resulted in product left in warehouses rather than on the shelves.

In such cases it is the logistics provider which usually gets the blame, although the true responsibility must lie with the client. It is therefore not surprising that where experienced logistics suppliers do not exist (for example in Southern Europe) shippers are not keen on relinquishing control of a critical part of their business. Even in highly developed markets such as the UK, some specialist activities are still kept in-house as logistics suppliers have yet to develop the competency to deal with them.

Perhaps the most important part of the outsourcing process is trust, as without it the relationship between client and supplier becomes adversarial and strained. In the worst case, the supplier will then start hiding mistakes, or the client will start to stretch the scope of the contract without advising the supplier.

The level of the logistics supplier's involvement will influence the point at which it is introduced into the sales process. Many clients will use a consultancy to undertake supply chain re-engineering, and then manage the tender process to find the logistics company with the best fit to the solution which has been developed. This type of approach often relegates logistics providers' input to providing rates for volumes on certain routes, with price a major factor in the decision-making process. For this reason many of the larger logistics companies are shunning the tender process as it diminishes their value add, and hence reduces their margins.

Some of the more proactive suppliers aim to contact potential targets at the beginning of the sales process, demonstrating the benefits which they could bring to the company in terms of inventory reduction. As inventory accounts for a much higher proportion of costs than pure transportation, any gains which a logistics company can help the client make will have a greater proportional benefit.

This will also impact upon the type of contract which the client agrees with the supplier. Logistics companies can potentially make higher margins where there are elements of risk and reward in the make-up of the contract. However, when such agreements are made it is essential that they are backed up by objectivity and transparency of key performance indicators (KPIs). A breakdown of trust is inevitable if there is protracted wrangling over whether targets have or have not been met by the logistics supplier.

Most outsourced contracts lie somewhere in between, with one of the biggest decisions for the client being whether to choose a dedicated or shared user solution. This will depend not only upon the volumes and scope of the operation, but also on the level of specialization required. For example, security is a major issue in certain high-value electronic sectors.

Having defined the overall outsourcing strategy, the client is in a position to review the wide variety of suppliers in the market. The metrics against which they will draw up a potential shortlist range from the 'show-stoppers' to the 'nice to have'.

One of the first issues which the client will look at is the financial standing of a potential supplier. Given the critical nature of the logistics function to the client, it is essential that the logistics provider has a strong balance sheet, particularly in today's difficult economic environment. A company which has financial troubles is more likely to focus on its own problems than the needs of its clients. In a worst case scenario the failure of a logistics supplier could be catastrophic to its client.

Allied to this is the robustness of the supplier's management structure, as well as the key points of contact which the client will have with the supplier. Communication will be fundamental to the success of the contract in over-coming the inevitable teething problems and it is important that the logistics supplier can demonstrate that it has in place the necessary systems for issue resolution. These must be backed up by commitment from senior manage-ment and assurances as to long-term allocation of account managers. Changing key personnel regularly is disruptive to the running of the contract, and is usually indicative of deeper-rooted problems of staff turnover.

Another priority, albeit not completely essential, is the level of experience which the logistics supplier has in the client's sector. This provides a level of reassurance to the client that the supplier will not have to go through a learning process at their expense. It also means that the supplier will under-stand their needs and will be offering a similar price to that which is offered to its competitors. However, this is not necessarily the only option for the client. If they want to go beyond matching the performance of their peer group, they may be tempted to work with a logistics company with expertise in a different sector. This can introduce new levels of innovation and cost saving to a sector which may have become overly complacent. An example of this was the way in which Ford worked with UPS in the United States to bring the same level of efficiencies to the distribution of finished vehicles as to bar-coded packages.

A look 'behind the brochure' is also a prerequisite, especially with multinational contracts. Few logistics suppliers are in a position to offer consistent levels of service across a range of geographies, despite claims. The client should look at the level of resources which the supplier has in each country; where applicable the agreements which it has in place with subcontractors or agents, and if feasible actually visit the operations and facilities on the ground.

Technology is also an important factor in making an outsourcing decision. Many companies look to their logistics suppliers to provide them with the latest technology which will save them from having to make the invest-ment themselves. However, there is evidence that over the last five years technology has become less of a competitive advantage for logistics suppliers than it was. The number of companies with sufficiently competent IT cap-abilities has grown as the cost of the technology has reduced. Companies with highly specialist IT needs (a large multinational for example) will often opt to keep the capabilities in-house to reduce reliance on a supplier. This will enable them to disengage more easily from a supplier at the termi-nation of a contract.

Cultural issues must also be addressed in the outsourcing process. The logistics supplier must demonstrate an awareness and understanding of the business philosophy of the potential client. Sensitivity to different working practices and the sharing of the same priorities is essential in making the relationship work.

Finally, and to many clients most importantly, is the issue of cost. However, although surveys continue to show that price is still the major factor in awarding contracts, undue emphasis on this element is misplaced. The potential for making savings throughout the total supply chain far outweighs squeezing the transport and warehousing element of the logistics system. Losing focus of other issues outlined above such as quality, innova-tion, technology and operations can be counterproductive. It can also reduce the process from a highly strategic exercise providing the company with competitive advantage to purely a cost-cutting exercise delivering short-term benefits only.

Financing contracts

One reason behind a company's decision to outsource its logistics to a third party is the desire to take assets off balance sheet and thereby free up capital to be invested in other areas of its business. This is not the case in every contract, as for instance many manufacturers and retailers actually prefer to own the distribution centres, whilst contracting out the activities (and the labour force). This decision is primarily taken for reasons of control, as it facilitates disengagement at the end of contracts. However, many other companies welcome the opportunity to effectively sell off these logistics assets.

A transfer of assets effectively means that the logistics provider becomes a provider of capital to its clients, a role to which it is not necessarily suited. The logistics provider is limited in the level and cheapness of funds it can provide to its client, and there are other specialists in the market who are much more competitive in terms of financing. For example, for vehicles, the truck manufacturers themselves have major finance divisions and for warehousing there are companies such as ProLogis and Goodman. 3PLs now usually work in partnership with these specialists, effectively outsourcing this element of their business in the same way as their clients have outsourced their logistics requirements.

However, when the client requires it, logistics providers are able to take on this role as provider of capital, even though it will be more expensive than some other options. The industry as a whole has become more sophisticated in this role, especially at pricing the cost of capital into new contracts and making sure that when logistics assets are provided they limit the level of exposure. An example of this is making the lease of distribution centres coterminous with contracts, reducing the level of assets on their balance sheets.

However, logistics providers are still required to invest working capital in contracts and this typically results in contracts being 'front-end loaded' with costs as shown in Figure 6.1 below. The costs incurred prior to the contract and at the outset will include elements such as information technology, supply chain solution design, project teams, facilities investment etc. The greater these costs the longer the contract needs to be, in order to pay back

FIGURE 6.1   Contract life cycle costs

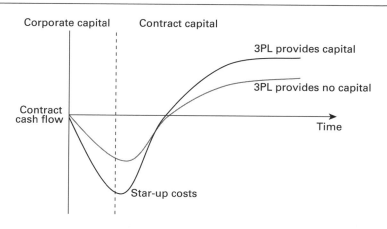

the investment and make a reasonable level of return. This is not so necessary where an open-book contract is agreed, as these costs, and other running costs, are paid for directly by the client. However, where a closed-book contract exists, the onus is on the logistics supplier to balance the risk and reward successfully. As also illustrated in Figure 6.1, when the logistics company provides capital it should be seeking a greater return than if it did not.

Sales cycle times

Sales cycle times vary considerably, depending on whether a logistics provider takes a 'product' or 'project' approach. A product, which has easily identifiable attributes, a repeatable format and a set price, should have a low sales lead time. An express parcel service or shared user network is an example of the product approach. Effectively the client makes a decision to trade off flexibility and customized solutions against speed of implementation, and a lower price.

The project approach requires a much longer lead time in order to come to fruition. The client decides that its needs are so specific or of a magnitude which rules out sharing common attributes with other clients of the logistics provider, that it requires the development of a dedicated, customized solution. Due to the size of the revenues involved in such a deal many logistics companies are keen to win such 'big ticket' contracts. However, there are many risks involved in pursuing this option rather than choosing to focus on selling low sales cycle time products.

One of the greatest risks is that the actual contract price does not fully reflect the true cost of all the resources which have been spent on winning the deal. In some cases it can take two years or more from point of first contact with the client to implementation of the logistics solution. In the intervening period, teams of sales, finance, administrative, consultancy as well as implementation personnel will have worked on the deal in its various forms and iterations. Over such a long period it is inevitable that some key figures – on both the client and provider side – will change, which increases the likelihood of key elements of the solution requirements also changing. This increases the possibility of 'scope creep', ie changing parameters of the operation, and this has to be effectively managed by the logistics provider.

However, this form of sales approach is still preferred by many companies to the tendering procedure, which many manufacturers and retailers adopt through the use of consultants. By working with the client at the very outset of the deal, the logistics provider has far more say in the eventual outcome, and is able to develop value-added elements which will increase its margins. Also after a long period of solution development it is unlikely that the client will be able to walk away from the eventual deal as this would mean starting from scratch with another provider and setting back implementation even further.

If their wish is to be able to pre-empt the tendering process, logistics companies need to have highly proactive sales forces which have been able to 'capture' the client at an early stage after it has made the initial decision to review its supply chain requirements. In order to assist with the targeting process, the most sophisticated sales divisions utilize financial analysis software, which allows them to identify potential clients which have the most to gain from supply chain innovation. Usually this takes the form of analysing the levels of inventory in a company's supply chain as well as cost of capital and comparing it with sector benchmarks. The logistics provider is therefore able to make a case for change and demonstrate the value they can bring to the organization.

Contracts and relationships

One of the fundamental, perhaps defining, areas of contract logistics is the nature of the relationship between logistics service providers and customers. Relationships in this sector are very rarely on a fixed-price basis. Rather, the contractual relationship between provider and customer can take several forms:

- open-book – this discloses all of the costs encountered by the LSP in fulfilling the contract and sets a fixed profit margin;
- closed-book – a set price for the contract is agreed and the LSP has to manage the costs;
- a compromise between the two.

The management of these different contract types is fundamental to the success of any logistics service provider. In truth, although the above categories are extensively used to define business, contracts are very frequently bespoke to each customer and situation. For example, if a LSP has an existing facility in a locality, its cost structure is likely to be a competitive advantage and this may well be something it wishes to conceal from customers.

However, if a contract demands investment, it may wish to demonstrate to a customer the level of investment it is making, leading it to prefer an open-book relationship. The success of any contract logistics provider really depends on its ability to manage this activity.

Profit margins

Table 6.1 shows the average contract logistics operating profit margins earned since 2006. The impact of the recession is seen clearly. The industry then regrouped in 2009, with improved margins, and made a further gain in 2010.

TABLE 6.1 Sector-weighted average operating profit

Year	Operating Margin
2006	3.1%
2007	3.6%
2008	–0.9%
2009	1.2%
2010	3.0%

Enhancing value through deeper relationships

Longer-term relationships between customer and logistics service provider afford a host of opportunities unavailable in a short-term, purely transactional relationship.

A major strategic goal of many transport companies has been to increase their engagement with clients and, as illustrated in Figure 6.2, deliver integrated logistics solutions which leverage their core competencies, such as IT and intellectual skills.

A deeper engagement allows a logistics company to better understand the needs of its client, and develop more innovative solutions. This, in turn, de-commoditizes its service offering, and increases its capacity to enhance margins.

FIGURE 6.2   Moving up the value chain

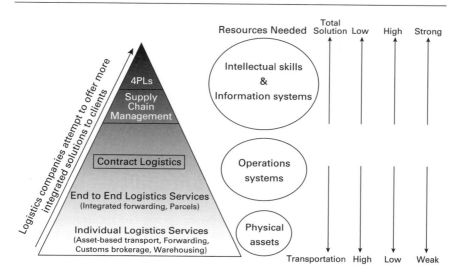

However, one of the major challenges which asset-owning logistics companies have to overcome is the innate tension between the need to utilize their assets efficiently, and the need to optimize a solution for its client. A 4PL (fourth party logistics), a term first coined by consultancy Accenture, was originally developed as a completely asset-free solutions provider, although the concept in its purest form has never really taken off. Most shippers expect their logistics providers to own assets, although at the same time they are suspicious that the solution which they develop will be in the logistics provider's interest and not their own.

There have been some successful incidences of 4PL relationships, but these have tended to be hybrid – a combination of the logistics provider's operations, assets, technology and networks together with a range of third party providers.

07 European road freight

Drivers of growth and profitability

Road freight is one of the most fragmented sectors of the transport and logistics market. The 'endless' supply of owner-operators and smaller providers, with tiny overheads and margins, limits opportunities for market dominance by big players.

The economic crises have made operating in a challenging market exceptionally tough, particularly for small/medium-size players, although larger players have shown much more resilience.

Demand in the road freight sector is derived from economic performance. That is to say that growth in volumes is directly related to the strength of manufacturing production and retail sales. At various times in the past decade it has been observed that growth in the road freight sector has become 'de-coupled' from economic development (although perhaps a more accurate description is 'weak de-coupling' where both economies and road freight output both grow, but the latter at a lower rate). This de-coupling had been difficult to explain, but was attributed to several factors. These include:

- changing distribution patterns (less centralization of inventory);
- the reduced importance of manufacturing in developed economies;
- increasing fuel costs and freight rates;
- offshoring of manufacturing.

However, much of the observed de-coupling has been as a result of the influx of foreign operators, especially those of Central and Eastern European origin, competing with domestic and international hauliers, and is not actually 'real'. Official statistics only reflect the output of operators based in the reporting country. Therefore, the true implication of the statistics is not that road freight output is flattening whilst economic growth continues, but that a large proportion of the derived demand is being met by foreign operators, taking market share from locally based rivals.

There is also another interesting conclusion which can be drawn from the road freight statistics. The alleged de-coupling could indicate that road freight has been switched from heavy goods vehicles, which are measured in the statistics, to light commercial vans, which are not. The trend towards the reduction in size and weight of shipments (so-called 'dematerialization'), increased shipment frequency in line with JIT supply chain strategies and the explosion of internet shopping has meant that a larger proportion of goods travel in smaller vehicles.

The issue of whether de-coupling is real or not is more than academic. As part of their sustainable transport policies, governments in Europe have been keen to find ways of breaking the link between economic growth and road freight output. Obviously, suppressing demand is not an option, especially in today's challenging financial environment, and so any sign that economic growth would not result in a proportional growth in transport emissions was welcomed.

However, according to research carried out by research company Transport Intelligence, comparing data over the last seven years, the correlation co-efficient is 0.83. This would suggest that the relationship between GDP growth and output in the road freight sector is as strong as ever.

FIGURE 7.1   Y-o-Y economic growth (GDP) and road freight output (tonnes)

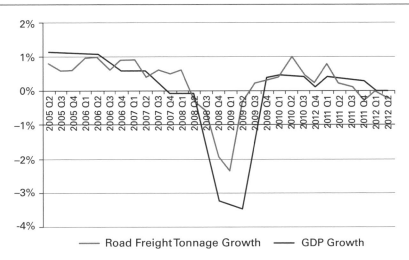

Road Freight Tonnage Growth ——   GDP Growth

Another important driver of the freight industry has been transit traffic. This has been due to the advent of the Single European Market and then the accession of the Central and Eastern European countries to the EU. This has increased considerably the level of transit traffic, not least because manufacturing became integrated on a regional rather than national basis. Increased production in countries such as Poland and Czech Republic was often fed by tiers of suppliers located elsewhere in the EU. Centralization of stock holding also became a key supply chain strategy, and this balance of inventory versus transport has characterized the European logistics industry for the past two decades.

Not all markets have been so affected. The periphery, the UK for example, has largely missed out on the impact of transit traffic.

The structure of the European road freight industry

The road haulage industry can be segmented in several different ways. The following are some of the most common.

'Own account' and 'hire and reward'

Also known as 'in-house' and 'third party' this categorization draws a distinction between road haulage carried out by a manufacturer or retailer for its own products on its own vehicles, and that undertaken by a professional provider for a range of clients. This distinction was previously recognized by many countries in law, with own account operators having a lower regulatory burden than hire and reward.

In Europe, the latest Eurostat figures show that, for most of the key European countries, own account operators comprise 15–30 per cent of the overall market, with hire-and-reward operators providing the remainder. By far the most own account haulage takes place on a local basis (less than 50 km), with specialist haulage companies undertaking movements with a longer average distance. For international movements, their share of the market is in excess of 90 per cent.

The outsourcing trend for transport varies on a country-by-country basis. Germany has shown the highest outsourcing growth rates in the past seven years. Since 1999 the number of vehicle metric-tonne kms (mtkm) undertaken in-house has dropped by 21 per cent. However, in the UK and in Spain the reverse is true, with the in-house market growing.

There are several reasons why companies retain control of their own transport fleets. In some cases it is because management views haulage as a key competence or at least too important to entrust to a third party haulier. There are also times when their needs are highly specific and specialist vehicles or operations are required (eg some types of chemicals or fragile goods, such as sheet glass). However, the most frequently cited reason is that on many occasions deliveries can be undertaken more cheaply by an in-house fleet than by an external hire-and-reward operator.

Conversely, there are many benefits from using a third party haulier. Asset ownership is transferred, reducing the level of investment in a function which many companies believe to be non-core. Road hauliers can also bring with them expertise in information technology and people management. Using a shared rather than dedicated network will also bring benefits in terms of cost reductions.

FIGURE 7.2 European road freight: own account & hire and reward 2011 [mtkm]

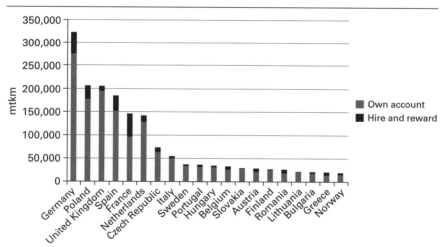

SOURCE: Eurostat

Segment by operation

Less than truckload (LTL)/groupage networks

Less than truckload (LTL) operators (also known as groupage operators) undertake the collation of consignments from a number of different sources to make up a full vehicle load. Services often depart on a set schedule, and therefore it is down to the operator to sell capacity on the vehicle in much the same way as a scheduled air cargo carrier sells space on its aircraft. LTL services take place on a point-to-point basis, with distribution of the consignments taking place from the destination hub. The market is highly competitive, due to extreme fragmentation, and consequently margins are low. Asset intensity can be low, due to the predominance of using subcontractors to undertake line haul (or 'trunking') although some investment is required in facilities.

A more recent development has been that of national and European networks. These largely replicate the systems used to move parcels, except they are capable of moving much larger weights. They work on a hub-and-spoke system, with local hauliers delivering consignments into regional hubs. Shipments are then moved between hubs, usually overnight. The advantage of using a network rather than a point-to-point system is the increased frequency which they provide. However, they require a critical mass of consignments to be viable and this has favoured the major players such as Schenker and DHL Freight.

The development of European road freight networks has come as a response to a number of macro-economic trends. The Single European Market (SEM) has enabled the seamless movement of goods cross-border and this has allowed the network concept to develop. Prior to the removal of border controls, customs delays were endemic, which resulted in unreliable transit times. Secondly, the SEM has enabled manufacturers to establish pan-European distribution models, which have reinforced cross-border supply. Networks with intensive coverage can also provide a way in which to mitigate the effects of the European Working Time Directive (WTD). Driving time will be reduced, which will require shorter trip distances between delivery points.

Full truckload (FTL)

A full truckload (FTL) is defined as any consignment which fills a whole truck. Operators usually undertake the movement of truckloads on a point-to-point basis, direct to the customer from the consignor. This requires less sophistication of operation, as there is less administration and fewer clients moving larger loads. Many of the larger players offer both services to clients.

In between LTL and FTL there is a further classification of part load or semi-truckload (STL). This bears more of the characteristics of the FTL model than LTL, with each vehicle undertaking a small number of drops.

Segment by speciality

Further segments exist by categorizing the road freight market by speciality equipment:

- temperature controlled (eg refrigerated, frozen and thermo);
- bulk (eg liquid, powder);
- air cushioned (eg high tech sector);
- finished vehicle transporters.

In each of these cases, a distinct industry segment has developed with highly specialized operating practices. This provides some level of differentiation from the rest of the market, to some extent reducing competitive pressures.

Segment by geography

Road haulage can be further segmented on the basis of the geographic scope.

Intra-regional and local transport

Most road haulage takes place on this basis under 50 km.

Inter-regional or national

Fewer goods volumes are moved on a region-to-region or national basis. This therefore, requires a (relatively) more sophisticated groupage or part load operation to make operations economically viable.

International

Only a small volume of consignments are shipped internationally. Prior to the Single European Market, international shipments required documentation which increased complexity and administration. Now barriers to market entry are very low in terms of technical capabilities, and this has encouraged hauliers from Central and Eastern Europe to take market share (especially when bidding for return loads).

Segment by consignment attribute

The parcels sector is increasingly important to the transport industry, not least with the emergence of e-commerce. The sector is dealt with in more detail in Chapter 8.

Parcel (< 35 kg)

There is no single definition of a 'parcel' in terms of weight. However, materials handling equipment in sorting hubs is designed to move shipments less than around 35 kg in weight. There are also difficulties offloading heavier consignments by hand.

Pallet (unitized shipment > 35 kg)

The pallet has revolutionized the movement of goods in the road freight sector in much the same way the container did for the shipping sector. It is a convenient way of unitizing goods in a form which facilitates movement by materials handling equipment (eg front-lift trucks).

In recent years 'pallet networks' have developed, using advances in materials handling technology to treat pallets in much the same way as parcels. The UK has been at the forefront of this trend, which is now spreading throughout Europe. The result has been the development of hub-and-spoke operations, with next day delivery the industry standard.

Segment by service attribute

A further method of defining the market is by the level of service which can be offered by road hauliers for either parcels or freight. Supply chain compression has driven trends towards same and next day delivery.

Express (day definite or time definite)

Express companies usually undertake to deliver consignments by a specified day and even by a specified time. In Europe and domestically, 'express' usually means next working day. Some companies have a more stringent definition: to qualify as express it must be delivered in the morning of the following day.

Standard (non time-definite)

Where price is more important than time, delivery is usually on a non-specific two to three days basis or longer and the service is also referred to as 'deferred' or 'standard'.

Segment by level of asset ownership

The road freight market can also be divided between asset-owning companies ('road hauliers') and those which manage subcontracted road hauliers ('ground freight forwarders'). Although in most cases there is some element of crossover between the two categories, the market forces affecting each are very different.

There are arguments both in favour and against asset ownership. Many of the largest companies, such as DSV and Schenker, decided specifically to reduce the number of vehicles which they own in order to utilize subcontractors. There are a number of reasons for this which have become compelling in recent years.

For those companies which have pursued the asset-light approach, the benefits are:

Flexibility

One of the major benefits of using a subcontracted fleet is the increased level of flexibility which this allows. If a company is able to build a large supplier pool it is better able to match supply to demand. This means it is always able to cope with peaks in demand without the need to maintain a fleet of vehicles which are underutilized at certain times of year.

Employee costs

With the increase in the payroll and social costs associated with employees, haulage companies have been keener to use self-employed subcontractors. This limits the company's liability in respect of a whole range of regulations and responsibilities including holiday entitlement, working hours, tax, as well as redundancy and severance pay.

Asset costs

A further compelling reason for the use of subcontractors is the positive effect on companies' balance sheets. Asset-light companies are able to provide a much higher return on capital employed, as subcontractors' operating costs are regarded as 'above the line' – a factor which is very important to many shareholders. The subcontractor effectively provides the capital on behalf of the contracting company. Although in theory the subcontractor should be able to build the cost of the capital into its pricing, there is little doubt that in practice this does not happen.

Maintenance and repair

As part of the responsibilities of the subcontractor, the roadworthiness of their vehicle must be ensured in order to comply with legislation. Any downtime whilst the vehicle is off road is cost absorbed by the subcontractor.

Countercyclical model

As mentioned above, for the asset-light model to work effectively, there must be a large pool of suppliers which can be tapped by the contractor. With very few barriers to market entry and exit this pool has been augmented in recent years, especially in times of economic downturn. With high levels of unemployment in many countries, the prospect of self-employment with the relatively low investment in transport assets required has allowed this model to flourish. What is more, contracting companies have benefited from the low levels of commercial awareness of these new market entrants. With relatively few exceptions, owner-drivers are less able to build into their pricing the full life costs of their vehicles, including depreciation. Most are more likely to set their prices too low in a bid to win business rather than at a rate which the market will actually stand. Likewise, they are less able to respond to increasing costs which often erode whatever profits they are making. Finally, they are likely to work for an income which they would never sanction from a formal employer, whilst not placing funds in reserve for the renewal of the vehicle at the end of its life, maintenance costs or even tax liabilities.

Inevitably, this basic inability to deal with commercial reality leads to a high turnover or 'churn' in the supplier pool as businesses become non-viable. However, whilst those dropping out are replaced by new owner-drivers at a comparable rate, the subcontracted model will continue to operate.

As a corollary to this situation, the costs of subcontracting rise during times of economic upturn. Subcontractors become scarcer as higher-paid employment is available elsewhere, and therefore rates rise, leading to what has been termed a countercyclical market. This is discussed at greater length below.

Business risk

One of the risks of using subcontractors is the possibility that the end client may approach the subcontractor directly. Although this is unlikely to happen where the contractor has sufficiently differentiated its offering from its smaller suppliers (as in the case of the large European networks such as Schenker and DHL Freight) this is a constant problem for local or regional operators.

For those companies which have invested heavily in assets, there are also benefits.

Availability of supply

One of the greatest benefits of using subcontractors is the reliability of supply, which can be ensured through the ownership of vehicles and employment of drivers. Subcontractors may work for a number of other clients and will not necessarily be available whenever required. (The best asset-light operators will utilize a large pool of suppliers with an element of built-in redundancy.) At peaks of demand there is more likely to be a problem with supply as subcontractor capacity will be at its lowest.

Reliability of supply

For many companies to make a profit, the asset-light model relies on 'burning out' suppliers who do not pass on the full costs of their operations. This can result in vehicle failure or longer-than-necessary downtime. Companies which run their own vehicles can ensure that sufficient maintenance is carried out, or in fact have their own in-house workshops.

Quality of personnel and vehicles

The role of the driver is crucial to how a company is perceived by its clients and the public at large. Companies can ensure that their workforce is fully trained to appropriate levels as regards both driving skills and customer contact. The state of the vehicle being used is also important to how the brand of the contracting company is perceived.

Route knowledge

Although transport telematic systems have grown in sophistication, many haulage companies rely on the knowledge of their drivers to ensure fast and efficient navigation on a local, national or regional basis. Maintaining this level of training is easier when drivers are working consistently on the same routes. This is certainly possible with subcontractors, but it requires developing longer and deeper relationships with them.

Asset utilization

Companies which employ multiple drivers have the opportunity to more efficiently utilize their transport assets by ensuring longer periods of vehicle usage. This can be achieved by using several drivers for a single vehicle, ensuring round-the-clock usage after any one driver has used up their allotted working time.

Cost of capital

In the late 1980s there were double-digit interest rates, which meant that repayments on money borrowed to invest in assets were very high. Occurring at the time of dramatic falls in volumes, this led to large numbers of corporate failures, driven by companies' inability to downsize quickly enough.

However, in recent years interest rates across Europe have been at historic lows, which means that owning or leasing vehicles has become much more attractive. So, large companies were more likely than smaller subcontractors to be able to acquire capital for investment at a competitive rate, providing them with one of the few economies of scale apparent in the industry. This changed in the latter part of 2008 and early 2009, since when, despite the lowest interest rates ever recorded, lending institutions have been reluctant to lend.

Defensive business model

Those companies with their own fleets are less vulnerable to the impact of tightening capacity on prices during increases in volumes. Whilst asset-light companies end up being squeezed between their suppliers and clients unwilling to absorb the full cost of price rises, owned fleet operators are not so badly affected in terms of margin erosion.

Of course, in reality many road hauliers and ground-based freight forwarders operate a mixture of the two models. Subcontractors are used to augment owned operations and are called in on an as-and-when-required basis.

The link between fuel costs and rates

Fuel costs constitute an important proportion of freight transport operators' costs. Since the bottom of the first recession in 2009 there has been a steady increase in the cost of diesel, as shown in Figure 7.3. The UK remains the most expensive market, 25 per cent more costly than Spain. Over the last three years the cost of diesel fuel oil has risen by up to a half.

Using a Road Freight Price Index (see Figure 7.4) provided by Eurostat, it can be seen that European road freight rates have now surpassed the peak seen in 2008, just prior to the recession-related downturn. It may be slightly surprising, given the second element of the double-dip recession, that rates have not shown renewed weakness. However, industry sources put this down in part to a reduction in capacity seen at the time of the first recession, which has yet to be replaced. Another reason may be the influx of cheap freight operators from Central and Eastern Europe.

It is generally assumed that rising fuel costs are not helpful for road freight operators, as they find it difficult to pass these charges on to customers. Generally the increases are handled better by the larger players, many of whom have agreements in place which result in surcharges being

FIGURE 7.3   European diesel prices

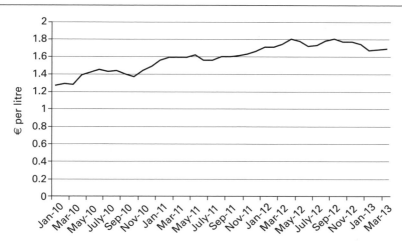

SOURCE: European Commission

FIGURE 7.4   Road Freight Price Index – EU (27)

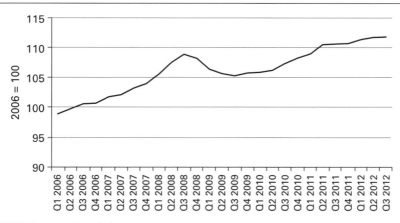

SOURCE: European Commission

passed on directly. Smaller players either do not have these mechanisms in place or do not have the bargaining power to increase their rates in line with fuel pump costs.

One way in which it is possible to test how well freight operators are able to pass on fuel cost increases to their customers is by examining the correlation between fuel costs and rates. If rates rise in line with changes in the price of diesel it could be concluded that freight operators are successfully passing on these costs to their customers. In fact, from the high correlation (0.85) this does indeed seem to be the case.

FIGURE 7.5   The link between fuel costs and freight rates

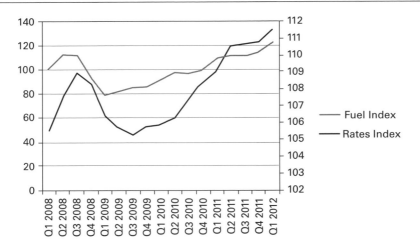

This is not to say that freight operators do not bear any pain. There are significant cash flow implications (especially for medium-sized or small players) which have to outlay significant sums of money up-front for diesel fuel. The greater the proportion of their cost base which fuel makes up, the larger the problem, as it can take up to 90 days for a haulier to recoup from customers the amounts paid out.

However, despite this, as we shall see in the next section, fuel costs do not play a significant role in company failures.

What causes transport company failures?

The rising cost of fuel is one of the biggest political issues which transport operators and governments face. In the UK it was the reason for a wave of fuel strikes in the early 2000s, with operators making the point that increases in the oil price through market forces and taxation were driving companies out of the market.

However, in reality there seems little evidence for this. Using official company failure statistics from the UK government and a diesel pump price index there does not seem to be a link between fuel costs and company failures. The correlation co-efficient is −0.25 which indicates only a very weak negative correlation. A strong positive correlation would have been expected if indeed the price of oil was a major factor in transport company bankruptcies, ie an increase of diesel would be expected to result in an increase in company failures.

FIGURE 7.6   Index of company failures and diesel fuel price

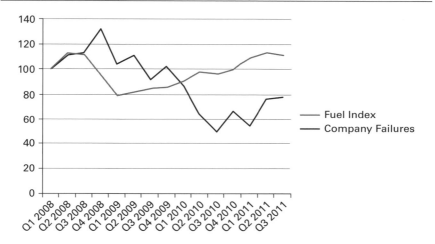

Testing out the reasons behind company failure further, a link with interest rates was investigated. Many road freight operators are highly leveraged, leasing road transport assets or borrowing finance to buy them outright. Hence, they are exposed to fluctuations in interest rates.

In recent years there has been considerable divergence between official central bank interest rates and those which transport companies can obtain on the open market. Therefore, company failure rate was set against an index of retail bank rates.

This resulted in a much stronger positive correlation of 0.6 – suggesting that a rise in interest rates did indeed result in higher company failures. The low interest rate environment may well be one of the key reasons why company failures are around half of what they were four years ago.

Rather than solely concentrate on the link between cost pressures and company failures, the relationship between fluctuating freight volumes and bankruptcies was also tested. As it is very difficult to get accurate information on freight volumes (due to the highly fragmented nature of the industry), a 'proxy' indicator was used, in this case retail sales. The logic of this is that the higher the throughput of goods through retail outlets the greater demand for freight transport throughout the entire supply chain as goods are replenished. Retail sales also take into account demand for imports, which an indicator relating solely to domestic manufacturing output would not.

It transpires that there is indeed a high inverse correlation between retail sales and transport operator failures (−0.73). The conclusion of this evidence is that road freight transport company health can be directly linked to volumes. Although the economy has been stagnant, retail sales have continued to grow, and hence freight operators have seen low levels of failure. They have coped with higher oil prices by passing these on through higher rates, and a low interest rate environment has proved benign.

FIGURE 7.7   Index of company failures and retail sales

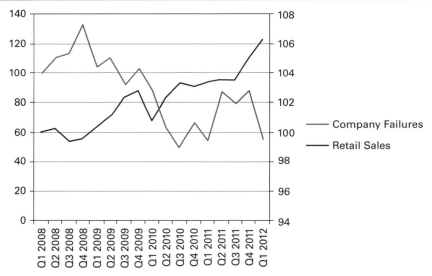

SOURCE: UK National Statistics

Margins and cost increases

Looking at the margins of four of the largest road freight operators in Europe, there is a moderate negative correlation between margins and price of diesel. This suggests that there is some likelihood that margins are negatively impacted by rising oil prices, but that there is no clear-cut relationship. The correlation is −0.48.

However, there is a stronger correlation between operating margins and retail sales volume growth (see Figure 7.8). The correlation in this case is 0.63. It seems that, mirroring the link between volumes and company failures, the most important factor for freight transport companies profitability is freight throughput.

The reasons for this are clear. Freight operators are able to make money once a 'break-even' point has been reached on each vehicle or on a network. This break-even factor is of course influenced by input costs and freight rates. Our research seems to show that operators are good at managing the break-even point by passing on costs to customers through higher rates. However, they are less able to control volumes, especially when the industry is impacted by wider economic crisis. This seems to be the major reason behind fluctuations in profit margins.

FIGURE 7.8 Operating margin and growth in retail sales

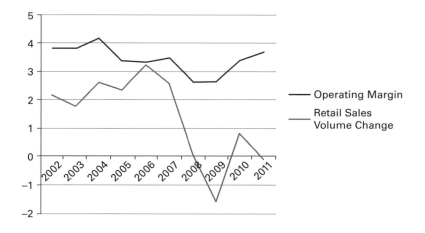

08 Express parcels

The origins of the express parcels industry

The express parcels industry has grown rapidly over the last 30 years. At the outset it fulfilled a need for faster, more reliable services, which also provided customers with an increased level of supply chain visibility. Its ongoing success has been based upon the systemic changes which it has been able to facilitate in global manufacturing and its associated supply chains. Whilst it has led the way in the modernization of the transportation sector, as much as in attitudes as in technological and process developments, it has enabled and benefited from trends such as globalization, e-commerce, lean inventory management, Just-in-Time and customization of mass production.

Its impact on the global freight industry has been dramatic. Freight forwarders, which had until the 1970s enjoyed a monopoly on the control of international freight movements, rapidly lost market share in the lucrative small parcel sector to the express parcels companies. In Europe, international and domestic freight haulage companies and groupage operators also lost out to cheaper and faster express parcel companies.

The express parcels industry is widely acknowledged as having been developed in the United States by companies such as UPS and FedEx. This was aided by the development of a country-wide interstate system (from 1956), deregulation of the air industry (1978) and interstate trucking laws (1980 and 1994). FedEx was the first company to introduce the hub-and-spoke model, which revolutionized the way in which parcels could be distributed around the United States in a fast and economic way.

In Europe, TNT's UK operation is generally credited with creating the first next-day parcels service, back in 1980. Prior to this, three-to-four-day parcel services had been the standard. TNT was the first company to utilize advances in communication technology to create a flexible, national network. Across Europe, development of the industry has taken place at different rates, complicated by the regulatory nature of many of the markets. Until liberalization, which in some cases is still ongoing, post offices controlled much of the market for parcels and the express industry had difficulty in breaking through the monopolistic regime.

Market definitions and structure

There is no single definition which encompasses the parcels and express sector. A wide variety of companies operate in the market providing services to a number of different segments. Over the last decade international air express operators have entered the domestic road-based market and ground networks have also started to provide international air services, often through partner companies.

However, it is possible to make some broad-brush definitions which relate to the following attributes of service and consignment.

Time sensitivity

Traditionally, there has been a separation in the market between 'parcels' and 'express' services. The most obvious differentiation between these services is the level of time sensitivity involved. Express companies usually undertake to deliver consignments by a specified day and even by a specified time. Domestically, 'express' usually means next working day. Some companies have a more stringent definition: to qualify as express it must be delivered in the morning of the following day, and even by a particular time. For users of 'parcel' services the time attribute is not as important, usually with cost being the overriding consideration. Delivery is usually on a non-specific two-to-three-days basis, or longer, and the service is also referred to as 'deferred' or 'standard'.

The difference between these services has blurred in recent years and is no longer all that useful. Most parcels companies offer express services, and due to improvements in systems, overall delivery times have become compressed.

In the United States there are more 'hard-wired' distinctions related to time sensitivity. UPS and FedEx both offer 'Next Day Air' and 'Deferred' (also air) package delivery services which are categorized as 'Express' services. However, they also offer 'Ground' package delivery solutions, which would be defined as 'Parcels'.

In Europe both DHL and TNT have sought to segment the market into 'Time definite/Day definite' categories and 'Economy', the former roughly relating to 'Express' and the latter to 'Parcels'.

The situation is complicated further when comparing international with domestic services. A two-to-three-day delivery time for a package from, say, China to the United States would be seen as falling into the express category. However, two-to-three-day domestic delivery service would certainly not be, demonstrating the problems related to trying to define a service by duration of transit.

Size of consignment

Traditionally, the maximum weight of a parcel (whether express or not) is usually considered to be about 31.5 kg (70 lbs). This is an estimate of the maximum weight that can be handled by one man. This was important, to ensure that the standardized procedures which are essential to the profitable running of a network are maintained. A large reliance is placed on the quick and efficient collection and delivery of parcels, as well as automated sortation at a sorting centre or hub. Parcels which are non-standard, too heavy, out of gauge, or with other attributes which require specialist handling (hazardous, perishable, etc) diminish the overall efficiency of the network. Such consignments are often termed 'non-compatible' and either attract a heavy surcharge or are refused.

However, definitions have evolved over the years and now the main integrators segment their volumes in different ways. TNT regards anything under 50 kg as a parcel (over is freight) whilst UPS and FedEx use 68 kg and DHL 70 kg. This is a sign that the integrators have been able and willing to penetrate further into what was once considered to be the 'freight' segments.

At the other end of the scale, express companies have been keen to prioritize volumes of documents. They take up little room on board a van or airplane relative to the revenue which they can generate. They also require comparatively little handling, which can be more easily automated. They can be collected and delivered by smaller capacity vehicles which do not require highly trained staff (thereby reducing costs) and are quicker and more flexible than larger vehicles. This allows greater volumes to be processed in a single day.

Business to consumer (B2C)/business to business (B2B)

This is one of the key differentiators between post offices and express or other parcels companies which specialize predominantly in business-to-business deliveries. An express or parcels company will typically operate on a door-to-door basis providing services to business clients.

Although in recent years many companies have started to offer B2C services ('home delivery'), these have specialist requirements owing mainly to the fact that it is often impossible to effect a delivery as, unlike businesses, many people are not in during the day to receive goods. A non-delivery will impact on the efficiency of an operation as it will either require redelivery or else follow-up by a customer service agent. In many cases procedures have not been designed for this eventuality.

Post offices, on the other hand, have established systems which can deal with non-delivery of consignments, usually by leaving a parcel at a local post office. Their dense networks of local drop-off points provide them with a competitive advantage over other companies, which can only take the undelivered consignment back to a regional depot.

Many large B2C operators have been spun off (or in some cases are still owned) by large catalogue, and more latterly, online retailers.

International/domestic

The express and parcels industry is broadly defined by domestic, regional or international destination. Although in many cases the operations are similar, for instance with hub-and-spoke networks, there are some major differences. Domestic express services are normally road-based, whereas international express can require multimodal transport. Domestic or regional operations are highly competitive due to the lower barriers to market entry. The international air express operators, often owning or leasing aircraft, use their scale and resources to offer higher levels of services over longer distances. Some companies, such as TNT, use a further segmentation, segregating the intra-European market (where it is market leader) from intercontinental volumes.

The difference between the prices which a domestic parcels player can charge and those of an international air express operator are significant. The average revenue per piece for the packages which UPS moves domestically, in countries such as Germany, is around $7. Its corresponding revenue per piece for international parcels is around $35.

Express market leading companies

In the last five years, boundaries in the market have become blurred as express operators, parcels companies and post offices have started to compete against each other in order to offer clients a full service portfolio. For express companies, lower-value parcels business is also a way in which to increase utilization of transport assets and resources. To European parcel networks, such as GLS or DPD, express consignments offer higher margin volumes at premium rates.

The air express operators that actually own or lease the airplanes which carry the consolidated parcels or documents between corresponding hubs are known as 'integrators'. This is due to the way in which they have been able to seamlessly integrate all the various transportation segments by controlling the assets. Globally, there are four integrators able to operate in this way:

- DHL;
- TNT;
- FedEx;
- UPS.

Although they are well known for their branded air operations, most cross-border movements in Europe occur by road rather than air. In conjunction with major air hubs, they also operate hubs which feed major ground networks. In general, any shipment which has an ultimate destination of under 800 km (500 miles) will travel by road. However, in the Asia Pacific region, air is very important, due to the insular nature of many of the markets and the lack of a quality road infrastructure. This is gradually changing, with TNT leading the way in building an Asia Pacific road network. Road is obviously less time-efficient, but considerably cheaper.

The four integrators have developed different strengths. FedEx and UPS have traditionally focused around the delivery of documents and packages under 5 kg, whereas DHL has based its service around document delivery. TNT Express, on the other hand, has focused on heavier weight freight, which may be to its advantage. Pressure from electronic substitution will be stronger at the document end of the scale, affecting DHL more than the other carriers.

The alternative to owning the air transportation assets is to utilize those of established air carriers, such as Lufthansa, British Airways, Air France or KLM, within a multimodal solution. As an attempt to provide an alternative to the integrators most of these carriers now offer time definite services of their own with 'flown-as-booked' guarantees. Although these are not retailed to the consumer market, they allow companies such as Chronopost, the subsidiary of French Post Office, La Poste, to compete more effectively.

Express operating model – hub and spoke

All the major European (and global) express and parcels companies operate hub-and-spoke systems, which enable them to provide comprehensive regional and global coverage through the economies of scale which it provides. The system works through consolidating smaller volumes from local markets at a central hub and then trunking them to a selection of global gateway hubs, usually regionally based, where the process is managed in reverse.

FIGURE 8.1   Express hub-and-spoke systems

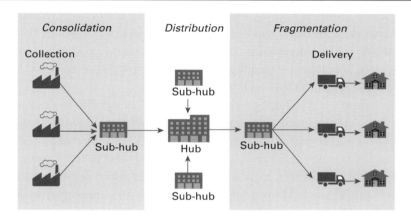

As an example, TNT utilizes nine sub-hubs (Northampton, Paris, Frankfurt, Helsingborg, Milan, Hanover, Brussels, Nuremburg, Madrid) and one main hub in Arnhem, Netherlands. Consignments are collected from the hinterland of each sub-hub, consolidated and then transported to Arnhem. Here they are deconsolidated, sorted and dispatched to the corresponding sub-hub where the reverse process takes place.

One of the benefits of the hub-and-spoke system is that it allows optimum utilization of assets and capacity across the network. The alternative, line haul between city pairs, is not as efficient, and although it may be quicker in terms of transit times, will be less appealing to clients, due to the lower frequency of service or higher costs.

One of the downsides of the network solution is that, when volumes become weaker the maintenance of a frequent service, and the fixed assets required to maintain hub and sorting operations, can make the entire network unprofitable.

Express economics

Cost structure

The global express industry is dependent on the development of comprehensive networks spanning regions. As with any form of network, this means that a substantial proportion of costs are fixed due to the investment in hubs and the servicing of fixed routes. Some research has shown that the fixed element can comprise up to 70 per cent of total costs. TNT estimates that 85 per cent of an air network's costs are fixed, compared with 65 per cent of the costs of a ground network. Consequently, substantial economies of scale exist in the industry, making volumes and pricing essential to the success of a network. A network requires a critical mass to make it profitable, over and above which incremental parcel volumes result in higher margins. Conversely, the capital expenditure required for fixed-cost networks compound the impact of falling volumes.

The industry is also highly labour intensive, although the automation of some hubs has reduced this dependence to a degree. Labour costs can account for 42 per cent of sales. In the case of UPS in the United States, they account for as much as 65 per cent of costs, mainly due to the dense nature of its network. However, there are significant variances dependent on the business model used. Many companies outsource to subcontractors much of the long-distance trunking between hubs, and others use a franchise system, thereby taking many employees off the payroll. In FedEx's ground network for example, which subcontracts out much of its transportation requirements, only 22 per cent of costs are employee related, whilst 43 per cent is purchased transport. Its air express operations are far more dependent on in-house staff, with 45 per cent of costs employee related.

Profitability

There is a wide variance in the level of profitability across the various express and parcels segments. This is due to a mix of asset utilization, cost control, pricing discipline and – importantly – the willingness of customers to buy high-yielding products (such as air over road). Table 8.1 shows the profits of some of the major express players.

The difference in performance of UPS and FedEx, on the one hand, and TNT and DHL on the other, is stark. TNT's low margins have made it vulnerable to takeover, as evidenced by UPS's abortive acquisition attempt in 2012. DHL,

TABLE 8.1   Average profitability of major express companies 2008–12

Company	Operating margin
UPS (Domestic US)	6.7%
UPS (International)	12.4%
FedEx Express (Air)	5.3%
FedEx Ground (Domestic US)	12%
TNT	0.8%
DHL	−0.6%

however, has managed to turn around its performance by shutting down or disposing of loss-making domestic express operations – particularly in the United States. Its margins are now in the high single digits.

The link between express parcels and economic output

Demand in the express sector is closely tied to performance of the overall economy. During the economic downturn volumes in the international express sector plummeted as customers switched from premium express to cheaper standard or deferred alternatives.

In order to retain the spend of migrating clients, companies such as FedEx have aggressively developed lower value ground operations in the United States to compete with the market leader UPS. However, the migration to lower value products at the same time as falling volumes has a multiplying effect on the revenues of the express companies. This means that troughs and peaks in the business cycle are lower and higher than GDP fluctuation.

Growth in the international express industry shows particularly strong correlation with growth in trade. Figures 8.2 and 8.3 show international package revenue growth for UPS and US export growth data. When testing the linear relationship between the two variables for the period Q1 2007 to Q4 2012 a correlation co-efficient of +0.96 is derived, indicating a very strong positive relationship.

FIGURE 8.2   Comparison of US GDP and international parcels revenue, quarterly growth year on year

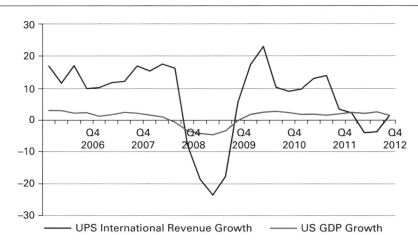

FIGURE 8.3   Comparison of US export growth and international parcels revenue, quarterly growth year on year

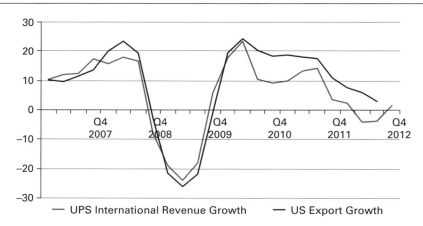

Long-term trends in the express sector

The growth of the express industry has been driven by the trend towards Just-in-Time manufacturing techniques. This has led to the increase in the demand for flexible, frequent and more reliable delivery services, which removes the necessity to store inventory on hand. It also allows the end user to source goods from remote locations, reducing costs. The development of sophisticated information and communication technology has given customers the ability to track and trace their consignments wherever they are geographically. This has allowed manufacturers to plan production with more certainty, integrating the express companies into their supply chains.

In summary, the success of the express industry has been based upon providing manufacturers and retailers with the following benefits:

- Speed. By transporting the product more quickly to the customer the shipper benefits from:
  - lower sales-to-cash cycle time;
  - lower total supply chain inventory levels;
  - better customer service.
- Reliability. Tracking and tracing technology, combined with guaranteed service levels, allows clients to plan schedules with confidence.
- Global service. Most parcels and express operators offer worldwide services, either through their operations or with partners.
- Price. The market is highly competitive both on an international and domestic basis. This provides the shipper with a number of alternatives and consequently value for money.

Express companies are well positioned for the global economic recovery. Some economists believe that when world trade rebounds, the value of trade will increase faster than volumes, which will favour higher value express products. The global express industry is also able to reach into emerging markets where trade is fastest growing, especially in sectors such as healthcare, spare parts and the movement of documents.

Key developments in the supply side

DHL in the United States

One of the biggest events in the express parcels sector of the past decade was DHL's ill-fated venture into the US domestic market. Such was the magnitude of the losses involved that it is worthy of a section in its own right. The episode has shown up many of the difficulties of breaking into a mature market already dominated by two strong players – UPS and FedEx.

Back in March 2003, as part of its global expansion strategy, DHL bought the ground operations of the US's third-largest parcel carrier, Airborne Express, for $1.05 billion. The air operations were spun off due to regulatory reasons. The acquisition was fought tooth and nail by UPS and FedEx, who tried to block the deal in the courts while at the same time vigorously lobbying Washington.

DHL carried on in the face of this opposition. Management said that the company could not claim 'global leadership' until it succeeded in the United States. However, losses were heavy right from the start, despite the integration of DHL and Airborne and attempts to cut costs. Operational issues impacted upon DHL's attempts to be seen as a low-cost alternative to UPS and FedEx, and the company started to lose market share, from around 8 per cent at its height.

In 2008 the decision was finally made to pull out of the domestic segment of the market. In total, the amount spent by the company in establishing a domestic presence in the United States is estimated to have been around €7.5 billion, including DHL's losses, reorganization costs and the expense of buying Airborne.

The episode was a disaster for DHL, and it has only been able to survive due to its extraordinarily large resources, and the profitability of its express operations elsewhere in the world. DHL still operates international services to the United States, but it is likely that the experience also prompted pull-outs from other non-performing domestic markets, such as those in France and the UK.

UPS and TNT

In 2012 UPS made a bid to acquire TNT, which many had felt was too small to compete effectively in the international express sector, and which had been coming under pressure for many years from its shareholders to improve its share price. The logic was to combine TNT's strong European ground network with UPS's global scale. The deal was eventually abandoned in 2013 in light of the likely veto by European competition authorities.

What appeared to be a straightforward – if rather large – deal to acquire TNT Express was made much more complicated by the behaviour of the European competition authorities. That UPS abandoned the bid, despite the hurdle of a €200 million termination fee, illustrated the magnitude of the obstacles that UPS perceived it was faced with to make the takeover work.

The pivot of the negotiations revolved around the competition authorities of the European Commission. The logic of its objections appeared to focus on the number of competitors in the market place. The Commission hinted that the removal of TNT Express would reduce the level of competition in the express parcel market. In suggesting remedies for this problem, they were drawn into dismembering the TNT and UPS network, a task which was doomed to fail as such assets are only worth anything as part of a network.

Of the main market players, TNT Express is now in the most uncomfortable position. The company stated that it would concentrate on the 'execution of strategy'. However, it has tacitly admitted that its businesses outside Europe have poor prospects and its core European business will have to work hard just to sustain its already squeezed margins.

UPS also has received a setback to its corporate strategy, although it is hardly a serious one. The company has huge financial fire power and will be able to consider alternative acquisitions in Europe should it wish to do so. Assuming this is regarded as a worthwhile prospect, the potential targets include GLS (owned by Royal Mail), which has a smaller, yet not dissimilar, road network to TNT Express. Yet, some people at UPS may be regarding the failure of the bid a relief, with middle management in Atlanta and elsewhere nervous about the prospect of integrating TNT Express.

DHL was probably the big winner out of the failed bid. The prospect of UPS creating a strong capability in DHL's home market can never have been welcome and now it appears to have gone for good.

09 Air cargo

Development of the air cargo industry

Air cargo is an integral element of many manufacturers' and retailers' global supply chains, allowing companies across a range of sectors to operate in lean inventory environments. Air cargo operations enable fast, frequent and predictable transit between many parts of the world as an increasing number of companies outsource to remote locations.

At an early stage of the airline industry's development, the spare hold space on passenger flights was used to carry freight. Since the early days of commercial flying, mail has also been transported on aircraft. As those aircraft became bigger, more efficient and more reliable, a wider range of goods was carried and freight volumes increased. Dedicated freighter aircraft and combined freight and passenger aircraft started to appear as volumes grew. In the 1970s, a new industry emerged using air transport to provide express parcel deliveries, and its major players – FedEx, UPS, DHL and TNT – have become household names.

Decreasing product cycles for high value, high tech goods have made fast delivery to market essential. Perishable commodities, such as foodstuffs or flowers, can be delivered into markets on the opposite side of the world in perfect condition. Periodicals can be delivered to readers worldwide while still current. Local companies have been able to develop into global traders, allowing consumers to buy all types of goods from any part of the world. In this respect, the air cargo sector has played an essential, although understated, role in the development of the global economy. Its continued development is key to the ongoing success of globalization.

The early years of air cargo

Air cargo services grew very rapidly during the 1960s; in fact, faster than passenger growth over the same period. This rate of growth slowed considerably in the early 1980s, although it was still around 9 per cent per annum. The early growth was centred in the United States and on transatlantic routes and the European and North American airlines were the dominant players until the mid-1970s.

Before the 1960s, air freight was considered a way of filling spare capacity on what were essentially narrow-bodied passenger aircraft. The high rate of growth in the 1960s, together with the introduction of wider-bodied passenger aircraft, provided the opportunity for many airlines to generate income from air cargo. Where cargo volumes exceeded the capacity available in passenger aircraft, there was an incentive to introduce scheduled all-cargo services. All-cargo aircraft enabled more unit loads and consignments to be carried and when these services were introduced they had the effect of further stimulating demand. The increased use of specialized handling equipment speeded up the movement of freight and the turnaround of aircraft. All-cargo aircraft were also able to fly at night to schedules which would not be suitable for passengers. This led to shorter freight transit times as well as adding extra capacity.

As the growth in the North American and European markets slowed in the 1970s, the Asian markets began the pattern of growth which continues to the present. In parallel came the rapid development of the East Asian and Pacific regional airlines – Korean Air Lines, Singapore Airlines, Cathay Pacific, Japan Airlines and China Airlines – which are now all among the top 10 cargo airlines in terms of route tonne kilometres (RTKs).

Cargo charter

Cargo charter airlines have existed from the early days of the industry and their development accelerated briefly in the 1970s, benefiting from freedom to operate outside bilateral agreements and the growing deregulation of freight operations to and from the United States, the UK and some other European countries. This growth was curtailed as the scheduled airlines began to take cargo more seriously with more flexible and competitive pricing. The latter were able to offer considerably more freight capacity as they introduced wide-bodied passenger aircraft on an increasing number of routes. Added to this was the restriction of charter operations by developing countries aiming to protect the interest of their own national airlines in the freight market.

Today, charter cargo carriers operate as an integral part of the industry, carrying regular as well as specialist loads.

The integrators

The most significant development in the air freight business has been the rapid development of the express sector. Express parcel services were pioneered by Federal Express (FedEx) in the United States. FedEx identified the requirement for door-to-door and overnight transport, which at that time was not normal practice in the air freight industry for either documents or urgent small parcels. Instead of selling on the basis of weight and price, convenience, speed and reliability became the principal product features. The express parcels sector in the United States boomed during the 1980s, with courier and express parcels companies following the Federal Express example and setting up their own air operations. By the 1990s, an international sector had emerged offering the customer a single provider of ground transport, air transport and the related clearance and documentation services. The providers of these services became known as integrators.

Market growth

The relationships between economic indicators and air cargo volumes have been well evaluated by several bodies, including Airbus and Boeing. There is a consensus view that air cargo market growth is closely related to economic development, tending to be higher.

The market for air freight is most commonly measured by revenue (or route) tonne kilometres (RTKs) – in other words, the sum of the revenue-earning cargo carried, multiplied by the number of kilometres for which it was carried.

FIGURE 9.1 Global air cargo industry output

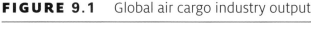

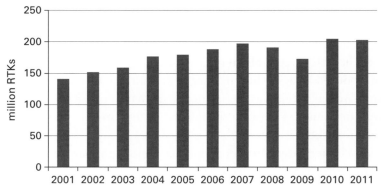

SOURCE: Boeing

This measure is sometimes expressed as FTKs (freight tonne kilometres) – or in the United States, in miles.

Market volume estimates for the 11 years to 2011, according to Boeing, are shown in Figure 9.1. Over this period there have been a number of factors that have stunted growth, notably the terrorist attacks in New York, the rising price of jet fuel and the economic downturn in 2008–09. Despite the recent loss of long-haul traffic to maritime channels, the underlying pattern of faster-than-GDP growth is seen as continuing over the longer term.

Industry players

The air cargo industry involves many different types of organizations, providing shippers with a range of inter-related air cargo services. These organizations include government bodies, privately owned concerns, or hybrids with a mix of state and private ownership. These operations function in a highly competitive market.

Airlines

Airlines provide and fly the aircraft on which air cargo is carried. Airlines range from the national passenger-carrying airlines to small operators with one aircraft. The main types of airline are as follows:

- Scheduled operators provide air cargo capacity principally in the belly holds of passenger aircraft. Some also operate freight-only aircraft on dense cargo routes. They principally work on behalf of freight forwarders, express operators (including integrators) and national post offices.

- Freighter operators operate freight-only aircraft and do not provide passenger services. Within this group are the larger airlines, which carry all types of freight; specialists, which concentrate on a particular type of freight or a particular route; and freight charter operators. Freighter operators give priority to the demands of the air cargo business and are able to operate on key air freight routes at times that satisfy customer demand.

- Integrators are operators which provide complete door-to-door services for the customers. Part of their service offering is the air freight component of any transit and these operators are now some of the largest airlines in the world.

● Passenger charter operators do not figure as major players in the air cargo market. Charter operators primarily operate on holiday routes. As with scheduled operators, they offer very limited freight capacity principally to forwarders, usually through general sales agents.

Within the airline sector there are a range of trading arrangements relating to aircraft ownership and operation. Some operators purchase their aircraft and operate them; others enter long- or short-term lease agreements with other airlines or aircraft owners. These can be on the basis of a dry lease (aircraft only) or wet lease (crewed, maintained, etc). There is also a great deal of trading between airlines to enable them to balance demand and cover a wider range of routes and share facilities.

Airline alliances

No single airline can cover all routes and all destinations, and 'alliances' of airlines have been formed. These alliances are mainly aimed at passenger operations where shared terminals, bookings, through bookings and transfer facilities provide advantages. There are, nevertheless, similar advantages in cargo systems. The three major groups are Star Alliance, Oneworld, and SkyTeam.

Integrators

Four major express parcel companies, DHL, FedEx, UPS and TNT, all operate their own fleets of freight aircraft and in their own right are some of the largest airlines in the world. As they combine the roles of freight retailers, wholesalers and carriers they are known as integrators. They normally contract directly with the shipper and provide a door-to-door service, usually using their own road and air network, handling and transit warehousing facilities.

The integrators started as express operators but have steadily increased the scope and scale of their offering until today they provide a full range of logistics services. In doing this they have taken market share from freight forwarders, first in the lucrative document and small package sector and then further up the size range. They now compete increasingly directly with freight forwarders and the airlines in order to maximize the capacity on their line-haul routes. However, whilst there is a degree of disintermediation, integrators are also reliant on freight forwarders to provide them with additional loads.

Airports

Airports provide the infrastructure to the sector, charging landing fees and parking fees to airlines and charging rent to service companies for cargo transit sheds, etc. A major cargo hub will have sophisticated handling equipment transhipment facilities, customs clearance arrangements and ground delivery arrangements. Typically, there will be a number of on-site providers of these facilities and many of the major airlines and integrators have their own dedicated cargo facilities at their main base and other airports of strategic importance to them. Smaller airports will offer a lower level of provision, with fewer (and sometimes just one) providers of services at that location.

Cargo flights are often run overnight or at off-peak times. This is for the benefit of shippers, for which an overnight delivery is often required, and for the airlines, which can more easily obtain landing and take-off slots at congested airports.

For many airports, noise and other environmental issues are increasing concerns, particularly in relation to night flights. For this reason, many cargo airlines are making increasing use of airports where there are fewer restrictions. The integrators have been the leaders in this trend in moving their hubs to airports where they can operate for 24 hours per day without restriction. One example of this is the move by DHL from Brussels, where there were an increasing number of regulations being placed upon night flying, to Leipzig, where there are none.

Air freight forwarders

Freight forwarders provide a service to manufacturers and other businesses which have a requirement to move goods internationally. The forwarder's role involves receiving or collecting consignments from customers and arranging transportation and documentation to either the destination or to a foreign airport.

General sales agents (GSAs)

General sales agents are utilized by many airlines as a marketing channel, to sell air freight capacity on their behalf. These organizations are normally used in geographical regions where it is not economically viable to set up a dedicated sales and marketing operation.

Transit warehouse operators

Transit warehouse operators provide a transit handling service for airlines and forwarders. Their function is to receive cargo from the aircraft, de-palletize and deliver to truck, or vice versa where customs clearance is required.

Customs brokers

A customs broker is an agent which arranges inbound customs clearance. This role is usually undertaken as a service provided by a freight forwarder.

Air trucking companies

Air trucking companies specialize in collecting and delivering goods between a shipper's premises and airport transit warehouses. These tend to be specialist companies with the appropriate security clearances and access to 'secure' areas.

Air truckers also provide road transport between airports. This need arises when freight is transhipped from one airport to another, either for onward shipment or, particularly in Europe where trucks are used as a substitute for aircraft, usually to a schedule.

Express operators

Express operators provide services for the movement of documents and small packages, where the timescales for transit are measured in hours, in contrast to forwarders, whose transit times are generally managed in days. The largest of these are the four integrators previously described.

Logistics providers

For many years, the integrators have provided an 'end to end' service for the delivery of parcels. As supply chains become increasingly complex, many organizations are looking for a provider which will provide the equivalent 'end to end' service for their supply chain and to which they can outsource supply chain management.

Services such as this are often branded 'logistics solutions'. They are provided by many of the major forwarders, most of which also have strong logistics capabilities; integrators which have developed strategies to offer logistics solutions, and others including '4PL' (fourth party logistics) companies, which provide supply chain management but subcontract all the transport warehousing and handling services.

The air cargo chain

Figure 9.2 illustrates the air cargo shipping process using traditional exporters, freight forwarders, air truckers, warehouse companies, etc.

The exporter will typically book the shipment with a freight forwarder which then manages the remainder of the process. Some freight forwarders have assets and facilities for carrying out some of the processes in-house, but many outsource all services.

The forwarder would typically use an agent at the destination to make the arrangements for customs clearance and delivery to the recipient.

There is a tendency for the major players in the business to expand the scope of their operations so that they are carrying out more of the functions in

FIGURE 9.2   Air cargo processes: traditional air cargo

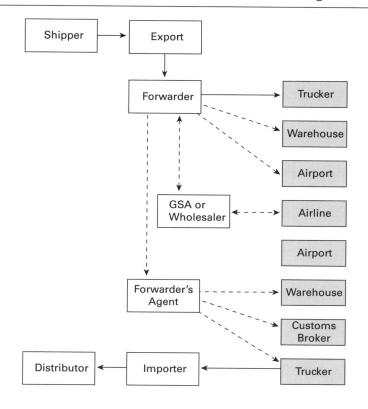

the chain themselves. This means that many of the asset-owning forwarders, whilst not integrators, are offering a more integrated service.

Figure 9.3 illustrates the process if the same consignment is shipped by an integrator. The integrator deals with the sender of the consignment, uses its own resource to provide all the various steps in the cargo chain and delivers the consignment to the recipient. As can be seen from the diagram, the possession and control of all the resources needed to make a shipment means that there are fewer steps in the otherwise very long chain of companies involved.

There is also a tendency to encroach into areas previously dominated by other operators. For example, DHL is now actively selling air freight solutions on its European Air Transport network. In the 'reverse direction', Lufthansa has recently begun to offer customers (forwarders rather than manufacturers) a time-definite express parcel and document service, taking advantage of the higher growth rates in that sector.

FIGURE 9.3 Air cargo: integrator process

Cargo types

Most air freight volume today is 'general' freight. This includes goods ranging from plant and equipment to cosmetics. International express comprises 11 per cent of overall air cargo. There is also a specialist air freight
charter sector catering for special needs and regular shipments. Within each
of these sectors, there are many specialisms, such as heavy lift capability,
refrigerated transport, cut flower transits, etc. Figure 9.4 shows the division
of the market.

FIGURE 9.4   Air cargo volumes by commodity

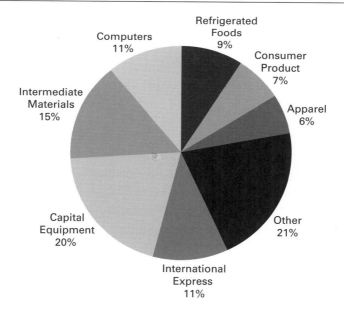

Freight aircraft

Cargo was originally seen as a means of filling spare hold capacity on
passenger aircraft. As the market has grown, aircraft partly or wholly
dedicated to the carriage of cargo have been brought into service. This is
particularly the case in the North American market in which over half the
world's cargo aircraft are presently deployed. Airbus estimates that 58 per
cent of the world's air cargo is now carried in dedicated freighters, with
the remaining 42 per cent carried in the belly holds of passenger aircraft.

Airbus also forecasts the dedicated freighter role to increase to 65 per cent by the year 2025.

With a substantial proportion of the cargo fleet deployed in North America, the main aircraft types are those with payloads of up to 60 tonnes, which are well suited to operations between North American cities. Many of these narrow-body or medium wide-body jets are converted passenger aircraft. This market segment is driven by express carriers, to whom the balance between the lower cost per tonne achieved by larger airplanes and the schedule flexibility of smaller airplanes is important.

Capacity on passenger flights has been expanding, especially as greater numbers of highly cargo-compatible airplanes, such as the 777-300ER, enter the global fleet. This increase in capacity will inevitably have an impact on freight rates, especially with the global economy so weak.

For intercontinental movements of goods there is likely to be a shift away from older designs towards larger wide-bodied jets as these are regarded as being operationally more convenient, with the integrators being cited as an example of a type of user that needs bigger aircraft with extended ranges.

Air cargo routes

The major air cargo routes are those centred on North America, Europe and Asia, and the major flows were East–West or West–East between and within these areas. Figure 9.5 indicates the major flows. The largest flows are between Asia and North America and Asia and Europe, with the North American domestic market the third largest grouping with 14 per cent of world air cargo traffic. In recent years, air cargo flows between China and the Middle East, Africa and Latin America have been growing quickly.

Leading air cargo operators

The 12 largest cargo airlines in the world carry over 86 billion route tonne kilometres (RTKs), which represents 48.3 per cent of the world's air cargo. That group comprises two integrators, eight scheduled passenger airlines and two specialist freight airlines. The volumes expressed in million route tonne kilometres are set out in Figure 9.6.

FIGURE 9.5   Major air cargo routes by volume

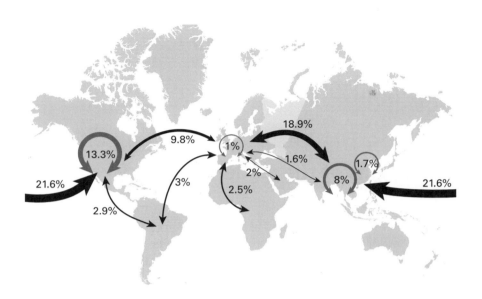

FIGURE 9.6   Top 10 air cargo carriers (freight tonne kms)

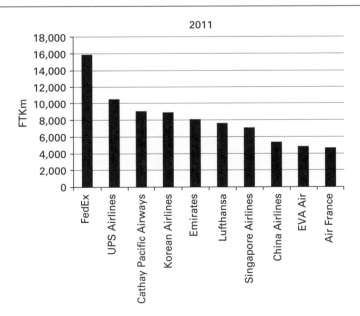

10

Container shipping

The origins of the modern industry

The shipping industry underwent a transformation in 1956, with the voyage of the first container vessel, the Ideal X from Newark, New Jersey. Since that time the major proportion of goods moving by sea (with the exception of bulk) have been unitized in standard-size boxes. This has created major efficiencies in terms of loading, unloading, storage and onward delivery of products. Intervention in, and interruption of, a consignment's movement has been minimized. It is estimated that just over half of seaborne trade in terms of value is moved by container ships, although still under one-fifth in terms of volume – the rest either being bulk or general freight – 'break bulk', as it is known.

In turn, this innovation had a major impact on the global economy. The falling cost of transport made it possible for manufacturers to source goods from remote locations on a much larger scale, despite barriers to trade such as tariffs. This has led to the globalization of industry and directly to the interconnected world in which we live today.

The size of container ships has risen rapidly over the last decade, in line with shipping lines' desire to optimize efficiency. Table 10.1 shows the growth in average vessel size in terms of 20 ft equivalent units (TEUs), a standard industry metric.

The increasing size of container ships has had a major impact on ports, as many can only dock at the major gateway ports, such as Rotterdam in Europe, or Port of Long Beach/Los Angeles in the United States. Ports have had to invest in large new cranes and information technology software in order to be able to load/offload the thousands of containers carried by each ship in an efficient and timely manner.

However, despite this revolution, the shipping industry has remained highly vulnerable to cyclicality. The most recent example of this was in the

TABLE 10.1   Fleet size and capacity

Year	Number of vessels	TEU capacity	Average vessel size (TEU)
2007	3,904	9,436,377	2,417
2008	4,276	10,750,173	2,516
2009	4,638	12,142,444	2,618
2010	4,677	12,824,648	2,742
2011	4,868	14,081,957	2,893
2012	5,012	15,406,610	3,074

SOURCE: UNCTAD

last recession of 2008–09, which occurred after a long period of economic growth.

One of the reasons for this is the relationship between supply and demand. In normal conditions, supply – fleet capacity – cannot be switched on overnight. For new-build ships, there are lead times of between two and four years, and these long lead times mean that orders which are placed in boom periods can be delivered after the peak has passed.

In other words, for long periods of the economic cycle there is often undersupply, due to shipping lines' inability to accurately predict demand, followed by oversupply when a large amount of extra capacity is finally introduced. This means that shipping lines' revenues are hit by the 'double whammy' of falling rates (due to overcapacity) and falling volumes (due to weak economic demand). As good load factors are essential for shipping lines to make money, when they fall beneath the break-even level, losses are very quickly racked up.

The shipping industry is regarded by many to be driven by derived demand, ie the faster that economies and trade grow, the higher the growth in container volumes. However, as mentioned above, there is very much a two-way relationship, with the fall in transport costs stimulating economic activity. It can be speculated that, during the 1970s, when containerization of goods was still being adopted, these cost savings had most impact (a paradigm shift, as it may be termed, from high- to low-cost transport).

There has been much research undertaken on the links between demand, shipping rates and capacity. In general it can be concluded that an increase in volumes and increase in rates has a positive impact on new orders of ships, and consequently on fleet size (and hence capacity). One piece of research claims that as a determinant of growth in capacity, volume growth is more important than rate growth.

However, the situation is more complex than might at first be assumed. Shipping lines have the option, in times of tight capacity, of extending the lives of ships (increasing 'Broken Up' age) and vice versa. They can also speed up or slow down the rate at which their ships move around the world (the latter, so-called 'Slow Steaming'). There is also the option of slowing the rate at which new-build ships are brought into the market, although in an upturn the reverse is not true.

These discretionary decisions make it difficult to gain an insight into the market, based on quantitative data alone. Consequently, forecasting of rates is impossible, even though at first sight this should be theoretically possible.

During the last recession, large amounts of capacity were taken out of the market as ships were laid up, and many shipping lines adopted 'super-slow steaming' speeds. It has been estimated that up to 10 per cent of the world's fleet was taken out of operation in one way or another. This capacity was brought back into the market gradually as the market improved, allowing the shipping lines to improve revenues and profits. This is in contrast to the more usual 'step change' in capacity growth caused by the introduction of new-build ships alone.

The structure of the shipping industry

The container shipping industry is characterized by three key attributes:

- it has a high level of fixed costs;
- there is little difference in the types of service offered;
- it is highly concentrated, with a few shipping lines accounting for the majority of market share.

Although the shipping industry was once regarded as a simple commoditized, point-to-point transport activity, this is no longer the whole story. The sector is now characterized by a complex eco-system of inter-related parties and processes.

Shipping lines

Shipping lines can either choose to service a route using its own vessels or collaborate with other shipping companies. Maersk, the world's largest container shipping line, exclusively uses its own assets on all the routes it operates. However, most of the other lines choose to share their capacity on the key routes. Managing space in this way mitigates the financial risk of capital investment, and allows them to invest in larger ships to create scale economies, whilst ensuring a frequent service for shippers.

Collaboration, in terms of capacity, has in fact always been an industry practice, through what were termed 'Conference' arrangements. Agreeing rates amongst the partners was also widespread, although this has now been outlawed in Europe following the implementation of anti-trust legislation. Formal conferences, where rate-setting still takes place, remain in several other geographies, including the United States, Japan and Singapore.

Ports

A port is an important node in the supply chain. It acts as a point of loading as well as a transhipment hub. With one of the major trends in the industry being towards larger ships, the number of ports which can receive the latest post-Panamax vessels (ie ships too big to transit the Panama Canal) has fallen. Thus the industry is more reliant on 'feeder' services which provide the 'spokes' to the port's hub. Barges play an important role in this system, as does intermodal freight.

Asia, Hong Kong and Singapore have important transhipment/hub ports and are retaining their importance despite the growth of ports, for example, in China's Pearl River Delta. Some shipping lines, such as Maersk, operate their own feeder services. Others work with specialist lines.

Terminal operators

Terminal operators work within a port, often on a long-term lease. The largest terminal operators are able to bring the latest technology, both in software and in handling equipment; operations know-how; and large-scale investment, which a port on its own would not have access to.

The ability to load/offload container vessels in a timely manner is a key competitive advantage for many ports. Shipping lines are very sensitive to delays to service schedule and this is one of the key criteria against which they will choose their ports-of-call.

Intermodal freight

With the growing importance of visibility and velocity in supply chains, the role of intermodal freight in the shipping process has become more critical, not least the ability of road and rail services to interconnect seamlessly and quickly with sea freight operations. This goes as much for ports in Asia, where most goods originate, as in Europe and North America, the gateway ports to the main consumer markets. This has led to high levels of investment over the years, especially in rail infrastructure links, which circumvent heavily congested roads.

Container relocation

One of the most challenging problems the shipping industry has faced is the imbalance in the flow of containers around the world. With most goods consumed in the West, but manufactured in the East, empty containers need to be repatriated. On the one hand, containers are expensive to build, buy or lease, and repair. On the other, moving 'empties' is costly in terms of backhaul or idle storage.

There are opportunities for shipping lines to work more closely with road, rail and other intermediaries to reposition containers.

Consolidation in the shipping industry

In a quest to increase economies of scale, the shipping industry has in the past seen plenty of acquisitions. Maersk was one of the main protagonists, building a position which would then allow it to price competitors out of the market. Sealand, Safmarine and finally P&O Nedlloyd were bought, producing a giant with an annual revenue of $50 billion. However, the last of these – P&O Nedlloyd in 2005 – proved disastrous.

The integration of the purchase of P&O Nedlloyd was handled badly, with Maersk spending €2.3 billion on the Anglo-Dutch container shipping company but failing to gain any market share from the business. These problems were compounded by internal issues around Maersk's IT systems. Since then, it has been content to grow organically.

Over one-third of container shipping capacity is operated by just three shipping companies, according to Paris-based analysis company Alphaliner. The clear leader remains Maersk, with over 2.6 million TEU. Next largest is Mediterranean Shipping Line (MSC) with 2.2 million TEU, with the third largest CMA CGM, with 1.35 million TEU.

TABLE 10.2   World's largest container ship fleets (TEU)

Shipping Line	2012
Maersk Line	2.62 m
MSC	2.19 m
CMA CGM	1.35 m
COSCO Shipping	0.72 m
Evergreen	0.70 m
Hapag-Lloyd	0.64 m
APL	0.60 m
China Shipping (CSCL)	0.57 m
Hanjin Shipping	0.56 m
MOL	0.51 m

SOURCE: Alphaliner

Maersk, MSC and CMA CGM have a clear differentiation in terms of size, with the next largest container shipping line, COSCO, not far off one-quarter of the size of Maersk. Below this group, the companies are generally regional operators, although they may serve individual global routes.

This differentiation by size is not a clear trend, however, as Maersk suffered a loss of market share after its takeover of P&O Nedlloyd. By contrast, MSC has more than doubled its market share in the past decade, whilst CMA CGM has almost tripled its share.

Despite reluctance to make acquisitions over the past 10 years, there is plenty of speculation about industry consolidation in the near future. Hapag-Lloyd has planned a future relationship with fellow German container shipping company Hamburg Süd, with a possible IPO slated.

One of the reasons behind the talk of a new wave of acquisitions is the hyper-competitive nature of the shipping market, fuelled in part by Chinese state-owned shipping companies. Klaus-Michael Kuehne, one of the investors in Hapag-Lloyd, has gone on record as saying he would like to add a Far Eastern line to the combination, specifically NOL.

There is also speculation about a merger of the three largest shipping lines NYK, Mitsui OSK Lines (MOL) and 'K' Lines. This merger would create the world's fourth largest carrier, with 7.5 per cent of the world's total fleet, just behind CMA CGM. In a sector that appears to be increasingly driven by economies of scale this is powerful logic.

Ship size

Increasing ship size is an essential element in ensuring that shipping costs on a per TEU basis are kept low. The first post-Panamax vessel was the MV Regina Maersk, launched in 1996 at 6,400 TEU. Within 10 years the MV Emma Maersk was launched with a capacity estimated to be around 15,500 TEUs. Now, however, ships as large as 22,000 TEUs are on the order books, so-called ultra-large container ships (ULCCs) or Malaccamax (the maximum size that are able to transit the Straits of Malacca).

The size of the new vessels means that they can only be used on certain main lanes, such as China to Europe. This excludes whole continents, such as Africa. These geographies will be served by the ships which would previously have worked the East–West routes. It also means that transhipment will become more important, adding time and cost to shipments from these developing regions.

Freight forwarders v shipping lines

One characteristic of the global shipping industry is the relationship between freight forwarders and shipping lines. Forwarders are both shipping lines' customers as well as their competitors, vying for the volumes of the major shipper companies, such as Walmart or Ikea.

The major forwarders have been very proficient in providing global shippers with end-to-end supply chain solutions. They are widely believed to have better customer service and IT systems which have been designed to provide requisite levels of visibility. The largest forwarders have huge buying power, and can be major customers in their own right; hence they are able to provide retailers and manufacturers with very competitive freight rates.

For these reasons it is believed that forwarders have managed to increase their market share over the past decade – 'owning' more customers than ever.

The overall global container trade has increased from roughly 55 million TEUs in the year 2000 to more than 120 million TEU in 2012. In 2012 forwarders accounted for about 33 million TEUs – a market share of 27 per cent.

Key growth lanes

The shipping industry, in terms of volumes of containers shipped, is now dominated by the intra-Asian trade, which accounts for around one in three containers shipped. For several years the importance of China–Europe and China–United States volumes has been declining. One of the main reasons for this is the development of virtual manufacturing networks, which have spread right across the whole of Asia. Japanese manufacturers, for example, have looked to unbundle and outsource parts of their production to lower-cost manufacturers, not least in China. Now that China's manufacturing is getting more expensive there has also been some migration of manufacturing to lower-cost producers elsewhere in the region.

TABLE 10.3   Top 20 containerized trade routes 2009–10

Destination	Origin	2009 TEUs (millions)	2010 TEUs (millions)
United States	Greater China	7.1	8.5
European Union	Greater China	5.8	6.9
Other Asia	Greater China	4.3	5.3
Other Asia	Other Asia	4.5	5.0
Middle East & Africa	EU	3.1	3.4
Greater China	United States	3.2	3.4
Middle East & Africa	Greater China	2.7	3.3
EU	Other Asia	2.8	3.1
Greater China	EU	2.9	3.1
Other Asia	EU	2.6	2.9

SOURCE: UNCTAD

The past few years has seen strong growth on so-called 'non-mainlines', including North–South (ie from North America to South America and Europe to sub-Saharan Africa), China–Africa and China–Latin America. This latter growth has been fuelled by Chinese investment in the extractive industries of developing countries. Such growth has been running in the high single digits, according to some authorities, compared with low single digits on more established routes.

One thing is clear: much more complex, sophisticated patterns of trade are emerging as a result of a nexus of new demand-driven trends. These also include the rise of the Asian consumer, which has meant the region has become a destination as well as an origin for containerized goods. This has been positive in terms of rebalancing supply and demand, with many more fully laden container vessels destined to Asia than before. This will eventually impact on prices, with 'backhaul' rates (ie Europe to Asia, for example) coming more into line with 'headhaul' (Asia to Europe or the United States).

A further positive trend for the sector is the migration to containerized shipping of commodities, which have traditionally been carried by other forms of transport. Many manufacturers of high tech goods, for example, which once would have used air cargo extensively, have in the economic downturn adjusted their supply chains to take advantage of slower, but cheaper, shipping. Also, some commodities are being shifted to containers from bulk shipping (such as foodstuffs and raw materials) where the economics of such a move allow.

One trend, which may well impact on the traditional mainline trades, is the effect of 'near-shoring' or 're-shoring' of manufacturing in the West, due to rising costs in Asia and fears of supply chain risk. It is still too early to judge whether it will have a material impact on shipping volumes, but it is certainly of concern to many shipping lines.

The European rail and intermodal sectors

11

The European Commission believes that rail – and the way it interacts with other transport modes through intermodality – is highly important to the future of the European transport industry. A white paper published by the Commission in 2011, on the transport sector, stated that the challenge was to ensure structural change to enable rail to compete effectively with road freight and take a significantly greater proportion of medium- and long-distance freight. To do this, considerable investment would be needed to expand or to upgrade the capacity of the rail network.

The white paper accepted that freight shipments over short and medium distances (below 300 km) would, to a considerable extent, remain on trucks. However, over longer distances intermodal freight could become economically attractive for shippers, if efficiency could be improved. According to the white paper, the EU needs specially developed freight corridors 'optimised in terms of energy use and emissions, minimizing environmental impacts, but also attractive for their reliability, limited congestion and low operating and administrative costs'.

In many respects the need for such statements reflects the lack of progress seen in the intermodal sector over the past few decades. Road is, and will remain, the mode of choice for most shippers. However, given the environmental priorities set by governments and administrators, this form of transport has achieved significant political importance, even if out of proportion with commercial realities.

The reason why there has been a push, at least at governmental level, for greater use of rail is evident from the European Commission's assertion that, whilst 1 kilogram of fuel is needed to transport 50 tonnes of goods 1 kilometre with a truck, the same amount of fuel can move 97 tonnes by rail and 127 tonnes by ship. However, it is estimated that intermodal transport represents only a small proportion of goods transported in Europe – somewhere between 2 per cent and 4 per cent of the total, although it is increasing by about 10 per cent per year.

What is intermodal transport?

The European Conference of Ministers of Transport (ECMT) and the United Nations Economic Commission for Europe (UNECE) have put forward the following definition: 'Intermodal transport [can be said to take place] when the major part of the journey is by rail, inland waterways or sea, and any initial and/or final legs carried out by road are as short as possible.'

Intermodal transport involves the carriage of freight using specially designed cargo-protecting units that can easily be swapped between several transport modes, eg road, rail, inland waterways, sea, air. The advantage of utilizing this method is that it reduces cargo handling, and so improves security, reduces damages and loss, and allows freight to be transported faster. It avoids unloading and reloading of individual items but results in a lower overall payload, due to the duplicated load-bearing elements of the rail vehicle and the load-carrying units. As a transport system, intermodal business tries to combine specific advantages of otherwise competing transport modes to achieve an overall gain for all partners involved. In some countries, road vehicles used mainly for intermodal transport get a tax redemption and these may carry a heavier load, thus commercially compensating for the higher deadweight of the units carried.

Intermodal terminals are the transfer points and are designed to take into account the very different properties of the transport modes involved, eg road with single load-units carrying intermittent traffic flows, as compared to transport by trains based on timetabled transport of consolidated loads. Some major ports have developed advanced freight terminals and good rail or inland waterway links that integrate the different modes of transport efficiently.

Europe's longest lorry trailer-carrying railway freight service started operating commercially in July 2007. The 1,060 kilometre-long 'piggyback' transit line transports trailers from Bettembourg in Luxembourg to Boulou (near Perpignan) in the south of France, close to the Spanish border.

The rail service needs about 14 hours to make the journey, so not only does it reduce road congestion and cut journey times (from around 20 hours) but it is also expected to reduce transport costs. Echoing the drive-on capability of EuroShuttle – the Channel train carrying cars under the Tunnel

– the Bettembourg–Boulou rail-freight line allows lorry drivers to load their trucks directly onto the train using a system of pivotal rail trailers.

Generally, freight benefits from the ability of different systems to operate together, particularly for container traffic, ship to rail. The role of combined road–rail transport in easing road congestion, for example, on the main north–south routes across the Alps to some extent depends on rail's ability to impact on infrastructure development. For example, Switzerland has developed its rail network with rail-friendly policies which have promoted a modal shift from road to rail. Rail now accounts for two-thirds of the volumes carried by Switzerland's trucks and trains and Switzerland aims to reduce the number of trucks on its roads further.

Who does what in intermodal transport?

Demand side

Companies involved in buying and managing services from rail/intermodal operators include:

- Shippers: Directly or sometimes on their behalf contracts are signed for the movement of cargo between locations. The shipper is the owner of the cargo.

- Forwarders: The forwarder calculates the best option for moving the cargo; decides the service required as well as handling all administrative procedures such as customs and freight document processing.

- Ocean Shipping Lines: Shipping lines buy services in order to move containers to inland clearance depots on behalf of their customers. The shipping lines not only ensure that their customers' requirements are met but also have to ensure that their container fleets are fully utilized.

- Logistics Service Providers (LSPs): LSPs manage or own assets including warehouses, cross-docking platforms, container freight yards, storage areas and transport equipment.

Supply side

Companies involved in providing services within the complex intermodal eco-system include:

- Terminal Operators (TOs): TOs tranship loading units between the various long-haul transport modes, such as trains, short sea vessels, inland barges and, of course, road. Their main assets are transhipment equipment as well as short-term storage for the loading units.

- Rail, Barge & Short Sea Transport Providers: these operators handle the movement of the loading units between terminals via rail, inland waterway or sea routes. Assets are railway traction as well as wagons, barges and short sea vessels.

- Road Transport Providers: within the intermodal process they operate trucks for local haulage between the relevant terminal and the consignor or consignee.

- Intermodal Transport Operators: intermodal operators obtain transport and transhipment services and either offer door-to-door or terminal-to-terminal transport. In addition, they also are able to assume the commercial risk of selling transport capacity from the transport providers as well as attempt to optimize the use of their own transport services.

Public supply side

Other parties involved in the process include:

- Infrastructure Providers: rail infrastructure providers (usually owned by governments) maintain the track, assign capacity (slots, pathways etc) to users and decide access charges.

- Port Authorities: not only do they manage the port area but in addition they develop services and facilities for transhipment, transport and often other logistics services.

- Regional Local Government: their role is similar to ports and they are frequently involved in logistics parks often with the express aim of developing and encouraging intermodal services and facilities.

How is the market structured?

It is not unusual for providers to have activities involving more than just one aspect of the intermodal process. This means that the industry is comprised of not only highly specialized providers but also those that cover all functions from logistics planning through to transport operation. This has resulted in a diverse market, with traditional providers operating alongside more hybrid providers, in a wide variety of partnerships and co-operations.

As a result, six market segments have emerged, all with slightly different aims and participants, and driven by differing market demands. However, there are many overlaps between segments; for example, it is often the case that the shipping lines and forwarders are each others' customers. Equipment used to transport and tranship is used by all the providers regardless of the segment, and many of the original road-rail operators now also handle containers.

The six segments are:

- carrier haulage;
- merchant haulage;
- seaport terminals;
- railway operator;
- continental short sea;
- continental rail-road.

Carrier haulage

Often shipping lines have the responsibility for carrying the goods into the hinterland ('line haul'). These costs are high in comparison to ocean movements over much longer distances. It is not unusual for shipping lines to have a stake in seaport terminals, which enables the lines to optimize the end-to-end supply chain. This becomes more relevant as the size of ocean-going vessels increases with the continuing consolidation in the shipping industry itself.

In addition, shipping lines have also taken stakes in inland terminals, particularly where these are the only point of entry for the hinterland. These terminals are often logistics centres, optimizing not only cargo consolidation but also container logistics, particularly where they can be combined with container depots to minimize empty runs, thus improving productivity.

Some shipping lines handle short sea-feeder services themselves, but most of this trade is handled by independent feeder operators with their own or chartered vessels.

When still independent, Sealand and P&O/Nedlloyd founded the intermodal operator ERS (European Rail Shuttle), mainly because shipping lines were dissatisfied with the existing services being offered. By 2003 ERS (now owned by Maersk) had also entered rail operations itself, giving the shipping line owners full control over transhipment and hinterland transport in and out of some of Europe's ports.

Merchant haulage

In this case it is the shippers, forwarders or LSPs that are responsible for carrying the goods (and restitution of empty containers) from the seaport terminal to the customer based in the hinterland ('merch haul'). This is traditionally associated with forwarders who have the specialized knowledge in intercontinental trade along with customs and administration skills.

In this market there are more providers and the average actual transport requirement is less in comparison to the ocean shipping lines' 'line haul'. As a result, vertical integration with seaport terminals is less likely, with a few of these providers linking only with feeder terminals.

Within the inland waterway segment both LSPs and forwarders are often owners or shareholders and often act as intermodal transport operators. Some of the forwarders are also involved in short sea feeder services and, as a result, are able to offer a more comprehensive hinterland and overland transport.

Seaport terminals

Along with the consolidation that is taking place in the shipping industry, a considerable amount of horizontal integration is occurring amongst seaport terminals. Today many of the largest container terminals serving the shipping lines are part of providers such as Hutchison Port Holdings, PSA and DPW.

By offering a network of terminals it makes it easier to co-ordinate and integrate supply chains on a global scale for customers as well as providing operational flexibility in handling demand and in spreading risk. The widening of the scope of the offer on a global scale has allowed the terminal operators to increase productivity, utilizing their terminal management and developing ICT skills. It is often the case that these operators also take shares or stakes in inland terminals, as well as intermodal hinterland transport services.

Railway operator

Historically, rail providers have been in a dominant position for providing hinterland transport, particularly when the European rail market consisted of national monopolies and integrated infrastructure, terminal development as well as terminal operations. It was not unusual for these rail companies to have shares in seaports.

As the rail market underwent reform and liberalization, infrastructure and operations were separated and freight operations were transferred to new operating providers. This opened the market for new intermodal transport providers bringing with them different types of providers and co-operation. This increased competition between rail and intermodal providers has not prevented new intermodal services being developed jointly, but the mix of parties varies greatly.

Continental short sea

These services are provided by ferry, ro-ro (roll-on/roll-off) or container operators and the market tends to be concentrated on a few larger providers centred on the North Sea, the Baltic and the Mediterranean. They tend to focus on this only, leaving other aspects of freight forwarding and overland transport to their customers. Some have their origins as ferry providers with road transport operators as their customers. Most of the door-to-door operators began life as freight operators in short sea shipping and extended their services, either into the hinterland or a full range of logistics services.

The scale of operations of a ro-ro provider often dictates that a terminal is dedicated to a single provider, with ownership of the port terminal usually remaining with the port authorities. It is unusual for container operations to be the domain of the short sea provider.

Continental rail–road

Most of these types of intermodal operators were founded by road and rail companies, with the latter always having a minority share. Railways provided traction, transhipment services, and often wagons, whilst road providers (or forwarders) had access to the customer as well as collection and delivery services. This meant that any additional development of logistics services was usually provided by the road companies and not the resulting alliance of the two. This development was of mutual benefit – road providers had access to large-scale rail transport and the railways access to cargo flows.

As the intermodal market opened up so other logistics providers entered the market and started their own intermodal operations. Often these were neither owned by nor associated with rail companies and these additional services became strategic assets that could be integrated with their existing logistics services, such as road transport, warehousing and storage, as well as other added-value offers.

Who decides what to use?

When transport management is outsourced by the shipper, the choice of mode is often left to the logistics provider, albeit some may express a preference for a particular supply chain solution. Whenever logistics service providers are involved with their own assets they try to increase their returns by utilizing them to their full optimization and intermodal services are offered as part of a portfolio of integrated services. They become very much part of the decision-making process and big influencers as to which services best suit the shippers' requirements.

Other intermediaries, such as forwarders who have little or no assets, manage transport for the shipper with a different agenda. They are interested in maximizing the margin above the actual procurement cost, albeit within the constraints set by the shipper. Intermodal transport is often utilized because of the potential to cut costs.

Shipping lines are often attractive to shippers as they can, in many instances, provide hinterland routes as well. Intermodal fits well into this because it adds to the overall scale of port terminal operations, thus providing additional opportunities for hinterland traffic and inland terminals.

CASE STUDY   Rotterdam's intermodal solution

Rotterdam

Rotterdam is Europe's largest port and as such the strategy which is in place to deal with the distribution of containers throughout its European hinterland is highly important.

In response to the growing pressure of congestion on roads around the terminal, the Dutch government invested $6.1 billion in the development of a freight-only rail line, connecting Rotterdam to Germany – the Betuwe Line. The project also involved the creation of two dedicated rail service centres, rationalizing previous operations in the port and run by a private company. A shuttle service links these two service centres with 100 TEU capacity per shuttle.

Using the Betuwe Line, a daily shuttle links 37 European destinations with Rotterdam with a total capacity of 7 million TEU per year, although the line is not confined to container traffic – chemicals and bulk dry are also important.

Overall, intermodal rail in the Netherlands has been eclipsed by intermodal barges. Rail accounts for just 5 per cent of volumes to Rotterdam, compared with 48 per cent by inland waterway. However, destinations such as Italy will benefit most from the rail link.

Internationally, 15 per cent of cargo moving to Germany through Rotterdam goes by rail; this compares with 13 per cent of volumes to Belgium; 14 per cent to France.

Largest domestic intermodal operators

According to the UIRR, the industry body representing the leading intermodal operators, German company Kombiverkehr is the largest national player (ie not including international shipments) in terms of tonne kms. It is followed by the largest players in Italy (Cemat) and in France (Novatrans).

Taking into account purely international shipments, Kombiverkehr is still the largest intermodal player, accounting for 9,189 million tonne kms. Swiss operator Hupac is the second largest, followed by Italy's Cemat. Both these players are very active in the transalpine market.

Intermodal solutions in the automotive sector

The rail market has played a very important part in the distribution strategies, both inbound and finished vehicle, of all the major vehicle manufacturers (VMs). The automotive industry, unlike geographically dispersed light industry, is still focused around major industrial plants which are large enough to support investment in railheads and have the necessary level of volumes. However, changes in the industry over the last 20 years has meant that even in one of the last remaining heavy industries, rail has become increasingly marginalized.

Rail is inherently less flexible than road freight, and this became a major problem when VMs started to implement JIT supply chain management techniques. Manufacturers moved from the stochastic flows of components,

FIGURE 11.1   European rail providers national traffic volumes

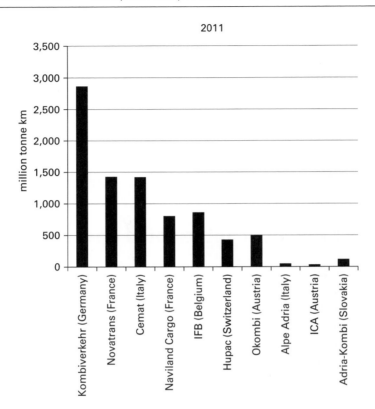

SOURCE: UIRR

to a model based on more frequent deliveries in smaller batch sizes. Inventory holdings have also been reduced, making delivery times more critical. Rail's reliability issues have therefore become another reason why volumes have been driven from rail to road.

In Europe especially, rail has not been able to benefit from the trend towards centralization of production in fewer plants. It may have logically been assumed that rail's competitive advantage over longer distance against road would have given it an edge, especially as production has migrated to the peripheries of the European Union, ie Spain, Italy, Central and Eastern Europe. However, the fact that Europe's railways continue to operate largely as nationalized and domestic focused organizations, mitigates against efficient international operations. There are also practical problems, such as difference in rail gauges in Spain and the rest of Europe. Russia has the same problem.

FIGURE 11.2 European rail providers international traffic volumes

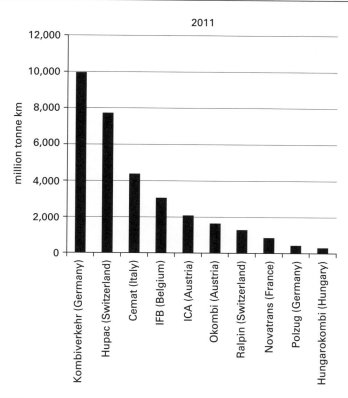

SOURCE: UIRR

There is a much larger market for intermediaries in the United States than in Europe, focused on the intermodal sector. Forwarders such as Yusen Logistics and the Hub Group, working with the railroads, guarantee capacity, recommend rates and routes.

The US railroads have also been much more proactive in developing services, especially on the inbound distribution side. Norfolk Southern runs a 'JIT rail network' for both GM and Ford. It works with a partner, Innovative Logistics Group, to provide daily milk runs from JIT rail centres in all the key hubs. Norfolk Southern also works with Penske Logistics for Ford, developing new services and more efficient rail equipment.

Given below are summaries of the rail strategies of some of Europe's leading auto manufacturers.

PSA Group Peugeot-Citroën

The handling of finished vehicle logistics from both PSA brands is handled entirely by French logistics subsidiary, GEFCO, which uses a mix of rail and road transport, with most trunk routes for the movement of vehicles being by rail. For example, although GEFCO does not use the Channel Tunnel to move finished cars into the UK, it does use rail in order to move cars to its central storage area in the English Midlands.

GEFCO also benefits from exploiting its relationship with French railways (SNCF). It has a major intermodal business which is built upon the scale of traffic moved by GEFCO for Peugeot-Citroën, giving it access to an infrastructure and – just as importantly – a relationship with the state-owned SNCF.

Ford

Ford has traditionally been a heavy user of rail services, although recently it has moved strongly away from its reliance on rail. First of all, it redesigned its finished vehicle logistics operations out of Cologne and Saarlouis. These are now heavily reliant on barge traffic to Vlissingen and Antwerp. Secondly, it has redesigned much of its finished vehicle movements from other plants to use short sea shipping. Major product flows to Scandinavia, the UK and countries in the Mediterranean now use short sea shipping rather than rail. This not only reflects annoyance at poor service from national rail systems in France, Italy and elsewhere, but also a greater concern for reliability and transparency from finished vehicle logistics providers.

Volkswagen

The origins of Volkswagen lie in its German Wolfsburg plant. Located in the centre of Germany the plant dates back to the 1930s when it was built around rail transport. As a consequence, the Volkswagen Group in Europe is still a heavy user of rail services. VW Logistics' operations in German rely on a structure of 'Gebeitspediton' (area transport) at its core. This is a series of logistics companies who use road transport to collect materials from VW's components suppliers. These components are then loaded onto trains at rail terminals and taken to the relevant VW Group plant. For the distribution of finished vehicles the process is reversed. The main exception to this is the delivery of components from suppliers located near to assembly plants, which use road transport. The companies used to do this are dominated by German LSPs, notably Schenker.

DB Cargo is fundamental to the 'Gebeitspediton' operations. This system covers a high proportion of components supplied to VW Group as VW has less supplier park developments than are seen at other VMs. Even bulky items such as seats and interiors are drawn in from suppliers some distance away (for example, much of the seating for the Golf is now sourced out of Belgium). Transport into VW Group plants outside Germany is more complex, but generally the same system is used, with plants in Poland, Spain, Czech Republic and Slovakia being heavily reliant on rail freight.

General Motors (GM)

In the past few years, GM's European rail activity has been rationalized. Its supply chain, particularly for inbound, has a very localized 'Gebeitspedition' system, which generally delivers around 70–90 per cent of all components. However, as GM's production geography has changed, the supply chain has stretched. Some suppliers, even of major engine components, are only located near one plant. As GM 'flexes' its production schedules, a need has arisen to move components between plants. To do this, GM has once again moved to use rail services, creating a dedicated daily 'block-train' travelling between its plants in Spain, Belgium, Germany, Austria and Hungary. The volume moving on this 'OTELLO' service are quite substantial and illustrate that GM frequently looks to rail to achieve economies of scale in logistics.

For finished vehicles again a 'Gebeitspedition' system, with local road-based car-carriers interfacing with rail trunking services, is used. This service has been consolidated to achieve the highest volumes possible, including consolidating Fiat loads as well as GM's Vauxhall, Opel, Saab, Chevrolet and Daewoo brands.

Renault-Nissan

Renault's inbound logistics is dominated by road freight with the close location of suppliers precluding other options. Outbound still has a strong rail element, particularly between Spain and France, but also within France. The company, however, has sought to reduce its exposure to rail transport for long-range trucking movement of finished cars, as rail was found to be too unpredictable and lacked 'transparency'. This has led to the increased role of short sea shipping.

BMW

In terms of modal choice, BMW shows a substantial preference for rail over road. In large part this is due to political pressure in Germany and Austria against road transport. Rail is used both for inbound material flow, but even more so for the movement of finished vehicles. Whilst local and some 'trunk' movements are still made by road, long-distance markets are increasingly served by rail. Large amounts of rail traffic include:

- vehicles for export to the UK and non-European markets;
- mini exports from Oxford UK through the port of Purfleet, UK;
- vehicles to Italy and other Southern European markets by rail from its assembly plants.

The trend towards rail transport in Germany and certain other Western European countries is likely to continue.

For inbound the question is more complex. As ever there is a trade-off between the capability of rail to handle high volumes of material and the flexibility of road freight to handle smaller batch quantities. In a slight departure from the norm, engines from the Hams Hall engine plant are moved to Germany by road. However, much of the rest of BMW's major component flows within Germany, and between plants, use rail.

Mercedes Benz

Mercedes Benz is a more modest user of rail than the other German VMs. The fewer production locations and lower volumes mean that suppliers tend to be located nearer to assembly sites and therefore the need to move large quantities of inbound materials over long distances is less.

Important exceptions to this are the movement of finished vehicle and components for 'Complete-Knock-Down' (CKD) exports out of Germany to non-European locations via the ports of Bremerhaven and Hamburg. Bearing in mind the proportion of production exported from its German assembly plants this is an important aspect of Mercedes Benz's overall logistics activity. The company has collaborated with Deutsche Bahn to create new designs of covered rail wagons which facilitate more efficient use of rail for finished vehicle distribution to German ports, within Germany and into other European markets. Like most European VMs, Mercedes Benz feels under pressure to increase its use of rail as opposed to road freight and it is assumed that projects like this will continue.

Supply chain dynamics of vertical sectors

12

Automotive manufacturing logistics

Since the 1980s, the global automotive sector has been widely regarded as the benchmark for logistics excellence. The introduction of supply chain concepts from Japan, such as Kanban and JIT, had been adopted by many European and US vehicle manufacturers. In turn, this had led to cross-fertilization across other sectors, with its focus on quality and lean supply chains.

In Europe, the onset of the Single European Market allowed vehicle manufacturers previously rooted in high labour cost markets, such as Germany, to exploit lower cost production locations, first in Southern Europe (such as Spain and Portugal) and then when the EU extended further, in Central and Eastern Europe. In North America a similar pattern has been followed, with many vehicle manufacturers sourcing goods from or even locating in Mexico.

The sector hit a major roadblock in the credit-driven recession of 2008–09. Big ticket purchases, such as cars, were postponed by consumers in Europe and North America wary of the uncertain economic conditions. However, this trend was not shared in developing markets, with consumer spending in China, for instance, continuing to increase dramatically. This led to a major strategic shift in focus by the vehicle manufacturers.

This had implications for logistics service providers, who were now being asked to provide services to support production in Asia markets, as well as continue to serve them as export destinations.

Since then, a further layer of complexity has been added. German vehicle manufacturers (VMs) have continued to do well, exporting to Europe and the developing world. However, other mid-market brands have suffered as the region enters a double-dip recession. This has led some to dispose of assets, consider pooling logistics purchasing or change the geography of their supply chains.

In addition, the US market has seen demand recover robustly. This has resulted in substantial investment in new capacity in North America, which implies future demand for logistics services will continue to grow at respectable rates. Similarly, German vehicle manufacturers are also investing heavily in their German-based assembly capacity, even as General Motors (GM) and possibly Ford face problems making money in Europe.

A further change concerns the relative competitive position of vehicle manufacturers. Chinese VMs are looking much less strongly positioned than previously. Despite being exposed to a market capable of growing at double-digit percentages they do not appear to be prospering; rather, it is the global VMs that are reaping the benefits. Indeed, German 'premium' manufacturers continue to export very substantial volumes into the market. The prospect of the increasing influence of global VMs in the Chinese market has very significant implications for logistics as it is beginning to result in a demand for higher quality logistics provision.

These VMs have become far more global in their supply chains, with both finished vehicles and major components moving between continents in order to improve utilization and reduce costs. Fundamental to this has been a move to increasingly globalized vehicle platforms by many VMs. This is a globalization model driven by the need to survive rather than by choice, with the leading VMs resisting this move.

The consequences of these changes for logistics service providers are sizeable but difficult to grasp. For example, the market for automotive logistics services in China is likely to develop rapidly. However, overcoming the barriers to doing business in China will be a real problem for many automotive logistics service providers not already strongly present in the market.

Indeed the ability to provide for VMs in emerging markets will be one of the key issues for LSPs in the near future. It is one thing to provide shipping and forwarding services to a port, another to be able to design and manage transport networks and other aspects of logistics in these markets. Yet, if big Western LSPs want to access the growth available that is what they are going to have to do.

The automotive world looks like it is emerging into one dominated by a few large global VMs with operations in markets such as China, Brazil, Russia, India and elsewhere integrated into supply chains heavily rooted in North America, Western Europe and Japan. Providing the logistics systems to support this structure will be the main challenge and opportunity for automotive LSPs from now on.

The reason for the importance of logistics for the automotive sector lies in the size of capital investment in production plant and vehicle design. Vehicle manufacturers' assembly plants can easily cost €500 million and there is intense pressure to utilize this investment to its maximum extent. The automotive sector is still driven by economies of scale and this means that the most successful companies are those who have the biggest plants with the highest levels of utilization. This can be characterized as 'production orientation'. To maintain high levels of utilization, raw materials and components need to be fed into the assembly plant and co-ordinated with the production schedule. This has been perceived as a core logistics task in the automotive supply chain and one that in the past was given to production engineers. Over the past decade, however, specific logistics management structures have been evolved to manage this process.

Production concepts in automotive logistics

In order to reconcile the imperative for economies of scale with the desire of the market for a wider choice of products, many VMs introduced 'flexible manufacturing'. VMs such as Ford, Honda or Nissan have the ability to vary the type of model being produced on a single assembly line. This means that demand can be better co-ordinated with supply by switching production capacity to the more popular models. This approach fits well into the 'platform strategies' that most VMs have adopted for the design of their different vehicles' types. This is now fairly standard practice in the sector, although with widely varying results in terms of profitability for VMs.

The next development has been the evolution of 'build-to-order' systems within more flexible 'order-to-delivery' production environments. Systems such as BMW's KOVP and GM's 'order-to-delivery' have reduced lead times for the delivery of product and increased the ability of VMs to make the sort of product that customers wish to buy. These systems are now well established. However, the Japanese, and some German producers, have not felt the need to adopt such an approach, although even they have striven to control customer delivery lead times more aggressively. Over the past two years the predominant focus for many vehicle manufacturers has been to cut costs. Many – notably the American 'Big Three' – have amputated huge parts of their companies and this has had enormous effects on their management systems and purchasing strategies.

This has precluded much innovation in logistics systems. Even the more healthy companies have sought to wring cost savings out of their existing systems. The result has been greater emphasis on reducing purchasing costs and increasing asset utilization.

Supply chain geography of the automotive sector

It is often said that the automotive sector is a global business. This is true only to an extent. Most of the largest VMs market vehicles on a global scale, although several of the largest produce in only one or two continents. However, vehicle production is not a 'globalized' activity, in contrast with some industries, such as electronics, consumer durables, clothing and furniture, which source their raw materials, semi-finished goods and finished product on a global scale.

This is a trend that has been amplified through the development of China as a production location. A good example of this is a large retailer such as Walmart, which has very large procurement and logistics structures located in China and feeding into its retail operations in the United States. The automotive supply chain is not like this. Most passenger vehicles are made near the market where they will be sold. Even components are manufactured near the assembly plant. The automotive sector does not have the geographically extended supply chain seen in many other sectors. Within Europe, for example, it is quite usual for 90 per cent of component suppliers to be located within 100 km of the assembly plant. These distances are greater in North America, although this is simply a reflection of the larger geography of the Midwest of the United States in particular.

This supply chain geography is so pronounced that the car industry has created specific locations, known as 'supplier parks', for component suppliers next to its assembly plants. These ensure reliable communication between the component supplier and the vehicle manufacturer's assembly plant, easing the implementation of systems such as Just-in-Time/Just-in-Sequence production techniques.

Key to local sourcing is the need to reduce foreign exchange fluctuations. The automotive sector finds it hard to manage fluctuations in the value of finished product as it is so focused on the management of capital investment. Therefore, it prefers to locate assembly facilities in areas of the same currency as it is selling its products. As a consequence there is a constant process of adaptation to the growth of new markets. High levels of imports mark the early stages of a market, often followed by the use of 'Complete-Knock-Down', that is, components loaded into shipping containers and taken into the market to be assembled. However, the attractions of local production are so substantial that if a market grows to any significant size vehicle manufacturers will want to establish assembly plants in that market. The consequence of this is that the automotive sector's material flows remain predominantly local or intra-continental. Intercontinental and global material flow is likely to remain a much smaller proportion of traffic. Exceptions to this local supply geography are not frequent but are important. For example, finished vehicles are imported in noticeable quantities from Japan in particular.

Having said this, the movement of finished vehicles and components from continent to continent has been growing, as VMs respond to a larger global demand. China imports large quantities of car components as its parts suppliers cannot provide VMs (Chinese and Western) with the quality required. This again may change in the near future as large component suppliers open facilities in China.

Location and size of assembly plants

Although automotive production is remaining local to large markets, there is also a contrary trend towards larger, more centralized assembly plants. The volumes going through assembly plants have increased, generally, to a point that big plants will often have production of over 500,000 vehicles (eg Honda at Maryville, OH, or the PSA Peugeot-Citroën plants at Mulhouse and Sochaux). The reasons for this are obvious in that bigger plants mean higher economies of scale. However, the trend pulls against both the desire to produce a larger number of different model types and the need to keep production within a currency area. Other industries solve this problem by moving to global production centres; however, the automotive sector uses flexible production techniques (see above) to attempt to deal with this apparent contradiction.

The impact of new production trends on transport demand

All of these developments – flexible production lines, build-to-order systems, leaner production – in automotive logistics over the past 20 years have one thing in common. They increase the demand for transport. The realization of the cost of inventory, flexible scheduling of production assets, and shorter lead-times that are characteristic of contemporary logistics operations on the automotive supply side, imply a trade-off between inventory and capital costs against transport costs. Although the dynamics of this trade-off are well known, VMs are reluctant to admit to it. Most will attempt to limit the increase in transport utilization through new management organizations or new methods of purchasing.

Despite this, the improvements in productivity coming from ideas such as JIT rely on the power of cheap transport. The sourcing of components, aggressive management of inventory, the centralization of inventory for the aftermarket, all depend on the availability of cheap transport. Potentially one of the most important developments in the future is the relocation of production to low-cost regions such as Central Europe or even China. If this happens, it will not only depend on the availability of transport resources, but particularly in the case of China, availability of transport will also drive choices of location. Therefore, although transport is perceived to be a relatively unimportant resource within the automotive industry, it is in fact one of growing influence which is increasingly affecting the nature of production in the sector.

Dealerships, retailing and logistics around the world

Despite attempts to reform automotive retailing and 'after sales' service sectors in both Europe and the United States, the sector remains an anachronism. In most other sectors, any analysis of logistics would start at retailing. However, the traditional 'production focus' of the automotive sector has had a big impact on its retailing structures.

Almost all contact with the customer is through the franchises which purchase the right to sell vehicles on behalf of one particular brand or VM. Vehicle manufacturers have in the past valued control of their assembly facilities higher than contact with their customers. Not that they have been willing to accept a free market in retailing their products. Dealerships are very much client companies of the vehicle manufacturers, who are controlled by the VMs' ability to withdraw the franchise.

That this structure is the product of the wider imperatives of the automotive sector is illustrated by the replication of similar retailing structures across the developed world. In no major market are there large independent retailers with autonomous purchasing and marketing strategies and independent logistics systems. In the United States, whilst the approach to automotive retailing is different to that in Europe, retailers are still franchises dependent on the instructions of the VMs. In the United States and the rest of the Americas automotive retailers have traditionally been holders of stock.

Larger operations, although dedicated to one brand, will hold several months' worth of stock-turn.

The reason for this is that the US consumer is more orientated to 'impulse purchases' than in Europe or Japan. The length of ownership in the United States also tends to be shorter. This difference in approach to retailing has its effects both on the nature of the product (which is traditionally of a lower quality than, for example, in Europe) and to approaches to production. Production batches in the United States are usually much larger and vehicles produced with higher equipment levels than in Europe.

Vehicles are then sent out to dealerships where customers expect to drive away a vehicle on either their first or second visit. In Europe it is very different. Although countries vary, the largest single market, Germany, has a strong orientation to 'build-to-order' (BTO). Customers put in an order for a new car many months in advance, expecting to keep the car for many years.

The ability of the VMs to control retailing activity is of increasing importance due to the spread of BTO production systems. In most systems of this type the specification of the car is set within the dealership, with the dealership staff inputting data into the VMs' order capture IT systems. If the market were to revert to a free-market these complex systems would have to be redesigned. The above types of build-to-order systems are distinctively European and specifically German in approach.

Although GM and Ford have different production/supply chain management/retail systems in the United States, they have moved appreciably towards the German BTO model, not least due to the cost benefits it offers. On this basis it is reasonable to assume that this trend will continue and the model of dealerships holding large quantities of stock will be phased out. The exception to this approach is Toyota, Honda and the other Japanese VMs (with the exception of Nissan which is influenced heavily by Renault). The Toyota Production System (TPS) does have similarities to the increasingly influential KOVP at BMW; both are designed to optimize capacity on the production line, for example.

Different types of inbound logistics operations

The nature of inbound logistics operations does vary to a degree. Whilst all need transport and consolidation services, the manner in which this is delivered does change. For example, suppliers feeding into German VMs in Germany tend to have a requirement for consolidation centres near the VM assembly plant.

This is very much the case with Mercedes Benz (MB) passenger car plants, where suppliers usually opt to hold inventory in a consolidation centre near the plant to facilitate immediate availability of stock. This is further complicated by some major suppliers having assembly facilities within the MB plant. In contrast, in Toyota plants this is not the case.

Here, Toyota's LSPs will collect from suppliers and consolidate components at a dedicated facility at the plant. Toyota will require the supplier to set aside part of its loading bay for Toyota-destined supplies, but the supplier should be operating under the Kanban system and therefore should not need any further inventory management systems.

FIGURE 12.1   Dynamics of Toyota component feed

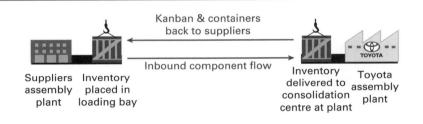

SOURCE: Transport Intelligence

FIGURE 12.2   Mercedes Benz passenger cars component feed

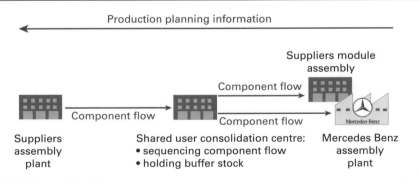

SOURCE: Transport Intelligence

Component suppliers are also faced with contradictory demands from vehicle manufacturers. VMs want suppliers to invest in logistics or assembly facilities near assembly plants. For example, Mercedes Benz passenger cars/Smart wants suppliers to have on-site assembly capabilities. This of course requires investment by suppliers; however, VMs are unwilling to commit themselves to suppliers for long enough to ensure that the investment is covered.

The reasons for this are:

- The increasing trend for VMs to have several different types of vehicle produced at one assembly plant.

- Continuing variability in sourcing of similar components leading to variability in the volume of component feed to an assembly plant over the medium term.

- Frequent changes in vehicle model/design affecting the volume of component feed.

Consequently, there is a danger that suppliers will be left with facilities at or near the VM's assembly plant which are redundant or underused. Many LSPs view this as an opportunity for outsourcing, with several suppliers sharing facilities owned and run by the LSP. This appears logical; however, it conflicts with the unwillingness of many suppliers to outsource assembly operations which they regard as core-competences. Logistics is usually one of the core functions of such 'near-plant' facilities.

For example, the main function of 'Sequencing Centres In-line', usually referred to as 'SILS' or 'Regional Assembly Plants', is to break-bulk and feed components into the VM's assembly plant in sequence, dictated by the production schedule. This would suggest that LSPs are well positioned to offer such services within shared user facilities. This is certainly the case in many plants. However, many larger suppliers are very aware of the importance of logistics as a core-competence and are unwilling to relinquish it to LSPs on a large scale. As a consequence, the market for such centres may appear more promising for LSPs than in reality.

Pharmaceutical logistics

An industry in transformation

Economic and globalization trends are having a major impact on the pharmaceutical drug manufacturing sector and hence on the associated logistics industry. Whilst multinational drug manufacturers struggle with rising costs, expiration of blockbuster drug patents and changes in government legislation within their largest markets, Europe and the United States, opportunities are increasing within Asia and South America. These trends have resulted in manufacturers re-engineering their supply chains' strategies.

In the past, little attention was paid to supply chains as manufacturers were focused on drug sales and development. In particular, the changing government role within the pharmaceutical drug industry, especially in the European and US markets, has meant that manufacturers are now faced with supply chains that are not effective in a sector that is in transformation.

With the globalization of the drug-manufacturing sector, companies are targeting emerging markets, such as China and Brazil, as locations not only to sell to but also as locations for outsourcing such operations as manufacturing, research and development, and clinical trials. However, an array of issues, such as security, intellectual property and knowledge of government legislation within these emerging markets, has resulted in manufacturers turning to logistics providers for assistance.

Valued at almost €43 billion, the pharmaceutical drug logistics market is expected to grow a little more than 12 per cent in 2011 to €47 billion, with the largest increases noted in Asia and South America. Logistics providers are expanding their service offerings and their geographic reach to meet the needs of the sector. To prove successful, however, logistics providers will need to demonstrate an understanding of the special needs of the pharmaceutical industry. Many manufacturers within the industry have shied away from using logistics providers in the past, due to their lack of industry knowledge. To counter this, market leaders, including FedEx, DHL and UPS, have sought to demonstrate their knowledge and understanding of the pharmaceutical drug manufacturing industry by introducing specific solutions. For example, the growing demand for biopharmaceuticals has resulted in the need for temperature-regulated transportation. Logistics providers have introduced special temperature-controlled containers and monitoring systems to ensure temperatures remain constant. Also, the need for temperature-regulated warehousing is also developing.

Along with the introduction of temperature-regulated solutions, logistics providers are also providing consulting services to assist manufacturers with such issues as trade and compliance concerns, as manufacturers expand into the fast-growing emerging markets of Asia and South America. Also, management of clinical trials, samples, returns and recall management and management of marketing materials are some of the additional services logistics providers are offering to the drug manufacturers.

Pharmaceutical manufacturers are faced with numerous changes within the sector. These changes must be addressed with an updated, proactive supply chain in order to be competitive. By partnering with the right logistics provider, manufacturers will prove successful in this changing industry.

The global pharmaceutical logistics market

The global pharmaceutical logistics market is in a state of change. In the past, supply chains were neither flexible nor cost-effective as many pharmaceutical manufacturers appeared to be little concerned about the efficiency of their supply chains. However, facing mounting government regulations and increasing competition, they are now assessing their supply chains in order to remain competitive in this changing market.

In the blockbuster drug model, oral solid-dose pills were shipped to a small number of wholesalers that then moved them on to retailers. However, as the market shifts towards personalized healthcare, an increasing focus is on a narrower group of individuals. Many of these newer drugs require more complex manufacturing and distribution processes than shelf-stable pills. Also, the push for safety in the supply chain is a factor in requiring backward visibility to manufacturers' suppliers and suppliers' suppliers in a robust and real-time way.

Fluctuation in demand for branded and generic products, and changes in distribution channels, are also driving the continued evolution of supply chain models. For example, the loss of patent protection is impacting the supply chains of both manufacturers and large retailers. In the United States 70 per cent of generic drugs are now delivered direct to retailers compared with just 10 per cent of brand-name drugs. This volume of generic drugs now sold through the retail channel is leading many large retailers to work directly with manufacturers to integrate products into their own distribution network for less complexity and cost. New direct-to-patient, high-cost specialty therapies are also causing manufacturers to reconsider how they take products to market in order to better respond to consumer demand.

The growth in emerging markets adds another level of complexity. Global pharmaceutical outsourcing has become increasingly prevalent, but is creating a complex and risky supply chain environment. This global expansion is making it more difficult for pharmaceutical manufacturers to manage their supply chain. The need for a flexible supply chain is great as the industry undergoes changes in product mix, manufacturing routes and distribution channels for different kinds of products.

Many manufacturers have grappled with these changing supply chain needs and are beginning to realize the benefits of outsourced logistics partners. Companies see the benefit of shifting responsibility to a global LSP that is likely to have access to more facilities and resources, and consequently, a greater capability to quickly respond to changing business needs.

Pain points in the pharmaceutical supply chain

As the pharmaceutical manufacturing industry adapts to its changing environment, its supply chain will need to become more flexible in order to respond more quickly to these changes. Based on surveys conducted by logistics providers and the pharmaceutical industry, some of the identified pain points include information technology, legislation, regulation and security of products.

To address the issue of various government regulations and security issues, the pharmaceutical manufacturer must have near-complete visibility of its supply chain. However, as the manufacturer expands its operations throughout the world it becomes difficult to connect to not only its primary suppliers but also to its suppliers' suppliers. According to some manufacturers, the primary method used to gain visibility into suppliers' practices is a periodic audit. Many still manually aggregate the data.

Many industry executives are also concerned about the willingness of suppliers and distributors to provide information to address regulatory requirements. Hurdles exist in implementing the necessary technology including cost, the difficulty of implementation, lack of industry standards and lack of regulatory requirements and guidance.

Progress is being made as a variety of industry consortia have been established to address these issues. Many logistics providers offer visibility solutions that could benefit manufacturers. They also have introduced specific industry solutions to address visibility of products while in transit, particularly for those products that require temperature monitoring. For example, Schenker offers an RFID solution to monitor products' temperature as well as to track the cargo from origin to destination. Both FedEx and UPS offer bar-code solutions.

Logistics and transportation service offerings

Cold chain

Growing global demand for complex drugs is increasing demand for cold chain solutions. It is estimated that at least 25 per cent of all healthcare products are temperature-sensitive, meaning they require refrigeration during transportation and storage. Further, these products may also have a short window of viability, which makes rapid transport essential.

According to the Biopharma Cold Chain Sourcebook, the pharmaceutical cold chain market was valued at almost $6 billion in 2009. Growth is expected to average around 8 per cent over the 2009 to 2015 period. Logistics spend for cold chain products will be driven by increased volumes of products and by faster pharmaceutical market growth in emerging economies.

FIGURE 12.3   Pharmaceutical cold chain market

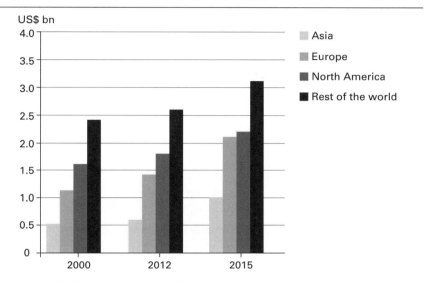

SOURCE: 2011 Biopharma Cold Chain Sourcebook

Airlines have increasingly developed products to make the transit of pharmaceutical products more reliable. For example, British Airways World Cargo's offering, 'Constant Climate', in 2009 launched an SMS customer update service and broadened the scope of its service to include passive temperature-controlled packages and shipments. Its SMS offering updates customers by text message or e-mail at key milestones through the air freight journey. For Constant Climate Active shipments using Envirotainer, the exact temperature inside the unit and the condition of the battery are included in the update. In 2011, American Airlines expanded its cold chain service, ExpediteTC, to include a solution for the requirements of cold packaging during transit.

The solution, called ExpediteTC Passive, supports ambient temperature control using cool rooms, expedited handling processes and high-visibility monitoring to ensure cargo is handled within desired temperature ranges. This offering augments American's current service, ExpediteTC Active, which utilizes dry ice and battery-powered containers to actively regulate temperature levels, regardless of ambient conditions. Customers are able to access online tracking and receive notification alerts via e-mail or mobile phone.

Ocean carriers are also announcing cold chain solutions for the pharmaceutical industry. For example, APL announced the SmarTemp system for monitoring onboard refrigerated containers via satellite communications.

Packaging technology is also continually evolving. CryoPort Systems Inc and FedEx Express announced the signing of an agreement to provide an 'innovative and breakthrough' frozen shipment solution for the life science industry. The solution allows for products to remain frozen at temperatures below −150 °C for up to 10 days, unlike dry ice shipping which often requires re-icing during transit.

In late 2011, UPS announced it would offer a new air freight container for healthcare products. The PharmaPort 360 addressed a key industry issue of safeguarding healthcare shipments in the supply chain by enabling near real-time monitoring and maintaining product temperatures in extreme outside conditions.

The PharmaPort 360 container, manufactured by Cool Containers for UPS, maintains strict temperatures by utilizing both heating and cooling storage technology, allowing it to tolerate a significantly wider range of extreme ambient temperature changes. The container more effectively maintained temperatures critical for protecting medicines that need to stay within the required 2–8 °C to prevent spoilage. The PharmaPort 360 also sustained its protective temperature range for more than 100 hours, which is an important factor as more supply chains extend globally and healthcare products need to travel farther to reach markets.

Envirotainer is a provider of air cargo cold chain transportation solutions. The company works with both pharmaceutical manufacturers and logistics companies to provide a variety of packaging, container and other cold chain solutions. The company also developed an industry accreditation and certification programme to acknowledge those service providers are capable of properly managing cold chain shipments. Accredited air freight forwarders are Agility, Cargo-Partner, DB Schenker, DHL, FedEx, Kuehne + Nagel, Panalpina, Uti, World Courier and Panther. Accredited airlines include Air France/KLM, American Airlines, British Airways, Korean Air and Emirates.

Distribution services

Distribution and warehousing services within the pharmaceutical logistics market can be complex due to government regulations, security and safety of the products. As such, inventory management is more than just ensuring adequate inventory levels to meet demand. For example, a temperature-sensitive drug arrives at a distribution facility prior to receiving government approvals to market the drug to the public. This inventory must be isolated and data must be collected from temperature loggers within the shipment and communicated back to the manufacturing plan. The product cannot move from the quarantine area to a primary storage location until the plant indicates that temperature readings were satisfactory to ensure product safety and compliance and government authorities have approved the product for sale. Also, packaging and labelling is regulated and often differs from one market to the next.

Reverse logistics

The proper management of recalls is very important. The ability to implement reverse logistics, including recalls, in an organized manner is critical to containing the potential damage from an incident. Products not properly reclaimed and destroyed may end up being resold illegally. The Healthcare Distribution Management Association (HDMA) estimates that 3 per cent to 4 per cent of products that leave pharmaceutical warehouses ultimately are returned. Of the estimated 3 per cent to 4 per cent of products returned, it is also estimated that about 1.5 per cent to 2 per cent of pharmaceuticals manufactured will be destroyed.

The majority of major logistics providers offer reverse logistics services, however, there are niche players such as Genco that provide returns and recall management solutions specifically targeted to the pharmaceutical drug industry.

Consumer goods and retail logistics

The consumer and retail industries are hugely important for the global logistics industry. In the contract logistics industry, they account for over half of all revenues. Although most movements of consumer goods (which include food and drink) take place on either a local or national basis, an important and growing segment takes place increasingly at a regional and global level.

Consumer packaged goods (CPG) manufacturers have complex supply chains. Not only do these companies produce a range of foodstuffs, beverages, cleaning products and beauty goods (a number of which may be classified as hazardous), they also operate in a range of temperatures (from ambient, through various levels of chilled, to frozen). Add in a mix of national production and overseas production and the logistical requirements are vast.

In Europe, the consumer goods industry was transformed by the advent of the Single European Market. This allowed manufacturers to exploit the lower labour costs of the peripheral members of the EU (such as Spain and Portugal) whilst being able to export unfettered to the rest of the region. Improving infrastructure meant that transport costs were comparatively low, which allowed manufacturers to centralize their distribution.

Meanwhile the migration of consumer durables manufacturing to the Far East meant that sea and air gateways to Europe evolved into important logistics nodes for the distribution of imported goods.

At the same time as this, the manufacturers' relationship with retailers changed, as retailing became much more centralized. There was a shift in the balance of power in the supply chain which, as we will see, resulted in the imposition of several logistics initiatives, not least Factory Gate Pricing (FGP).

General food and drink production and distribution still largely takes place on a local or national level. It is undertaken by a range of contract logistics or local hauliers, with high levels of competition in a largely fragmented market.

However, at the consumer packaged goods (CPG) level (dominated by manufacturers such as Procter & Gamble and Unilever) supply chains are far more regionalized. Production locations have been centralized with a focus on economies of scale. Whereas many food types are produced for local tastes, consumer packaged goods (such as razors or toiletries) have across-the-board appeal.

Global supply chains exist where the production emphasis is on cheap labour. Goods falling into this category include toys and other durable goods (including consumer electronics). Freight forwarders and shipping lines have a much bigger role in these intercontinental movements of goods. However, global 3PLs can also play a part in providing value-adding services, for instance in consolidation centres (see below). Goods often come through major gateways (such as Rotterdam or Antwerp in Europe) and are then stored and distributed from European distribution centres (EDCs) often based in Belgium or the Netherlands. Others are moved from the gateway ports directly to national distribution centres (potentially owned and managed by the major retailers).

It is impossible to look at the consumer sector in isolation from developments and trends in retailing. Supply chain strategies of the major manufacturers have necessarily been influenced by the growing power and leverage of international retailers such as Walmart or Tesco. Retailing is now being transformed by e-commerce and this is described in more detail below.

Consumer packaged goods (CPG) sector

The CPG market is highly fragmented, comprising many different product lines requiring different distribution chains. The products falling within this sector include food (ambient, chilled and frozen), dairy products, beverages (dry and wet), healthcare (soaps, deodorants, etc), household products (cleaning products often hazardous) and cosmetics.

The market for consumer packaged goods has changed hugely over the past 10–15 years. Once, it was dominated by national 'champions' who also had a global presence. It is now dominated by global brands and is one of the most influential in the world.

The sector has experienced a series of challenges, including the economic downturn, increased competition, food scares and new consumer trends. While these challenges pose a threat to some companies they can be an expansion opportunity for others. In response to these new challenges, CPG companies are improving competitiveness by restructuring and intensifying the fight for market share through product differentiation and/or the development of new food products.

Amongst the traditional leaders in the sector – Procter & Gamble and Unilever – there has been a clear shift towards products with greater complexity and added value. Both companies have seen a transformation in their product line: Unilever has sold many of its key frozen food brands; Procter & Gamble has bought Gillette and both have increased their involvement in health and beauty products.

This illustrates that there has been a shift away from:

- products dependent on access to basic raw materials, such as fats;

- products very dependent on low cost/high volume production;

- products wholly dependent on access to large distribution capabilities;

– and a move to: high value added products with an aspect that strengthens the brand – for example beauty products; complex products such as 'over the counter' pharmaceuticals or razors.

The supply chain of the consumer product sector and its associated production activities has traditionally been affected by the high volume and commoditized nature of the products being sold and the need to source raw materials/ingredients.

The big CPG companies used to be highly orientated towards basic household items such as soap. These were delivered in different forms but they were consumed rapidly and in large quantities. Consequently, it made sense for production not to be too far removed from the area of consumption.

The result was a strong orientation towards national-based companies. Whilst the sector did not suffer from the 'national champions' syndrome seen, for example, in the car industry, most consumer products consumed in a country were produced in that country. Therefore, up until very recently CPG companies were organized on a national basis.

This is changing remarkably slowly. Indeed for many product categories within the consumer goods sector it remains the case that product is manufactured near to the market.

However, CPG companies are now beginning to change: their relationship with the customer has changed as the sophistication and power of retailers has increased; their products have changed, especially their dependence on fat-based staple food and cleaning products.

Therefore, while we still see a substantial volume of 'in market' production in sectors such as soap powders and highly commoditized food products such as spreads, production of stronger food brands, for example chocolate, is more concentrated on a regional/continental scale (although this varies with related items such as ice-cream). Health and beauty products also have a more regionalized production approach.

One must, therefore, be cautious about making any generalizations regarding the dynamics of any CPG supply chain due to the broad differences between the products.

A further qualification about the supply chain dynamic is the issue of inbound raw material. The traditional 'staple' products were heavy users of agricultural commodities, in particular various types of fats. These were sourced globally with tropical agricultural products being sourced on international markets and shipped to production locations usually located in major seaports. Again, whilst this model still applies to many product lines, many of the new product categories are quite different and do not use these raw materials.

An intermediate type of product, however, includes the category of petrochemical-based cleaning products. These use a variety of chemicals, but primarily ionic-surfactants. Therefore, facilities which are largely concerned with blending and packaging these products are increasingly becoming centralized. To a lesser extent this also applies to health and beauty products.

A further observation should be made about the coherence of CPG supply chains. A key imperative is to 'get closer to the customer'. This means organizing marketing activities at a national level, as most market idiosyncrasies are expressed nationally. These activities are generally concentrated around advertising and marketing issues related to product design.

In addition, the question of relations with retailers is usually handled at the national level.

Regionalization of supply chain geographies

Originally the supply chains of CPG companies were dominated by the need to obtain raw materials for their products. Consequently, manufacturing facilities were often located near ports. This is now changing. Inbound logistics is less important; 'outbound' logistics, that is the management of finished product, is now the dominant concern. That said, the utilization of production capital assets has also become a more important cost driver leading to important redesign of the supply chain.

However, the dominant feature of the CPG supply chain is the focus on retailing. This, combined with the high volume, low value nature of most of products sold, means that production and inventory management locations cannot be too far from the consumer.

There is a clear trend amongst all of the major producers to improve the cost base of their supply chain by consolidating production facilities. This trend is also reflected to some extent by a centralization of inventory. This should not be exaggerated as most products need highly distributed inventory near retail locations (although this is complicated by the varying role of the retailer in managing stock). Nonetheless, the major companies are creating larger warehousing complexes serving national markets. Crucially these are served by more intensive road freight services.

Durable goods

Whilst CPG companies largely utilize regional supply chains, durable goods are mainly manufactured in the Far East and moved by ship to consumer markets in Western Europe and North America. The phenomenon of globalization has been examined in much depth elsewhere in the book, but consumer goods have been the major beneficiary.

The bulk of consumer goods are bought for sale by the major retailers. Traditionally they have worked through purchasing companies and of these Li & Fung is the largest. It sources goods for companies such as Walmart, Target and many others.

However, one of its largest customers, Walmart, appears to be making several changes to its purchasing strategy. In January 2013, the company announced plans to 'significantly' boost its sourcing by $50 billion from domestic suppliers over the next decade. According to data from Walmart's suppliers, items that are made, sourced or grown in the United States account for about two-thirds of the company's spending on products for its US business.

Walmart's international sourcing may also change. Last year, Li & Fung announced that Walmart would not be executing its option to buy a global sourcing business, Direct Sourcing Group, set up by Li & Fung in 2010 to solely support Walmart's international retail sourcing operations. That led many to say Walmart was planning to cut out the sourcing middleman.

Not only is Walmart perhaps looking to cut costs by removing or reducing the use of the sourcing middleman, but also the desire to have more visibility and knowledge of its vast supplier network is increasing. In November 2012, Walmart was the recipient of intense negative publicity due to a fire in a Bangladesh manufacturing facility used by a supplier. As a result of this, Walmart has adopted a 'zero tolerance policy' for violations of its global sourcing standards, and plans to sever ties with anyone who subcontracts work to factories without the retailer's knowledge.

Other companies such as Apple and Nike have also received negative press due to manufacturing practices and as such are working towards corrective measures. Improvements in visibility and collaboration are needed and are increasingly being adopted by retailers.

For many, the re-shoring trend has been beneficial as these companies are perhaps more adept at managing domestic suppliers. Still, a good bit of retail manufacturing will continue in Asia and companies such as Li & Fung provide valuable knowledge and assistance for companies that are in need of such services.

Consolidation services

One of the best ways in which retailers and manufacturers can save money on shipping costs is to consolidate less-than-container loads from multiple suppliers to make up full container loads. These are then shipped to distribution centres in Western Europe or North America. Consolidating shipments into a single unitized load reduces the overall transportation cost per unit as well as increasing efficiency.

The point of consolidation is usually at the port of origin. Ports in southern China are particularly important, due to their close proximity to Chinese exporters, although some shippers use major transhipment hubs such as Hong Kong or Singapore. In these cases bringing together shipments from multiple countries of origin considerably increases the levels of complexity, as containers can be held up due to inbound shipment delays or customs issues.

Although consolidation has been around since the 1970s, it is becoming an increasingly important strategy, not least because of the proliferation of products which retailers are importing. This has led to smaller order levels which would ordinarily increase the per unit transportation costs. The economic downturn has also reduced retailers' order sizes, which has had the same effect. Rather than wait for sufficient demand to fill a container, consolidation services can ensure that containers are shipped in a timely fashion, thus reducing inventory holding costs as well.

Some importers have also implemented so-called distribution centre (DC) bypass programmes which avoid the use of a DC in the end-user market. By sorting and consolidating at the point of origin and shipping direct to the customer, distribution costs and transit time can be reduced. Using local labour, consolidation centre services can be undertaken more cheaply than in a developed market. There is also the opportunity to carry out quality control closer to the vendor rather than when it arrives in end-user market when it is too late to rectify a problem with the order.

This element of control which consolidating at origin provides to shippers is also useful in balancing supply with demand. With the rise of the Asian consumer markets in particular, shippers are often supplying markets not only in Europe and North America but also throughout the Far East. Using an upstream consolidation centre gives them the ability to allocate inventory at the latest possible moment and avoids accumulation of stock in national/regional warehouses.

Hong Kong is probably the best known location for consolidation services. As a deepwater port it originally attracted shipments from the Pearl River Delta special economic zones as the local ports were not able to accommodate large container vessels. Although this included the transhipment of containers, it is estimated that 75 per cent of goods transiting Hong Kong were consolidated. As its competitive advantage has dwindled over the years with the development of deepwater ports throughout China, Hong Kong has sought to position itself as a key location for value-adding logistics services.

Challenges in developing countries

Downstream CPG supply chains are expanding rapidly into developing markets, and this is providing manufacturers with considerable challenges, as well as the evident opportunities.

One of these challenges relates to the different levels of development in retailing structures. Although in China and India major grocery retailers are growing fast, in many areas of the Indian subcontinent in particular 90 per cent of sales are through very small general retailers.

In parts of Asia, poor road infrastructure has resulted in a high degree of supply chain uncertainty and this has had a big impact on CPG manufacturers' cost structure. It has created an environment in which transport spending is a much higher proportion of overall logistics costs than in the West, driven in part by the fragmentation of the transport supplier base as well as the weakness of the transport infrastructure. In contrast, lower labour costs have resulted in cheap warehousing, although this is often not effectively used to reduce transport costs.

That situation is quite distinct from the one facing companies in Europe and North America, where many are rethinking their supply chain's intensity of transportation use, driven by the cost of fuel and an increasing need to reduce carbon emissions.

However, the centralization of production and inventory in Asia Pacific is nuanced, with certain aspects of the supply chain being centralized whilst others remain regional.

The influence of oil prices

Many CPG supply chains were designed, developed and implemented in the 1980s and 1990s, when capital spending was fairly high and oil was very cheap. This led to the centralization of production locations and warehousing and the reliance on intensive use of transport to supply geographically dispersed markets.

Post-recession, this situation has been turned upside down and this has resulted in a reversal of many companies' thinking on supply chains. Both Procter & Gamble and Unilever have stated that they are looking at reducing their use of transport, which of course would necessarily have an impact on inventory holdings and their locations. It could be an important factor in the creation of regional, rather than global, supply chain structures.

This is likely to be a long process as networks, both manufacturing and logistics, take years to restructure. One senior executive of a major CPG commented that the tipping point would occur when the price of oil surpassed $150 per barrel. Although the oil price in the last three years has not gone over $125, any sign of global economic recovery could see costs shooting up.

In any case, with companies' present distribution networks designed when the price of oil was $20 per barrel, it is clear that they need to start seriously re-evaluating their supply chain networks, both in terms of major infrastructure such as warehousing locations as well as individual elements such as pallet sizes and delivery frequencies.

Collaboration within consumer goods supply chains

The term 'collaboration' can be used to describe partnerships between different types of companies at many supply chain levels. However, in the consumer goods sector it refers to co-operative relationships between manufacturers, merging their shipment volumes and distribution networks to achieve a range of logistics efficiencies. One of the most compelling reasons why collaboration is an important supply chain initiative is that it has been shown to bring fast and measurable benefits, and is relatively cheap – an important factor in a harsh market environment.

Within the warehouse environment, combining inventories can increase distribution centre utilization. It has been used to good effect when, for example, a supply chain re-engineering project has resulted in the reduction of stock held at centralized facilities. This then leaves an underutilized warehouse which usually has to be disposed of, incurring property and employee costs. By inviting another manufacturer to share the premises, these costs are avoided and efficiencies are increased.

On the transportation side, there are also benefits. By co-loading shipments there are obvious synergies to be gained, especially where the product is being distributed to similar retail outlets. One particular project between two collaborating companies found that 80 per cent of their delivery locations were the same and that a saving of 31 per cent in transportation costs could be achieved.

However, collaboration not only benefits warehousing and transportation operations. It can also enhance customer service by providing a critical mass which allows increased frequency of deliveries. That is to say, shippers do not have to weigh up the benefits of increasing the number of consignments to customers against the cost of dispatching half-empty vehicles. Co-loading with a partner ensures that vehicle break-even points are met.

The last major benefit in terms of bottom line is the leverage which shippers can gain in terms of negotiating freight rates. Consolidating shipment volumes can ensure small and medium-size manufacturers can compete in the market on the same basis as larger rivals.

Collaboration works best if the products and distribution profiles of the collaborating companies are similar. Even if the products themselves do not need to be identical, it certainly helps if handling characteristics, life cycles, inventory velocity and seasonality as well as environmental control and security needs are compatible.

Some examples of successful collaboration include the following:

- Global consumer goods giants Kimberly Clark and Unilever have collaborated to build a joint warehouse to supply retailers' distribution centres in the Netherlands.

- Reckitt Benckiser, Johnson and Johnson, and Colgate-Palmolive manage a facility in Unna, Germany, to distribute goods on a shared-user basis.

- In France, Reckitt Benckiser, Kimberly Clark and Colgate-Palmolive co-operate in another distribution centre operation.

Retail trends

The consolidation of the retailing sector has had a fundamental influence on the development of the associated consumer goods industry, which has become more regionalized/globalized as a result. In most cases, manufacturers have been able to rationalize the number of distribution centres they operate as they no longer need to make multiple deliveries over large geographic areas. This has had significant consequences for the logistics industry.

National retail markets have been transformed in many developed countries over the past 30 years. The large grocery multiples – such as Tesco, Carrefour or Walmart – have driven consolidation in the market through highly efficient distribution channels. Prior to this the retail sector was characterized by a three tier model – manufacturers, wholesalers and retailers. These days in many markets the wholesaler has largely been driven out and this has had major implications for supply chains and logistics providers.

In 1982 the Institute of Grocery Distribution in the UK estimated that retailers were responsible for about 32 per cent of final deliveries to stores. After decades of restructuring relationships with their suppliers, and cutting out the role of the wholesaler, almost 100 per cent of deliveries are made to stores through retailers' own distribution centres. This has resulted in a step change of cost reduction – for both manufacturers and retailers. One UK consultancy, Logistics Consulting Partners, estimates that logistics costs fell in real terms by 70 per cent over a 25-year period. This increased the grocery multiples' competitive advantage, placing even more pressure on high-street retailers.

Another key dynamic driving change has been a focus on retailing space. Adopting supply chain concepts which were being employed by other sectors such as Just-in-Time, allowed retailers to eliminate in-store stock holding, maximizing display space and reducing inventory. This obviously relied upon fast and efficient replenishment and the sophisticated logistics required to facilitate it.

Although the major changes to retail distribution channels occurred mostly in the 1980s and 90s, more recently supermarkets have introduced Factory Gate Pricing (FGP) which had been pioneered in the fashion and automotive industries. Under FGP, products are no longer delivered at the retailer distribution centre, but collected by the retailer at the 'factory gates' of the suppliers. Owing to both the asymmetry in the distribution networks (the supplier sites greatly outnumber the retailer distribution centres) and the better inventory and transport co-ordination mechanisms, this results in major cost savings for the retailer.

The major grocery multiples found that the move to FGP was able to:

- reduce product cost and inventory;
- achieve supply chain visibility and control in vehicle planning, scheduling and utilization through enterprise compatible systems throughout the product supply chain;
- reduce waiting time at supply and delivery locations;
- decrease empty running through backhaul capacity (it is estimated that up to 35 per cent of all truck miles are run empty and that truck utilization could be increased by FGP on average by 15 per cent);
- improve vehicle performance in time, load and distance;
- increase product visibility through the supply chain;
- utilize buying power and supply chain knowledge in 'partnership' negotiation;
- reduce carbon emissions.

In some respects the implementation of FGP is the logical conclusion of the centralization of distribution strategies employed by retailers in the 1990s. By absorbing the costs of establishing these new supply chain structures, including the increased transportation element, they had unwittingly reduced the logistics costs of their suppliers as well. The implementation of FGP allowed the retailers to unbundle product and logistics costs, reducing suppliers' margins and finally obtaining a contribution towards the cost of distribution.

Diversification of retailer product offering

Growth in the supermarket sector across Europe is being driven not by sales of food but rather by the ever-widening range of non-food goods being made available by retailers. In the UK, the trendsetter as far as European retail is concerned, supermarkets are now attracting 62 per cent of shoppers to regularly buy non-food items from them, collectively spending over £19.7 billion, compared with only 45 per cent of shoppers five years ago.

Specialist stores are coming under severe pressure from the multiples, right across Europe, as retailers look to tap into general merchandise as a way of increasing new sales growth on top of a more mature food market.

The growth of non-food sales has been driven by a number of developments, including:

- the growth of the hypermarket format;
- the drive to make space in supermarkets work harder;
- the development of non-food dedicated store formats, ie Asda Living and Tesco Direct.

Healthcare, toiletries and household products are as important to a supermarket's core offer as food, and therefore, it is important that the range and pricing meet shoppers' expectations.

The expansion of the range of products being offered by the major supermarket chains has created opportunities for logistics service providers to bid for major new contracts with existing clients. The larger players generally benefit from consolidation within the retail sector, with the supermarkets taking market share from the more fragmented high street stores. The latter offer few opportunities for the major LSPs in terms of contract size or complexity.

High tech manufacturing

The global high tech market is undergoing a vast change. Globalization has given rise to increases in competition and new products, both of which have had profound effects upon the high tech supply chain. Companies within this market compete on tight margins resulting in many turning to their supply chains for a competitive edge.

As cost management and operational efficiency are top priorities for high tech companies, the ability to operate the leanest, most cost-effective and adaptable supply chain usually results in success. Apple has proven this over the past few years and its supply chain is considered an example for many companies to strive towards.

As a result of the industry's quest for cost management and operational efficiency, manufacturing has moved away from the mature markets such as the United States and Europe and into Asia. Today, over 90 per cent of all high tech goods are manufactured in Asia. However, as costs such as raw materials and labour rise, Asian companies are now looking for alternative sourcing locations. A major shift of supply sourcing is now occurring within the region and this is expected to increase, resulting in the growth of intra-Asia trade lanes.

Although eastern and western China are expected to remain the top sourcing locations for many high tech manufacturers and solutions providers over the next five years, Taiwan, Thailand, Japan and South Korea are likely to see increases as well.

Innovation in high tech supply chains

The global high tech industry is best described as one of constant innovation and change. Those companies that are the quickest to adapt and innovate are the ones to achieve market leadership in this highly competitive industry. As a result, consolidation persists as companies turn towards mergers and acquisitions as a means to acquire the latest technology or expand into a new service offering.

Not only has consolidation increased but the effect that Apple has had on the industry has been truly remarkable. The introduction of the iPhone and the iPad have changed both the PC and cellular mobile phone industries and have created a blurring of these two high tech subsegments.

As a result, the entire supply chain has undergone great changes – from the original equipment manufacturer (OEM) to the contract manufacturer, distributor, retailer and finally to the end customer. These changes have resulted in shifts in manufacturing locations and transportation modes as well as shifts in business strategies. For many OEMs there has been greater emphasis towards software as opposed to hardware.

Logistics providers have responded to these changes by introducing specialized solutions to meet the industry needs. Niche logistics providers have also emerged – those providers that work mostly with high tech companies. For example, due to the ever-shortening life cycle of high tech devices and increasing regulations that manage the disposal of these products, logistics providers and other partners within the high tech supply chain have introduced specialist reverse logistics operations as well as other after-market solutions.

Logistics providers have also launched targeted services particularly as shippers opt for less expensive means of transportation such as ocean and, in some cases, even rail services. For many air cargo providers, particularly those that operate along the Asia trade lane, there has been an overdependence on high tech product launches over the years, and, due to the rise of oil prices, the shift towards ocean freight and slowing demand, overcapacity issues have occurred.

High tech supply chains

The typical high tech supply chain is highly complex, characterized by fragmented distribution channels and remote manufacturing locations. The number of companies involved in different aspects of getting a product to market can lead to high degrees of inefficiency in the supply chain, resulting in either too much or too little inventory being stored at different locations.

As an example, an original equipment manufacturer (OEM), such as Hewlett Packard (HP) or Acer, is likely to outsource production to an electronic contract manufacturer (ECM) which may well be located in a remote, low labour cost market (such as China) and will have its own supply chain. The OEM will then deal with a distributor who will in turn deal with a reseller. Other parties supplying goods such as peripherals or software will also be involved.

Given the short product life cycles which are typical in the market (new releases and developments come out continuously throughout the year), it is critical that for a supply chain to remain competitive, information and product must flow as seamlessly as possible. OEMs have a short window of opportunity to make significant margins on a product before competition catches up. However, there is a trade-off between being able to take advantage of the initial demand and the risk of overproduction. In the 1980s many companies were guilty of overproduction which left them with high levels of redundant product. Since then the industry has attempted to work with very low levels of inventory, whilst keeping stock-outs to a minimum. Best practice will involve collaboration between supply chain partners in terms of data-sharing, with some companies providing visibility to real-time information.

Transport of high tech goods

Air freight has tended to be the transportation mode of choice for manufacturers to ship high-value, high-demand goods. However, when Steve Jobs returned to Apple in the late 1990s, planning for air freight took on a strategic and competitive edge for shippers – one that has benefited air freight providers and freight forwarders alike since. Jobs booked all available air freight space to ensure that the company's iMacs would be available in time for the holiday season, thus handicapping rivals who later faced a shortage of capacity.

A similar transportation strategy was adopted in 2001 for the company's iPod. Apple found it more economical to ship iPods directly from Chinese factories to consumers' doors, and again in March 2012 it utilized its freight forwarder, DHL, to ship its latest iPads via air from China.

However, the high oil prices and the slowing global economy have affected air freight. The sector relies heavily on exports to the European and US consumer markets, both struggling with economic woes. Official figures provide an insight into why China's air cargo sector has been struggling. In 2011, the export growth of China's electronic products slowed markedly to 11.9 per cent. The data shows that the growth rate was 17.4 percentage points lower than that of the previous year.

The export value of electronic products accounts for nearly 35 per cent of China's total export value, with computers and mobile phones being the top two categories of exported electronic products. In 2011, computer and mobile phone exports increased by 11.1 per cent and 34.3 per cent, respectively.

Likewise, the growth rate of imports of electronic devices saw a sharp decrease of 23 percentage points, in comparison with that of 2010. Despite this, it hit a new high of $468 billion, up 11 per cent year-on-year.

The official figures of course have to be adjusted for inflation – a statistic which is never reliable in China. However, the impact of the slowdown can be seen on the main airports and air cargo carriers in the region.

As a result of the high costs associated with air freight, companies such as Acer and HP are turning more towards ocean freight. Lower-value computer components such as keyboards and mouse devices have moved by ocean for a long time. Intermediate value components such as monitors have been migrating to ocean, though high-value components such as computer chips will more than likely always be shipped by air.

According to some industry estimates, based on value, 60 per cent of computers and related components are flown by air, and 40 per cent move by ocean. But on a weight basis, only 15 per cent move by air, compared with 85 per cent by ocean.

While the obvious advantage of ocean freight is the much lower cost of transportation, it also has disadvantages, in particular longer transit times. Computers shipped by ocean must be built four weeks earlier than if shipped by air. That creates the risk of a substantial decline in a product's value during the shipment period.

There is also the risk that an order might be cancelled while the goods are on the water, and there is a greater risk of damage. There are also higher inventory costs. Unexpected delays, such as the backlogs at ports can tip the balance of any cost-benefit equation.

In 2010, Dell, the global computer manufacturer, announced plans to revamp its supply chain. It revealed that it intended to increase the volume of Notebooks which it ships by sea, from 20 per cent (an increase from 5 per cent the previous year) to around 70 per cent by the end of its financial year 2013.

According to a senior director of Dell, shipping via ocean freight had already created a '$35 million benefit' as the company 'penetrated this opportunity', as he put it. It plans to ship up to 3 million units by sea. The core of Dell's new strategy, of course, is cost management – recession-related losses and fierce competition in the PC market have put an emphasis on cost-cutting.

This is a classic response to a market maturing and the effects of global price deflation in the technology sector. Dell appears to be trying to realign landed costs with the selling price in the market. The key way to do that is by shifting modes.

The decline in the price of laptops illustrates the cost challenges computer makers face. When they first became popular, they typically cost $3,000. Now they can cost as little as $400. But there has been little movement in the cost of air freight, meaning the cost of transportation as a percentage of the total selling price has surged. So a shift to ocean transportation, which typically costs one-tenth the price of air freight, is a logical way to cut costs.

Companies successfully utilizing an ocean shipment strategy have had a different supply chain structure. According to some within the industry, companies such as HP handled the longer lead times by building to a forecast, maintaining a finished goods inventory, having a large distribution network, and by offering very little customization. This is very different from Dell's traditional build-to-order strategy, extremely low inventories of finished goods, direct sales to customers and extensive configuration options.

HP is also working on a rail-sea link to move by rail, on a relatively expedited basis, to port in Shenzhen and then by sea to ports of Long Beach CA,

Rotterdam etc. According to HP, it takes 20 days transit time by ocean, port to port for a Notebook made in China to hit the port at Long Beach. It takes 39–40 days to hit Rotterdam.

The increasing need to cut costs but also to get products to its markets as quickly as possible has resulted in PC manufacturer Acer testing a new transportation method – shipping computers by rail via Chongqing in China through Kazakhstan, Russia, Belarus, Poland and into Germany. This takes 18–20 days, undercutting sea freight by about one week to ten days and though it costs more, it is still cheaper than shipping by air.

High tech logistics services

Besides the traditional warehousing/distribution services offered such as kitting, labelling and repackaging, a growing number of logistics providers are expanding their capabilities into aftermarket services for high tech companies.

Aftermarket

Long known as a way to promote a positive customer experience, after-market services also provide revenue streams for OEMs and logistics providers. According to various industry publications, the market for total aftermarket services is estimated at over €435 billion ($525 billion) with €66 billion ($82 billion) of this total spent on average each year on logistics related services.

After sales is also known by a variety of other terms such as reverse logistics and returns/services management. The processes involve the receipt of previously consumed products for the purpose of repairing or ensuring proper disposal. A host of components play into this service including returns, repairs, recycle, disposition, all of which are increasingly dependent on growing regulatory compliance (in its simplistic format, the after sales supply chain is demonstrated in Figure 12.4):

- An end-user returns a product such as a mobile phone or tablet via instructions usually from the store or e-retailer where it was purchased.

- The product can be returned via the store or directly mailed to a service centre. In many cases, service centres are part of a distribution centre. If the product is mailed, usually a printable pre-paid label is provided for the end-user – another measure to ensure proper customer service.

FIGURE 12.4   High tech aftermarket sales supply chain

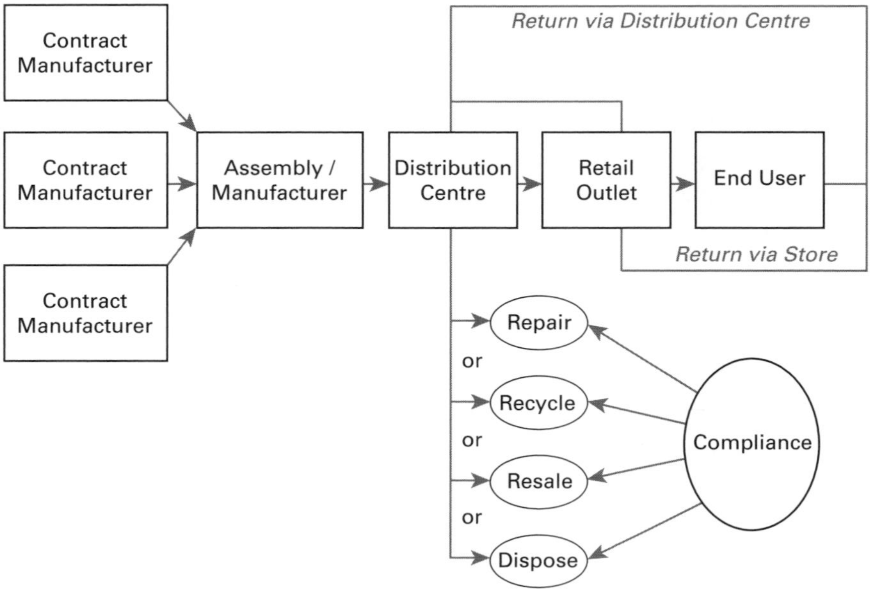

SOURCE: Transport Intelligence

- Once received by the service centre, the product is evaluated based on end-user's description of issue and may include the following:
  - return for replacement;
  - repair and return to end-user;
  - repair but provide end-user with alternate product;
  - resale;
  - dispose of product which may involve recycling and/or disassembling products and reselling components and lastly dispose of goods per government regulations.

Returns/repairs

As a whole, the electronics industry spends over $19 billion on returns every year. Warranty claims and repairs are a major part of the reverse logistics process, requiring varying methods for receiving, tracking, processing, repairing, and ultimately redelivering the product to the consumer. Over the years, the level of high tech returns has become increasingly apparent, resulting in a sub-industry dedicated to electronic repairs.

In the electronics industry, the average return rate on sales is 8 per cent but the return rate within subcategories can range from 4 per cent to 15 per cent – many of the returns are not even defective. It is estimated that the non-defective rate for consumer electronics hovers around 65 per cent of total goods returned, meaning only 35 per cent of the returns are actually defective. The non-defective product may be in perfect working order or slightly damaged by the customer but still repairable.

Logistics providers such as DHL, Kuehne + Nagel, New Breed Logistics and UPS provide repair services as well as specialized companies such as Brightpoint and contract manufacturers such as Celestica and Flextronics. All of these companies screen the products and analyse the status of returned products to determine the next processing step, whether it is to scrap the product or repair it.

Field service/spare parts logistics

A challenge for companies is that of stocking enough spare parts at all times. For those companies that need to service customers in the field, this is especially a concern particularly as contracts often dictate short lead times to dispatch a technician and/or required part for replacement. As a result, warehousing not only involves storage and handling in central or regional facilities but it also involves storage and time critical handling in strategic stock locations in order to get the part to its final destination in as short amount of time as possible.

Field service logistics is an estimated $26 billion market. Logistics providers such as UPS SCS, FedEx, DHL and CEVA all offer solutions for this market. CEVA, for example, has a network of strategic stocking locations that manage the delivery of 'mission critical' and scheduled parts to customers, field engineers or Pick Up Drop Off (PUDO) points.

13 Risks in global supply chains

Rebalancing 'external' and 'internal' risks

External threats to supply chains have received considerable attention following the well-publicized natural disasters in Japan and Thailand. However, understanding of these risks is at a very early stage. One survey, undertaken for the World Economic Forum, found that 30 per cent of respondents estimated losses of 5 per cent of annual revenue from supply chain disruption. However, over one-quarter of respondents were not able to place a figure on the financial impact of a disruption.

It is not that the risks themselves have become more acute. After all, there have always been wars and natural disasters. Rather, it is the evolving supply chain and production strategies of the major global manufacturers which have changed, leading to a rebalancing of the risks inherent within various parts of the supply chain.

One distinction which can be made is between 'internal' and 'external' risks. For example, in the 1980s the personal computer sector adopted traditional manufacturing practices involving the outlay of huge amounts of capital. The risks were clear as many of these companies quickly went out of business when their forecasts proved hopelessly wrong. From this period new business models were developed which allowed manufacturers to focus on design and marketing and let their supplier bear the risk of production.

This process has been referred to as 'unbundling' of production. In other words, in this example, 'internal' risks were outsourced to Contract Electronic Manufacturers. This, however, did not leave the OEMs risk free – rather the 'internal' risks were transformed into 'external', ie those which are inherent in extended supply chains. The risks have changed but are still there and are just as business critical.

The 'unbundling' of various production processes has led many OEMs to evolve into what are, in effect, managers of integrated and complex networks of remote but interlinked suppliers. In some cases this has produced greater levels of risk, and in others it has had the opposite effect. There is no doubt that extended supply chains are more vulnerable to external threats, but on the other hand, such networks have also dispersed risks to a number of markets by reducing centralization.

A small supply chain, for instance, with a single production facility is highly vulnerable to external events whereas a large, complex supply chain with multiple supplier options has the potential to be much more robust through a greater number of sourcing options. Each option may have higher supply chain risk attached, although – and this is the key point – the probability of overall network disruption is less than in a small supply chain (see Figure 13.1).

FIGURE 13.1   Global supply chain risk – probability of disruption

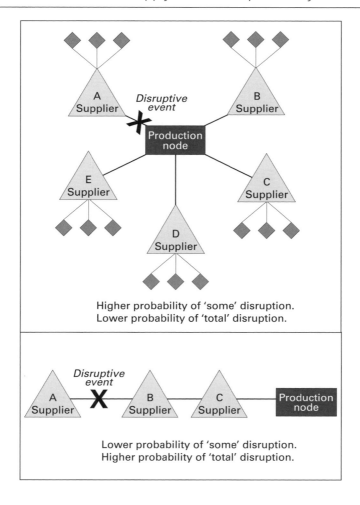

The move towards more complex supply chains has its own risks, related to a reduction of visibility and the development of sub-optimal networks. With Asia transforming from a production market to a consumer-led economy, this will only add extra layers of complexity into sourcing and outsourcing decisions for Western manufacturers. Timeliness, reliability, information sharing, quality and design, along with wider benefits resulting from shared labour skills and knowledge, all need to be weighed along with levels of visibility, management control and, of course, external risk.

Globalization has brought its own risks. Extended supply chains mean longer lead times (and less agile response to market conditions); more handoffs between parties; more challenging quality control as well as exposure to currency fluctuations, labour disputes, shipping costs, corruption, theft and natural/geopolitical instability. An understanding of this has led to many manufacturers adopting a hybrid strategy of remote production combined with near-sourcing.

The cost of transport (on which globalization is predicated) is also over-looked as a major risk. This not only includes shipping rates, which have been volatile over the past few years (in early 2012 shipping rates per TEU rose by $1,000 overnight on Asia–Europe trade lane) but also cost of fuel which has been driven up by tension in the Middle East.

Quantifying supply chain risk

Manufacturers usually adopt one of three strategies when dealing with risk:

1 Inventory management – build up buffer stock.

2 Sourcing – developing contingency strategies for specific suppliers or supply chain links.

3 'Acceptance' – doing nothing as costs of mitigation outweigh benefits.

Deciding on which strategy to adopt relies on understanding the cost implications of each approach.

One pharmaceutical company undertook a cost/benefit approach to working out how it should mitigate supply chain risk. They used insurance and industry data to estimate the frequency and duration of disruptions, and using scenario planning software they worked out how many weeks per year their production would potentially be affected. They were then able to set inventory holdings at a level which would minimize disruption. Of course the weakness of this approach was that although it minimized disruption, the strategy imposed huge additional costs on the organization, not only from the financing of the additional inventory, but also from the risks of redundancy of stock.

Modelling exercises also need to take into account the length of disruption as well as the probability. There are other variables: for example the length of time it takes for alternative suppliers to ramp up production. One other interesting factor which impacts significantly on the extent of disruption is the location of the event within the supply chain. The further upstream it occurs, the longer the disruption to supply. The reason for this is that downstream processing locations act as bottlenecks and take time to fulfil back-orders once upstream supply is switched back on.

In many respects, effective supply chain management is all about the trade-off of one set of risks against another. Keeping higher amounts of stock in various locations is not necessarily a good response to the threat of disruption as this is not only costly, but in high tech sectors, for example, where product life cycles are low, could be commercial suicide.

Lean supply chains are also a double-edged sword. Whilst they are working efficiently they have the potential to reduce inventory levels at the same time as maintaining/improving customer service. However, there is no doubt that they are less resilient to external shocks, as they do not provide a safety net when supply chains break down.

In effect, what has happened in the past is that inventory levels have been used as 'insurance' against risk. If there have been disruptions to supply or to transportation, 'buffer' stock has allowed production or sales to continue unaffected. Insurance companies which are now entering the supply chain risk market are allowing manufacturers to outsource this risk, whilst keeping inventory levels to a minimum. Quantifying the risk for insurance companies (as well as manufacturer) is a major challenge.

Types of supply chain threat

When people talk about supply chain risk, they usually mean 'external' threats. As we have discussed, though, the relation between external and internal risk is very close. For example, increasing inventory levels increases 'internal' risks (redundancy, wastage, financing etc) but mitigates external risks (the impact of a disruptive event on supply).

The reverse is also true; reducing 'internal' risks can increase 'external' risks. For example, the problems which Toyota faced in the United States relating to a malfunctioning brake pedal design were blamed on a supplier.

One estimate put the total costs of this supply chain catastrophe to Toyota at $2 billion, not including lost consumer confidence. With 60–70 per cent of a vehicle manufacturer's inventory managed by the supply chain, quality control is obviously a huge issue.

TABLE 13.1   Global supply chain risk – supply chain internal and external characteristics

Supply chain characteristic	Internal risk	External risk
High stock levels	High	Low
Lean supply chains	Low	High
'Bundled' in-house production	High	Low
'Unbundled' outsourced production	Low	High
Globalized sourcing	Low	High

This perhaps can be seen as the inevitable consequence of a trade-off between these different types of risk. However, one piece of research suggests that when outsourcing production (and risk), only 10 per cent of manufacturers undertake any sort of risk assessment.

Where external events have had most impact, this has been due to insufficient risk assessment. One such example was the floods in Thailand. Here the risk of centralization (which can occur in any geography) was transplanted to a remote region where risk was not fully understood. The high tech manufacturing cluster which developed in Thailand had comparative advantage in terms of leveraging a local production eco-system whilst offering low cost labour. The fact that this cluster developed in a region of Southeast Asia was not the problem; rather that a consolidation of specific competences had been allowed to develop in an exposed, flood-prone location.

External threats to supply chains can be divided into four main categories:

- Environmental
  These include a wide range of events including extreme weather, earthquakes, tsunamis, floods and even volcanic eruptions. The economic cost of natural disasters was estimated by insurance company Swiss Re at $194 billion in 2010. The supply chain

consequences are derived from not only the disruption of production but also the impact on transportation services and infrastructure. A WEF/Accenture study found that following the Japanese tsunami/earthquake the operating profits of 15 leading multinationals fell by 33 per cent in the subsequent financial quarter directly as a result of supply chain disruption.

- Geopolitical
  Tensions in the Middle East are a considerable source of risk for supply chains, especially affecting transit routes such as the Straits of Hormuz and the Suez Canal.

  Terrorism also falls into this category, the most obvious example being the events of September 11. A more recent example, described below, relates to the bombs placed in packages originating from Yemen. It should be noted that as regulators seek to limit the impact of a terrorist event, they risk increasing supply chain costs by high levels of security-driven regulations and procedures. This would seem to be counterproductive, but politically expedient.

  Piracy is also a major issue for supply chains, although the true cost of the disruption is largely hidden. Although millions of dollars are paid to pirates off the Somali coast each year, the real costs occur when shipping lines have to divert to longer routes to avoid the problem areas. Other costs include increased insurance; security and guards; increased steaming speeds; higher wages for seamen (danger money); not to mention indirect payments for military operations.

- Economic
  One of the most pressing supply chains risks from an economic perspective is what can be termed 'demand shocks'. An example of this is the disruption caused by the company failure of suppliers following the 2008 recession. This was particularly relevant to the high tech and automotive sectors where supplier bankruptcy was prevalent. Many of the problems were caused by manufacturers 'switching off' supply from remote suppliers, and although this had a short-term positive effect on inventories and balances, it meant that when demand picked up strongly in 2010, manufacturers were unable to meet demand.

  'Supply shocks' are less obvious, but a material threat all the same. The volatile nature of shipping rates could fall into this category. In early 2012 shipping rates on Asia–Europe routes increased by about $1,000 per TEU (from about $650 to $1,650) – a situation which most shippers would find difficult if not impossible to predict.

Manufacturers are ever more exposed to currency risks, given the globalized nature of their suppliers and customers. Due to the Greek debt crisis, and the impact this is having on the strength of the euro against the dollar, this risk is likely to have significant financial impact in the coming months and years.

● Technological
  Technology failure/outage is a major concern to shippers, although as yet there have been few significant incidents. A lot of money has been spent by agencies, such as the Pentagon, in assessing and planning for a 'cyber terrorist' attack, although minor disruption to date has come from power failures or accidents. More reliance in the future will be placed on information and communications networks as the supply chain industry becomes increasingly paperless, and this will only heighten the risks. However, actually measuring the true nature of the threat and robustness of information systems is difficult.

Even localized events can have a major impact on global supply chains. For example, an earthquake such as the one in Japan in 2011 may be very localized in geographic terms, but has worldwide implications for supply chains which depend on a large number of suppliers clustered in the affected area.

Shipping rates, in contrast, are a global phenomenon. They affect all supply chains, but although serious, have less of a catastrophic impact.

FIGURE 13.2   Global supply chain risk – external event impact on supply chain (illustrative matrix)

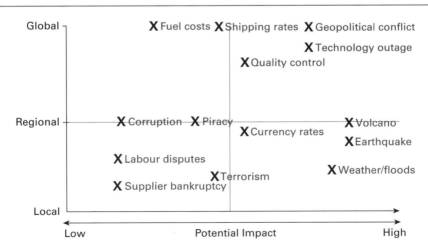

A geopolitical conflict, depending on where it takes place, could have a very serious, disruptive impact at a global level. A supplier bankruptcy, on the other hand, may be a local problem, and if contingency plans are in place, may not be serious.

Of course, the seriousness of each of these threats is very specific to each supply chain as well as the level of disruptiveness of the event in question.

Unknown unknowns...

The most disruptive supply chain events are those which have not or cannot be planned for. Therefore, it is perhaps more useful to, rather than look at past events in order to gain some insight into the future, identify weaknesses in supply chains instead. Addressing vulnerability is the best way to mitigate the impact of a disruption, although there still remains the issue of how much time and money should be invested on each perceived weakness.

The World Economic Forum's Supply Chain and Transport Risk Survey 2011 identified the least effectively managed supply chain components as rated by respondents. The top five are:

- reliance on oil;
- shared information;
- fragmentation along the value chain;
- extensive subcontracting;
- supplier visibility.

As the survey analysis points out, three of these components relate to visibility and control. Improvements in technology can mitigate this type of risk. For example, development of supplier/buyer communities and the use of social media technologies within supply chain communities could be one way in which risks can be reduced; 'Sense and respond' technologies allow for greater awareness of the location of products in the supply chain, and hence enabling better decision-making/re-routing.

The development of information technologies will play an important role in the mitigation of supply chain threats. There is little prospect that these risks will diminish – some may even increase. Therefore, the ability to react to events will become the key competitive differentiator, and technologies which enable an enhanced level of supply chain agility will become highly sought-after.

However, the adoption of more technology will also play a role in increasing risks. Increasing reliance on technology will leave supply chains open to 'cyber attacks' or even accidental outages. Whilst technology will lead to greater levels of efficiency, it will also mean that maintaining robust networks will be ever more critical.

Despite this it is the industry's reliance on oil which is of primary concern. Given the relation between geopolitical tension and the price of oil and the extreme volatility which this causes, it is clear that alternative strategies must be developed. This could entail a rebalancing of the inventory/transportation equation as shippers position stock in closer proximity to end-users. This will increase stock levels, but reduce transport costs. Of course, as mentioned above, this has risks in its own right and these need to be taken into account in a holistic supply chain management strategy. It could also entail a move from global supply chains to near-sourcing of products, especially utilizing less fuel intensive modes of transport.

Sector resilience to threats

The characteristics of some supply chains make them more vulnerable to supply chain threats than others. Figure 13.3 illustrates this point. The high tech sector, for example, relies heavily on global supply chains which are typically high value, lean and unbundled/outsourced. The pharmaceutical supply chain is much less globalized (although becoming more so), and

FIGURE 13.3   Global supply chain risk – sector threat resilience

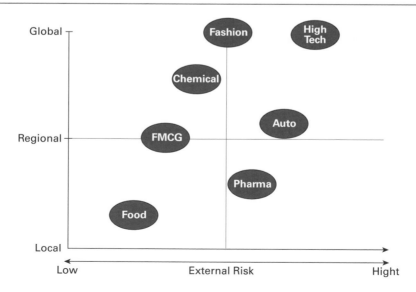

although there are intrinsic risks for the products themselves, the high level of in-house production/distribution mitigates many of these risks. With greater levels of outsourcing in this sector, the external risks are set to rise. Food supply chains tend to be local, characterized by low product value and, in most cases, have low levels of risks attached. However, the recent horsemeat scandal in Europe showed very clearly, for processed foods at least, that the sector was not immune to corruption and criminality involving wide-scale substitution. Food supply chains were shown to be complex and lacking in transparency, which ultimately created issues of security and process integrity.

Examples of supply chain disruption

Natural disasters

Japanese tsunami

The impact of Japan's 2011 earthquake and tsunami on global supply chains was dramatic with production across a whole range of sectors badly affected.

The Japanese electronics sector was amongst the hardest hit. Output of NAND flash memory, on which new consumer electronic equipment depends, was disrupted, albeit on a temporary basis. Many wafer fabrication plants, supplying the semi-conductor industry, remained closed whilst aftershocks continued to take place.

More surprising was the effects on other industries. The Japanese automotive sector traditionally has a highly localized supply chain, with mechanical component manufacturers located next to major assembly plants. Although these supplier parks were not affected, production was halted all the same.

One reason why these automotive plants were hit is the increasing number of electronic components in new motor vehicles. Already a huge part of the value of new cars, electronic component sourcing differs to that of mechanical parts. Increasingly, the more complex assemblies are sourced globally, with physically small yet important and expensive products often moved by air freight from distant production locations. This illustrates an emerging trend in the automotive supply chain.

Plants beyond Japan suffered as well. For example, Toyota's plant in the UK shut down production due to uncertainties over component supply. Renault's Samsung plant in South Korea also slowed output due to problems accessing its supply chain, part of which it shares with Nissan.

In fact, supply chains in the electronics sector, heavily dependent on Japanese production, were affected right across Asia. There were reports of key electronic components being in short supply as leading electronic manufacturers such as Sony, Sharp and Panasonic shut plants.

Japan has a large chemical sector much of which is located on the coast. Many of these facilities were damaged, with Dow Chemical reporting one of its facilities flooded.

However, things could have been worse. More widespread disruption was prevented by global supplies of flash memory on hand having built up over the previous two months. Manufacturers were also able to shift production from Japan to facilities outside the country.

It is believed as a result of the tsunami that manufacturers increased orders to buffer against future supply chain disruptions. Higher inventory could become the 'new normal' in the future, a calculated measure deployed to mitigate the disrupting effects of natural disasters.

The Thailand floods

In 2011 Thailand suffered one of the worst floods in five decades. The floods began in July, but steadily worsened throughout October, mainly limited to northern and eastern areas around Bangkok. However, these affected areas were home to hundreds of manufacturing facilities that were completely flooded. The automotive and hard disk drive manufacturing industries were among the hardest affected.

Japanese car makers that had just started to recover from the earthquake and tsunami now faced shortages of key parts made in Thailand. Toyota and Honda both had to halt production at facilities even in North America because their Thai suppliers were flooded.

The hard disk drive manufacturing sector was particularly affected. Thailand is the second largest country for production of hard disk drives after China. Toshiba, the fourth largest producer of hard disk drives, halted all of its production in Thailand. However, Seagate, the second largest producer of hard disk drives, did not have to stop production because its factories were in the north-east where flooding was less severe. Shortages of supplies lasted into the first quarter of 2012. Prices increased 20–40 per cent.

Subsequently, semiconductor chip manufacturer Intel warned that its revenues and profits would be lower than expected due to shortages of hard disk drives in the industry. Due to the closures, Intel's customers were not able to source sufficient volumes of hard disk drives to meet demand, and cut down on their microprocessor inventories. Intel warned that the shortages would continue into the first quarter of 2012.

Intel was not the only manufacturer struggling. Dell also missed sales targets in its quarterly results due, in part, to shortages of hard disk drives. However, management said that it had made strategic purchases of inventory elsewhere in an attempt to overcome this problem. This inevitably came at a cost.

Thailand supplies about 40 per cent of the world's market of hard disk drives. The supply chain problems which high tech manufacturers are facing reopened the debate over the wisdom of sourcing from suppliers clustered in such a vulnerable area.

Icelandic volcanos

The eruption on 14 April 2010 of Iceland's Eyjafjallajokull volcano (the second eruption in a month) caused havoc throughout Europe and beyond. The impact of this first eruption in 190 years continued even after airspace restrictions were lifted.

The regulators' decision to shut down airspace in Britain, Norway, the Netherlands, Germany, Austria, Belgium, Denmark, Finland, France, Germany, Latvia, Luxembourg, Poland, Slovakia, the Czech Republic, Bulgaria, Sweden and Switzerland cost airlines some $200 million per day from cancelled flights and caused the European economy to suffer massive losses in lost business.

The obvious reaction by logistics planners was to use other modes of transport for intra-European movements. The main problem was handling intercontinental traffic. As a contingency, freight forwarders and airlines set up hub activities in airports in southern Europe. For example, UPS flew some freight to Istanbul and moved it into Europe by road. Other providers used North African or even Middle Eastern airports.

The supply chain consequences were felt further afield than in Europe, and no more acutely than in east African markets. Here, perishable air cargo, such as fresh fruit and flowers, backed up at airports and, given the lack of appropriate temperature-controlled storage facilities, much of it was ruined. This caused considerable hardship to exporters and their employees.

Conflict and political unrest

The Straits of Hormuz

Tensions between Iran and the West increased in 2011, with sanctions imposed as a result of Iran's nuclear programme starting to bite. In response to the United States' and EU's further plans to block exports of Iranian oil exports,

Iran retaliated by threatening to close the Straits of Hormuz. This is the narrow passage between Iran and Oman, linking the Gulf with the Indian Ocean. Twenty per cent of the world's oil supplies pass through the Straits, as well as container vessels using the UAE's and other Gulf countries' ports.

Many analysts believe that Iran's threats were baseless, and that closing the Straits would be economically and politically damaging, not only to relations with the West, but with its powerful neighbours Saudi Arabia and the UAE. However, military activity in the area, a test of a new missile and warnings to the US Navy that its carriers should stay out of the Gulf, ratcheted up tension.

The consequences of any sort of military action in the Straits of Hormuz would be severe. Dubai is the ninth largest port in the world and the region has in recent years developed as a major hub for shipping, supplying Indian, Central Asian and African destinations with Asian-originating products. International sea-air business would also be affected, not to mention end markets in the Gulf itself.

Of more immediate concern to supply chains is the impact of the war of words on global oil markets. The possibility of the closure of the Straits, which acts as a transit for 17 million barrels of oil per day, was a factor in the rising oil price, despite the weak economic environment.

Economic/demand shocks

Cisco's troubles typify supply chain challenges

In June 2010, the Council of Supply Chain Management Professionals (CSCMP) asserted that the sharp destocking experienced during the recession had disrupted supply chains and that many organizations had had to resort to emergency measures to cope when demand picked up. This, according to the Council, was behind much of the boom in air freight seen in the previous few quarters as manufacturers desperately sought to source components and support increased production. What emerged were some examples of such supply chain stress.

Take Cisco, a huge company built on the design of the hardware that makes up the infrastructure of the internet. For much of 2010 Cisco was in crisis due to the malfunctioning of its supply chain. Its customers complained that the company could not deliver its products on time or, in some cases, even deliver them at all. Engineers maintaining infrastructure such as data centres were facing a wait of up to 12 weeks for basic switching components.

The origin of the problem clearly lay with Cisco's suppliers, many of them based in China. According to a statement from Cisco itself, the issues were, 'Attributable in part to increasing demand driven by the improvement in our overall markets… the longer than normal lead time extensions also stemmed from supplier constraints based upon their labour and other actions taken during the global economic downturn.' In other words, component suppliers laid off workers during the recession and reduced capacity. Consequently, there was not enough production capacity to fulfil demand.

It was also very interesting to see the reaction of customers to the worsening supply situation. According to Cisco, this led customers, 'to place the same order multiple times within our various sales channels and to cancel the duplicative orders upon receipt of the product, or to place orders with other vendors with shorter manufacturing lead times.'

In its statement Cisco said that, 'Our efforts to improve manufacturing lead-time performance may result in corresponding reductions in order backlog. A decline in backlog levels could result in more variability and less predictability in our quarter-to-quarter net sales and operating results.' This might be taken as typical 'squirreling' behaviour, where customers increase inventory levels in an environment of uncertainty. The result is 'lumpy' demand, with wild swings between shortage and overstocking.

The economic stress being visited upon supply chains led in turn to a failure to manage inventory properly. This in turn affected the management of transport. Or, in the words of Cisco:

> We have experienced periods of time during which shipments have exceeded net bookings or manufacturing issues have delayed shipments, leading to nonlinearity in shipping patterns. In addition to making it difficult to predict revenue for a particular period, nonlinearity in shipping can increase costs, because irregular shipment patterns result in periods of underutilized capacity and periods in which overtime expenses may be incurred, as well as in potential additional inventory management-related costs.

In other words, this statement meant Cisco, an erstwhile poster child of supply chain excellence, faced immense challenges in its logistics.

Terrorism and piracy

Yemen-originated terrorism

The placing of a parcel bomb on a Qatar Airways plane between Sana'a, Yemen and Dubai as belly-hold freight amplified the issue of security for the air freight sector. Whilst it was disturbing that terrorists were able to penetrate the networks of FedEx and UPS, the Qatar Airways incident in 2010 demonstrated that the whole of the air freight industry is affected by the problem.

Although freight industry organizations cautioned against an excessive security clampdown, politicians in Britain and the United States committed to security reviews. This reaction by the authorities has led to more inspection and scanning, possibly leading to the wider use of 'explosive detection systems'. These are complex pieces of engineering, which are both slow and very expensive, but they do offer better performance than x-ray systems against nitrate-based explosives.

In the latest cases the core problem is that the primary systems put in place to prevent the loading of explosive devices failed. Both the surveillance technology being used and the 'Known Consignor' system were either deceived or bypassed. It is worth observing that it was the express providers who were targeted as these systems are possibly more open to the general public and, therefore, may offer greater opportunity to hide the identity of the person placing the package in the system.

The lesson that the incidents appear to give is that the nature of the threat is dynamic rather than static. The individuals placing the bombs into the freight systems designed the devices to deliberately evade the security systems. This displayed both a knowledge of the security systems used and the ability to design a device capable of evading these systems. Therefore, any effective new security systems put in place by the air cargo sector is going to have to be both proactive and continually adaptive.

In truth, there is nothing particularly original about the approach taken in the most recent devices. The bomb on Pan Am 103, which blew up over Scotland in 1988, had strong similarities in design. However, the innovation of disguising explosive as printer toner illustrates an evolution in the nature of the problem. The air freight business systems must in turn evolve to anticipate such developments. It must achieve this whilst not crippling the operations of the business, either in terms of time to scan each consignment or cost. Either way, the cost penalty of developing such a response quickly and across the whole air cargo system is likely to be substantial.

The question is whether to approach the security with a risk-based strategy that relies on characteristics of a shipment to identify packages for increased scrutiny or one in which all shipments are subject to some form of physical inspection.

Proponents of comprehensive physical screening argue that it is the only way to ensure adequate security, while advocates of risk-based approaches argue that comprehensive screening is too costly and too time-consuming. Costs of implementing 100 per cent screening is estimated to be over $3.5 billion over a six-year period. Not only is this an expensive approach but probably an inefficient one, as shipping delays are likely to occur with this method.

Under the current air cargo security system, a number of risk-based strategies are being implemented and expanded to evaluate the security risk of air cargo shipments. Existing programmes, such as the Known Shipper Programme and the Certified Cargo Screening Programme, both of which have been in place for several years, are being studied for potential enhancements and expansions.

Another measure that must be taken on is technology. The United States' Transportation Security Administration (TSA) has approved a number of x-ray, bulk explosives detection systems and explosives trace detection machines for screening air cargo. However, these are variations of technologies used for screening checked baggage and carry-on items. Unfortunately, none of these devices are capable of effectively screening palletized or containerized cargo, which makes up 75 per cent of all cargo carried on passenger planes. Instead, screening must be done on individual cargo items.

As a result, the TSA is studying various new technologies. In 2010, TSA carried out a pilot programme at 18 locations to evaluate the effectiveness of selected screening technologies. The study concluded in August 2010. TSA is now assessing the performance of the various screening technologies and methods employed.

The US Department of Homeland Security and the TSA will also need to monitor and provide a solution for international air cargo entering the United States. Most of the focus has been on air cargo screening of out-bound domestic US cargo. Although the TSA lacks the direct authority to dictate screening requirements at foreign airports for US-bound cargo, it could potentially impose regulations on foreign carriers, as well as US carriers. However, enforcement overseas would be up to authorities in other countries. If they do not concur with the US approach, disagreement over security standards could complicate US foreign relations and potentially impact foreign trade.

Somali piracy

It has been estimated that pirates cost the world economy an estimated $6.9 billion (£4.3 billion) a year. In 2011, pirates reportedly raised $159.6 million from 31 paid ransoms.

Piracy off the coast of the Horn of Africa has been continuing for several years with not a great deal of sustained attention. However, the problem is a significant hazard to transport on one of the core global transport routes, even though since 2011 action by various navies has suppressed activity, with a recent report by the International Maritime Bureau suggesting a fall in the number of attacks.

Despite some successes for the campaign, attacks by pirates are ongoing. In May 2012, the Greek-owned oil tanker MT Smyrni, carrying 135,000 tonnes of crude oil, was hijacked in the Arabian Sea; the first successful attack on an oil tanker for more than a year.

One of the problems has been that captured pirates have been difficult to imprison or get to trial due to the lack of countries willing to take them. This has led many to be repatriated after a brief spell on a European warship.

In response to the problems, a private navy costing $70 million is being set up to escort merchant ships through the Gulf of Aden. It will comprise 18 ships, based in Djibouti, and will offer to convoy merchant vessels along the Internationally Recognized Transit Corridor (IRTC).

The initiative has been established by Convoy Escort Programme (CEP), a British company launched by the shipping insurers Jardine Lloyd Thompson (JLT) and the Lloyds of London underwriters Ascot.

In addition, the British government's endorsement of the use of armed guards on merchant vessels is another step towards the routine arming of ships passing through the Red Sea and Indian Ocean. The minister responsible for a policy which is effectively regulating the arming of cargo ships commented that 'by allowing the use of armed guards in a structured, legal framework we can move to a system where ship owners can provide an adequate deterrent against this scourge on the maritime industry'.

Conclusion

Although global supply chains have created mutual benefits for developed and emerging markets alike, these same supply chains have increased risk to the global economy. Reliance on production in markets such as China and the rest of Asia Pacific has put Western economies at the mercy of a series of internal and external threats to its extended supply chains.

Production in remote locations has brought with it increased exposure to environmental threats, such as the tsunami in Japan and the floods in Thailand, both of which have been important in raising the issue of supply chain vulnerability. These events brought massive disruption to automotive and high tech supply chains, but both could have been much worse. The first step for many manufacturers will be to accept that global supply chains bring with them risk. However, once the threats have been identified, quantifying them will be harder still.

The e-commerce logistics phenomenon

14

One of the biggest trends to impact on the global logistics industry over the past 10 years has been the emergence of e-commerce. Whilst the retail sector in the developed world has stagnated due to the economic situation, e-retailers have seen volumes grown significantly. The changing business model has meant that, whilst logistics and transport companies tied to traditional retailers have struggled, those which have been able to embrace the new distribution channels with a host of new services have prospered. Not least amongst these have been the parcels companies responsible for last mile 'B2C' deliveries. The phenomenon has also created a welcome new revenue stream for the post offices.

Not all retailers have been quick to adapt to this phenomenon. Long-time UK retailers, such as HMV, Jessops and Comet, have faced restructuring or even bankruptcy. Their inability to adapt to the rise in online retailing played a major role in their problems. E-retailers, such as Amazon.com and eBay, have brought a new business model to the retailing industry – stores open 24/7 via a consumer's laptop or mobile device, the ability to compare products and prices and delivery to the consumer's door.

Being able to adapt to a changing retail industry and respond to these changes with a flexible, agile supply chain is now a necessity for retailers to survive. As an increasing number of 'brick and mortar' retailers embrace e-commerce they will need to bolster their supply chain to provide a successful multichannel experience for the consumer.

International retailers, such as Tesco and Walmart, have been able to make the leap, as have several traditional catalogue companies, such as Germany's Otto Group and the Netherlands' Wehkamp. Pure-plays are also making headway. Asos, an apparel and accessories online retailer, has achieved success in not only its home market of the UK but it is now expanding into Europe, the United States and also has expansion plans for Asia. US-based retailers and pure-plays are expanding into the European market as well. In fact, Amazon is the largest European online retailer and eBay is right behind them in many European countries.

Logistics providers and postal services have responded to some extent to the needs of retailers, pure-play and brick & mortar alike, to compete effectively in the market. Many have tailored solutions for transport, fulfilment and returns and also additional value-added services. Logistics providers are also playing a role in many retailers' strategies as they expand services into new international markets.

However, although mail, express and logistics companies are benefiting from the growth of e-commerce, a large proportion of logistics functions are still not outsourced, as retailers believe that they are better positioned to undertake these operations themselves. Likewise the product range provided by carriers is very patchy – as is service quality.

What is e-commerce?

The term e-commerce can have a very broad meaning overall and refer to many different aspects of business, including selling online directly to customers using a virtual storefront.

Some of these models include:

- Business-to-business or B2B – B2B e-commerce involves the buying and selling of physical goods between businesses.

- Business-to-consumer or B2C – the most common type of e-commerce; many large electronic retailers or 'e-tailers' fit this model, including Amazon.com.

- Consumer-to-consumer or C2C – on this model, the online platform serves as a connection between two individual consumers who wish to make an exchange. Amazon.com can sometimes fit this model as they allow individual sellers to resell items (regardless of whether they were purchased on Amazon) to other individuals. Currently, the leader in C2C commerce is online auction site eBay.com.

UK retailers were early adopters of multichannel strategies but German retailer Saturn led the way in mainland Europe by launching a click and collect service bridging their online website with the offline in-store. As a result, the brand is experiencing much stronger customer engagement.

The ability not only to adapt to a changing retail industry but also to respond to these changes with a flexible, agile supply chain is now a necessity for retailers to survive. As more and more brick and mortar retailers embrace e-commerce they will need to bolster their supply chain to provide a successful multichannel experience for consumers.

The impact of e-retailing on logistics

Warehousing and fulfilment

E-retailers require distribution systems that often are more complex than traditional ones. Besides the need to manage an increasing number of suppliers and varying inventory, the management of multiple delivery options such as home delivery, in-store pickup, lockbox or elsewhere also becomes more difficult.

E-fulfilment centres are being built to manage the unique needs of this growing retail segment. These centres tend to be highly automated with service offerings ranging from basic order management and storage to pick and pack, returns handling and value-added services such as monogramming, gift wrapping and garment hanging services. Speed is very important – the quicker to fulfil and deliver an order, the greater the likelihood of a returning customer.

The size of these facilities also varies greatly. While Amazon operates warehouses that average 62,000 sq m, other companies use smaller facilities often located within urban areas close to where parcels are collected and also where customers can pick up their orders.

In the European and North American market many retailers are keeping warehousing and fulfilment in-house instead of outsourcing to logistics providers. This is due to not only the complex distribution requirements and limited supply of facilities but also to the still undeveloped range of services currently available by 3PLs.

As online retailing matures and retailers expand into additional countries, warehousing and distribution requirements will change and will likely include the adoption of outsourcing, particularly to those providers that adapt and introduce offerings for these changes.

Reverse logistics

The rate of online returns can average anywhere between 25 and 50 per cent. According to several retailers, customers are becoming more sophisticated in their online shopping – at one time they bought one item; now they buy two and return the one they do not like.

As such, many retailers are adding features such as panoramic viewing and virtual modelling to help minimize returns. However, these alone do not solve the amount of returns.

Other problems include regulations specific to online sales such as those relating to distance selling in the EU, which dictate that retailers have to offer cash for return rather than just store credit.

In any case, handling returns is expensive and difficult for retailers to manage. Some retailers charge a restocking fee while others offer free returns. Most, if not all, logistics providers, including fulfilment specialists, offer returns handling as part of their solutions. For many of these providers, the solutions involve the gathering of returned items; determining if the items can be resold or disposed of and then submitting the items into the proper channel of distribution. Because of varying individual country laws and regulations, much of this handling is done in the country in which the returns occur.

Courier, express and parcels sector (CEP)

The parcel segment has witnessed an impressive increase in volumes due to the rise in e-commerce. The industry's limited capacity for home delivery as well as the increased handling of returns amongst parcel carriers has allowed for the creation of new services as well as delivery and pickup points.

For example, in late 2012, DHL introduced its DHL Easy Return. The service allows for consumers to return goods across Europe. DHL's service is a standardized process across Europe. Distance sellers are able to use a special software platform and web portal to provide returns labels for their customers or customers can choose to create and print these labels themselves from a web portal. The portal is available in English, French, German and Dutch languages. It also offers the option for consumers to send their return parcels via DHL's network of 80,000 drop-off points. Transit times range from 3 to 12 days and the company plans to eventually expand the service beyond Europe.

In B2C, convenience and prompt delivery is expected. The increasing demand for such delivery services has put a strain on parcel delivery companies and post offices alike, and this has led to the greater use of self-employed drivers.

Alliances are also being created to maximize and expand the services of partners. According to TNT Post and Hermes, shippers in Germany want a partner that can provide the entire logistics solution. Consequently the two companies formed a delivery alliance in which Hermes will offer catalogue delivery via TNT Post and TNT Post will offer parcel delivery through Hermes – including access to the 14,000 Hermes parcel shops, charge-on-delivery shipment services, online identity verification and online real-time tracking.

As new delivery services increase, delivery points are also on the increase. Convenience and timing of deliveries are important to consumers when ordering online. To the parcel delivery company, additional delivery points may also assist them in maintaining fleet operations and thus keep delivery costs as low as possible.

Lockers

With Amazon's successful introduction of lockers to the United States, it introduced its locker pickup service to the UK market in 2011. Customers are able to choose to pick up goods from a locker location when placing their orders via Amazon UK's website. These lockers are typically located in various stores and there are also plans to expand the concept across the UK.

UK-based ByBox is a provider of a bank of such lockers that target field service engineers. It operates its own transport network, along with nine distribution centres to manage parts inventory and returns. Locations of these facilities are in London, Milton Keynes, Bristol, Haydock, Coventry, Doncaster, Newcastle, Glasgow and Thetford. The Coventry distribution centre is over 100,000 sq ft and is the national hub for freight sortation and warehousing. It also has a French hub located in Wissous.

The company has over 18,000 boxes in more than 1,300 locations across the UK. In addition, it operates 54,000 electronic lockers in more than 20 countries.

Parcel shops

GLS, DPD, DHL and many more parcel delivery companies have established parcel shops across Europe as a means for customers to drop off or pick up packages. Many of these shops are within other shops while others are stand-alone facilities.

Parcel shop networks in the UK include Yodel's CollectPlus network, with 5,000 outlets, Hermes' myHermes network has more than 1,000 outlets and Local Letterbox, a startup, aims to have 1,500 outlets by Summer 2013.

In Germany, there are 14,000 Hermes parcel shops, 4,000 GLS parcel shops and DPD plans to grow its 2,000 network to 8,000 parcel shops.

UPS recently launched its new network of parcel shops, UPS Access Points, in the UK. UPS is starting with about 500 outlets and plans to grow this to 1,500 by the summer of 2013. According to UPS, one of the attractions of convenience stores providing parcel services is that B2C parcels are converted into B2B parcels by parcel shops, meaning a more efficient delivery model can be used. Launching a new parcel shop network meant driving UPS further into the B2C parcel market without having to significantly expand fleet operations.

Click and collect

Bricks and mortar retailers, such as John Lewis, are now allowing customers the option of buying online and picking up at its stores. According to John Lewis, which has about 40 stores, this service includes its sister company, Waitrose, allowing the company to add an additional 300 outlets.

Asda, Tesco and Sainsbury also offer this type of service. According to Sainsbury's director of direct channels, over one-third of the supermarket's internet non-food sales already come through click and collect.

International commerce

Although the majority of B2C shipments are still domestic, international B2C is expected to gain importance as express providers build their cross-border networks. In the long term, larger e-commerce players will likely set up logistics operations in each of their key markets, which will convert international shipments into domestic ones. To cope with higher last-mile costs in this segment they will need to develop innovative solutions, particularly as e-commerce companies establish their own solutions.

The express segment continues to dominate in markets, with a perceived poor quality of standard mail services, such as in remote locations within Europe and in markets with high shares of volumes to or from non-European locations. Countries with more heavyweight business, and with central positions in intra-European trade and traffic, see more standard volumes.

As more e-commerce companies enter the market, the high levels of returned shipments, such as apparel, will need to be addressed along with the increase in parcels. CEP providers will need to either develop alternative solutions to cope with increasing costs or raise prices, although the latter approach is unlikely given the fierce competition and the aim to transport returns free of charge in most European markets.

The four major integrators, DHL, FedEx, TNT and UPS, have a distinct advantage: well-established air and road networks. FedEx and UPS have been keen to buy in the European market, although UPS's plans to buy TNT were thwarted by the European Commission on competition grounds.

However, in 2012 FedEx completed the acquisition of the Polish courier company Opek. Through the acquisition, FedEx Express gained access to a nationwide domestic ground network with an estimated $70 million in annual revenue and 12.5 million shipments handled annually.

In the same year FedEx also acquired Tatex, a French privately held company. The company has a nationwide network with a central hub at Lieusaint, just south of Paris, and 35 shipping centres including six regional hubs. The acquisition gives FedEx Express access to a nationwide domestic ground network which carried 19 million shipments and produced approximately €150 million in revenue annually.

The role of the postal services

Many of Europe's post offices are struggling due to varying degrees of privatization and declining mail volume. Unlike traditional logistics providers, many of Europe's post offices continue to be governed based on procedures dictated by inter-postal bodies. At the international level, the Universal Postal Union defines the postal standards applicable to all countries. At the local level, bodies such as the E-Parcel Group set the delivery time standards and the penalties postal services owe their foreign counterparts should they fail to deliver a parcel within a specific time frame.

As such, many are reinventing themselves, particularly as online retailing continues to grow and demand for parcel delivery solutions, e-fulfilment services and cross-border European solutions increases.

Along with the increasing selection of collection and drop-off points for parcels mentioned earlier in this chapter, post offices are also introducing additional solutions. For example, in Germany customers can choose to collect parcels 24/7 from one of about 2,500 automated Deutsche Post Packstations and receive SMS/e-mail notifications. They can also send parcels using a touchscreen automated process. About 90 per cent of Germans can reach a Packstation in 10 minutes.

A number of other operators have developed similar automated postal pickup solutions, including bpost, Cyprus Post, PostNord, Eesti Post and La Poste.

Austrian Post introduced 'Drop off Box' for 24/7 returns and 'Parcel Box' – parcels are placed in a secure box at select apartment buildings and a private access code is given with a notification card, which can be dropped into a personal mailbox.

In the UK, Royal Mail has trialled a 'Delivery to Neighbour' initiative, where a neighbour can receive a parcel if the intended recipient is not at home.

CASE STUDY   Amazon drives the market in Europe

Headquartered in the United States, Amazon.com began operations in 1995, entering the European market in 1998. The UK is Amazon's largest European market. At present the company has eight fulfilment centres in the the UK, one in Spain, four in France, one in Italy and seven in Germany.

Amazon's European fulfilment centres operate much like those in the United States. Employees are divided into four main groups. There are the people on the 'receive lines' and the 'pack lines'. They either unpack, check and scan every product upon arrival or they pack up customers' orders at the other end of the process. They place product wherever there is a free space. Employees use handheld computers to scan both the item they are stowing away and a bar code on the spot on the shelf where they put it.

The last group, the 'pickers', pick customers' orders from the aisles. Amazon's software calculates the most efficient walking route to collect all the items to fill a trolley and then simply direct from one shelf space to the next via instructions on the screen of the handheld satnav device.

As well as selling its own products, Amazon UK provides fulfilment services, whereby customers can store their products in Amazon's Fulfilment Centres, and Amazon staff will pick, pack and deliver them as well as provide customer service. Customers can also sell their products on other Amazon Marketplaces in Europe (Germany, France, Italy) and Amazon fulfils these orders from the customer's inventory stored in the UK.

Amazon has been experimenting with various delivery points and, in 2011, the company installed lockers throughout London through a deal with Land Securities, which owns several shopping centres in London.

Instead of delivering a parcel to a home or business address, the customer can select a locker location during checkout and pick up the parcel at a time that is convenient. Once the parcel is delivered to the Amazon Locker, the customer receives an e-mail notification with a unique pickup code. When the customer arrives to collect the parcel, the customer will touch the Amazon Locker screen until there is an option to enter the unique pickup code. Once entered, a message will appear with the parcel's locker number and the locker door will automatically open.

All parcels delivered to Locker locations must be picked up within three business days. If the parcel is not picked up within this timeframe, it will be returned to Amazon for a refund.

In 2012, Amazon introduced delivery to customers at nearly 5,000 convenience stores through collection network CollectPlus. More than 85 per cent of the UK population lives within one mile of a CollectPlus outlet.

Despite having several European website shops, Amazon still faces the issue of seamless cross-border service. However, in 2010, Amazon UK introduced free shipping for customers in various European countries. These countries are – Andorra, Finland, Gibraltar, Iceland, Liechtenstein, the Vatican City, Ireland, Spain, Belgium, Denmark, Greece, Italy, Luxembourg, the Netherlands, Norway, Poland, Portugal, San Marino and Sweden.

E-retailing in Asia

The growth of e-commerce amongst Asia-Pacific countries is rapid and the region is in the midst of becoming the largest as a percentage of global sales. According to market research company eMarketer, global e-commerce, which includes retail, travel and digital download sales and online marketplace transactions, grew at almost 22 per cent in 2012 to $1.1 trillion. Whilst North America is the largest geographic region, it is expected that Asia Pacific will surpass North America in 2013 as global e-commerce sales are expected to grow 19.3 per cent to $1.3 trillion.

Due to the growth, infrastructure is strained and is proving to be a hindrance to adoption. Much of Asia's infrastructure was structured to meet export demand. However, because of the need to balance exports and imports, infrastructure projects are under way to establish road and rail networks, improve delivery service options and to expand warehousing and distribution centres.

Payments are another part of the supply chain that has proven challenging for the region. Traditionally, Asia is a cash-based society and looks upon credit with suspicion. As such, e-commerce companies have had to make allowances for cash-on-delivery, which can slow the delivery process even further if frequent returns have to be made along with the prolonged financial payment cycle time.

The Asian e-commerce market is tempting for international e-commerce companies such as Amazon and eBay. While both are among the largest of such providers in North America and Europe, it has not been the case for Asia. E-Bay pulled out of the Chinese market in 2006 due to fierce competition but has operations in other Asian countries such as Korea and Japan. Amazon has had a difficult time in Asia as well. Although it is the second largest e-commerce company in Japan it only has about a 2 per cent market share within China's market. In India, it has had to partner with a local provider, as required by India's government.

China's Alibaba and Japan's Rakuten dominate Asia e-commerce and both of these companies are expanding into Europe and the Americas and could rival Amazon and eBay for international sales.

CASE STUDY   China's leading e-retailer builds its own logistics

The Alibaba Group has identified logistics as the major hindrance for Chinese e-commerce companies. Jack Ma, the founder of Alibaba, noted 'e-commerce sales are growing so quickly in China that logistics companies are in danger of being overwhelmed and unable to deliver merchandise ordered online to Chinese homes and businesses in a timely way.' As a result, it has partnered with investment company, Fosun Group, and banking group, China Yintai Holding Group, to develop a logistics network.

Since 2011, Alibaba has worked on a strategy to develop a logistics network connecting all of China and provide delivery within 24 hours anywhere in China. Named the China Smart Logistics Network, Alibaba's strategy is comprised of four parts:

- Its consumer-focused subsidiary Taobao will develop its logistics initiative, which consists of the 'Taobao supply chain management platform' designed to help merchants handle inventory, a logistics partnership network and an industry code of standards guiding logistics service providers.

- Alibaba will establish an integrated logistics platform at group level that aims to bring together all players in the industry from warehousing to delivery.

- Alibaba will also invest in the establishment of a nationwide warehouse network across China.

- The group will offer warehousing facility support to small Chinese exporters.

Prior to this announcement, merchants were responsible for their own warehousing and fulfilment needs. However, during a one-day promotional event on Taobao mall, over 21 million shoppers purchased more than US$146 million worth of goods. The unexpected volume caused the payment system to temporarily freeze and many merchants struggled to fulfil orders in the aftermath. Now, according to the founder of Alibaba, 'We are asking companies to keep their stock in our warehouses. We learned that their biggest concerns are goods storage and how to connect different parts of the logistics process.'

As such, Alibaba estimates the 10-year plan will cost over $15 billion, with the group investing over $3 billion itself to build a 'non-proprietorial' nationwide network of warehouses. In fact, the company plans to be a 'professional logistics property developer' with a centralized warehouse network dedicated to B2C services. Alibaba and its partners will establish the network in seven parts of the country – north-east, north, east, south, central, south-west and north-west.

Alibaba plans to expand its logistics network from 20 cities to 52 cities by the end of 2013. Initially, Beijing/Tianjin, the Yangtze River Delta and the Pearl River Delta areas were the first areas selected by Alibaba for warehouse construction because of their proximity to major population centres. It is expected that Shanghai, Tianjin and Guangzhou will have large warehousing facilities and an additional six to eight regional warehouse centres will be built.

E-retailing in North America

Of all North American countries, the United States clearly dominates the e-commerce market. Pure-clicks such as Amazon.com and eBay continue to expand their presence not only within their home country but within Canada, Mexico and globally. In addition, brick and mortar companies such as Best Buy and Walmart are leaders in B2C e-commerce abroad as well as at home.

In the United States, e-commerce growth has outpaced total economic activity year-over-year, and that trend is expected to continue as businesses shift operating models to take advantage of the benefits of e-commerce and the growing population of internet consumers.

Although e-commerce sales are steady throughout the year, holiday shopping in the fourth quarter is the busiest season; the increase of e-commerce shopping in recent years has led to the adoption of the term 'Green Monday', the Monday after Thanksgiving, which is supposedly now the biggest online shopping day of the year, similar to the 'Black Friday' day after Thanksgiving shopping holiday for traditional retailers.

The mostly undisputed leader of e-commerce in the United States is Amazon.com. Amazon, which began in 1994 as an online bookstore, is now the model many e-commerce companies wish to imitate. Amazon's growth for the past several years has outpaced the sales growth of the US e-commerce market as a whole.

Many traditional brick and mortar US retailers are learning that they need to embrace the e-commerce trend as brick and mortar retail sales continue to decline. Sales of Macy's, Best Buy, and others have declined as the e-commerce trend has taken off, and have only recently begun to invest in their e-commerce sectors.

The location of online retail distribution centres/e-fulfilment centres is an important consideration. The placement of e-commerce facilities varies among companies, depending on their growth strategy. Retailer Macy's, for example, has opted for a regional approach and has at least four fulfilment centres devoted to e-commerce. These facilities are large and are in excess of 1 million sq ft. Instead of a regional approach, however, Amazon.com has a different method, choosing instead to build facilities closer to its customer base and as a result facilities have proliferated.

When deciding upon a location for such a facility, key factors are considered, such as sales taxes and state incentives, close proximity to major markets, a good labour supply to utilize in normal and peak seasons and close to transportation hubs.

State taxes have been a major issue for e-retailers for years. In particular, Amazon.com has been a focal point as it has refused to locate a facility in such states that enforce sales tax on online purchases and has in fact pulled out of states that have imposed such a tax. However, as more states begin to implement a sales tax on online purchases, Amazon.com is rethinking its strategy and announced it would no longer fight the spread of sales tax on online purchases. Instead, the company has opted to work states as its strategy shifts towards one of numerous facilities that are closer to metropolitan areas in which there are larger concentrations of customers. Many within the industry view this as an attempt to offer same-day delivery.

Locating facilities close to transportation hubs is another important consideration – particularly as many e-retailers operate in a two-to-five-day delivery time frame. In order to achieve this delivery time, many facilities are locating to states such as Tennessee, Virginia, Ohio and Pennsylvania as these states are close to both UPS and FedEx primary hubs as well as to intermodal hubs. While many e-commerce orders are delivered via small parcel providers, such as UPS and FedEx, regional small parcel providers, the US Postal Service, trucking companies, rail and intermodal services are used as well depending on service level and cost.

Amazon and other online retailers often require distribution centres of 500,000 sq ft or larger and have different design requirements than those of traditional retail distribution centres. Quick turns and higher volumes of orders are typically the norm for online distribution centres.

15

3D Printing: the end of global supply chains?

'3D Printing', or 'additive manufacturing' as it is also known, has the potential to become the biggest single disruptive phenomenon to impact industry since assembly lines were introduced in early 20th-century America.

New technologies which are currently being developed could revolutionize production techniques, resulting in a significant proportion of manufacturing becoming automated and removing reliance on large and costly work forces. This in turn could lead to a reversal of the trend of globalization which has characterized industry and consumption over the last few decades, itself predicated on the trade-off between transportation and labour costs.

Globalization has benefited shipping lines, airlines and freight forwarders enormously as vast quantities of consumer goods are moved internationally to Western markets from the Far East. Consequently any challenge to globalization must be viewed as a threat to the global transportation industry. However, as with all disruptive technologies, it also offers opportunities. This chapter takes a look at the new technology, assesses the chances of its widespread adoption and examines its implications for the logistics industry.

What is 3D Printing?

3D Printing was originally developed as an automated method of producing prototypes. Although there are several competing technologies, most work on the basis of building up layers of material (sometimes plastic, ceramics or even metal powders) using a computer aided design. Hence, it is referred to as an 'additive' process; each layer is 'printed' until a three dimensional product is created.

The logic for using 3D Printing for prototypes is compelling. Traditional 'reductive' manufacturing techniques (where materials are removed) can take longer and are much more expensive. Mechanical parts, shoes, fashion items and accessories, and other consumer goods, can all be printed for review by the designer or engineers, and revisions printed equally as easily. Whereas mass production is viable due to economies of scale, it is uneconomical for 'one offs' and prototypes. 3D Printing will remove this differential, where every item produced is an original (or perfect copy) and tooling for one is as cheap as tooling for many.

The final 3D Printed product also has other benefits. Products can be lighter, but just as strong. There is also less wastage. In comparison, traditional reductive manufacturing is highly inefficient in the use of materials.

The way in which each product is individually manufactured means that it is ideal for 'mass customization' techniques. Consumers will, in theory, be able to have a much greater say in the final format of the product which they are buying, and have it manufactured to their precise specifications.

Can 3D Printing revolutionize global industry?

There is obviously an enormous leap between a manufacturing process which can presently produce one-offs and one that can replace large-scale manufacturing. However, in theory, there is no reason why advances in technology could not increase the speed of production and reduce unit costs.

If this were to happen there would be many consequences, bringing about relatively minor (and then potentially major) changes to the global manufacturing industry.

For instance, 3D Printing is already very good at producing products (even with moving parts) which previously would have required the assembly of multiple components. By eliminating the assembly phase there will be huge savings for the manufacturer in terms of labour costs, but also potentially in the removal of storage, handling and distribution costs involved in bringing together the relevant components.

However, systemic change will only occur if the automation of production rebalances global supply chain costs. The falling proportion of total costs made up by labour in the West would take away the rationale for producing goods in remote, low-cost markets (as relative transportation costs rise).

Instead these manufacturing facilities could be sited close to the customer in Europe or North America where there would be fewer quality control issues and more responsiveness to market needs. Lower batch quantities would consolidate these benefits.

3D Printing, combined with efficient manufacturing, will revolutionize the principles established in the first Industrial Revolution. Not only will local manufacturing re-establish itself close to end markets, but it will allow the flexibility to reconfigure in response to changing consumer demands. The nature of manufacturing will be very different from traditional models in which it takes established production plants months (or even years) to retool.

The philosophy of manufacturing, in which products are made precisely to customer demand, could have big implications in certain sectors. For instance, in healthcare vertical small 'one-off' production runs of drugs/compounds will reduce inventory holding costs. But this capability will also enable the rapid transport of entire production plants to areas where large amounts of drugs may be needed in times of emergency (ie pandemics or natural disasters).

Looking even further into the future, some household products could actually be manufactured in the consumer's home, once the cost of 3D printing technology has become affordable. This would have even greater implications for the logistics industry – this time on a domestic rather than international basis. This is not as far off as may be thought. 3D printers for consumers can already be purchased for just a few hundred dollars.

What are the implications for the logistics industry?

The implications of this new manufacturing technology for the logistics industry could be massive:

- Potentially a proportion of goods which were previously produced in China or other Asia markets could be 'near-sourced' to North America and Europe. This would reduce shipping and air cargo volumes.

- The 'mass customization' of products would mean that inventory levels fall, as goods are made to order. This would have the effect of reducing warehousing requirements.

- There would be fewer opportunities for logistics suppliers to be involved in companies' upstream supply chains, as manufacturing processes are increasingly rebundled within a single facility. Tiers of component suppliers are done away with, as is the need for supplier villages, line side supply, etc.

- Downstream logistics would also be affected. Build-to-order production strategies could fundamentally impact the manufacturer–wholesaler–retailer relationship. In the future, the shopping experience could also be vastly different. In some sectors, retailers will either cease to exist or become 'shop windows' for manufacturers, keeping no stock of their own. Orders are fulfilled directly by the manufacturer, and delivered to the home of the consumer.

- A major new sector of the logistics industry would emerge, dealing with the storage and movement of the raw materials which 'feed' the 3D printers. As 3D printers become more affordable to the general public, the home delivery market of these materials would increase.

- The service parts logistics sector would be one of the first to be affected. At present billions are spent on holding stock to supply products as diverse as cars to x-ray machines. In some cases huge amount of redundancy is built into supply chains to enable parts to be dispatched in a very short timescale to get machines up and running again as fast as possible. It doesn't take much imagination to understand the benefits for a service parts engineer of being able to download a part design from an online library, 3D Print it and then fit it within a very short time window. This would make global and national parts warehouses as well as forward stock locations unnecessary to fulfilling customer needs.

The logistics company of the future

The changing supply chain dynamics will lead to the evolution of a new type of logistics company resembling a '4PL', or service management company, as much as anything else. Their businesses will comprise a mix of software development, delivery services, partner relationship management, contract management and brainpower.

The new logistics company will design solutions comprising demand planning, manufacturing, delivery, market monitoring, service parts management and return and recycling services. In essence, they will become Product Life-Cycle Management service providers.

This is a big opportunity for the major industry players that have the resources to establish these new organizations.

The service parts logistics industry could be either transformed or de-cimated by 3D manufacturing. With small 3D Printing machines available, operations in remote locations – or even in an engineer's van – will only need electronic libraries of designs available to them on a local computer. They can then call up the design of the spare part required and immediately print it. Obsolete parts could simply be scanned in 3D, fixed in the computer's memory and the new part printed. The implications for inventory are clear.

Conclusion

If the new technology is to completely transform global industry, 3D Printing must be able to mass-produce goods in the same volumes as traditional manufacturing techniques. At present, the jury is still out on whether this is feasible. Some in the sector (such as global manufacturing group GE) foresee a time when a whole engine, for example, could be printed. Others believe that, at least in the medium term, hybrid solutions will develop, which combine new technologies with more traditional techniques.

However, what 3D Printing is certainly not is science fiction. Its ability to create strong but light parts has been identified by the aerospace sector; components for the automotive sector are already being printed and the technology is being adopted by the mobile telecoms sector.

It has been estimated that in 2012 up to 30 per cent of finished products already involve some kind of 3D Printing. By 2016, this is expected to rise to 50 per cent and by 2020 potentially up to 80 per cent.

At the moment the following areas are in line for transformation:

- Now:
  - production prototypes;
  - small manufacturing runs of high value/high complexity products;
  - dental/aural healthcare forms/aids.
- Soon:
  - almost all service parts;
  - complex high volume/high value forms;
  - products related to fashion/trends that have a high volume/short lifespan profile.
- Later:
  - mass-produced fast-moving consumer goods.

It is difficult to see that industry will undergo complete transformation for many years – probably decades – to come. What could happen, though, is that some sectors are penetrated by the technology at a much earlier stage, such as the manufacture of spare parts. In this case, the most enlightened logistics companies could even become early adopters of the technologies – investing in the 3D printers and providing facilities for engineers – rather than kicking against the progress. This would also provide a way of leveraging their capital and their own technological capabilities.

It is clear that, if the larger logistics companies delay or ignore the implications of this trend, they are vulnerable to new kinds of organizations or associations that will match or leap ahead of their capabilities for very little outlay.

INDEX